DATA STRUCTURES
AND
PROGRAM DESIGN
USING C

DATA STRUCTURES AND PROGRAM DESIGN USING C

A Self-Teaching Introduction

Dheeraj Malhotra
Neha Malhotra

MERCURY LEARNING AND INFORMATION
Dulles, Virginia
Boston, Massachusetts
New Delhi

Publisher: David Pallai
MERCURY LEARNING AND INFORMATION
22841 Quicksilver Drive
Dulles, VA 20166
info@merclearning.com
www.merclearning.com
(800) 232-0223

D. Malhotra and N. Malhotra. *Data Structures and Program Design Using C.*
ISBN: 9781683922070

Library of Congress Control Number: 2018938986

181920321   Printed on acid-free paper in the United States of America.

Dedicated to our
loving parents and beloved students.

CONTENTS

PREFACE

Data structures are the building blocks of computer science. The objective of this text is to emphasize fundamentals of data structures as an introductory subject. It is designed for beginners (students or professionals) who would like to learn the basics of data structures and their implementation using the C programming language. With this focus in mind, we present various fundamentals of the subject, well supported with real world analogies to enable a quick understanding of the technical concepts and to help in identifying appropriate data structures to solve specific, practical problems. This book will serve the purpose of a text / reference book and will be of immense help especially to undergraduate or graduate students of various courses in information technology, engineering, computer applications, and information sciences.

Key Features:

- *Practical Applications:* Real world analogies as practical applications are given throughout the text to easily understand and connect the fundamentals of data structures with day to day, real-world scenarios. This approach, in turn, will assist the reader in developing the capability to easily identify the most appropriate and efficient data structure for solving a specific problem.

- *Frequently Asked Questions:* Frequently asked theoretical/practical questions are integrated throughout the content of the book, within related topics to assist readers in grasping the subject.

- *Algorithms and Programs:* To better understand the fundamentals of data structures at a generic level-followed by its specific implementation in C, syntax independent algorithms as well as implemented programs in C are discussed throughout the book. This presentation will assist the reader in getting both algorithms and their corresponding implementation within a single book.

- *Numerical and Conceptual Exercises:* To assist the reader in developing a strong foundation of the subject, various numerical and conceptual problems are included throughout the text.

- *Multiple Choice Questions:* To assist students for placement-oriented exams in various IT areas, several exercises are suitably chosen and are given in an MCQ format.

Dheeraj Malhotra
Neha Malhotra
May 2018

ACKNOWLEDGMENTS

It is our pleasure to take this opportunity to sincerely thank the people who have extended their kind help and support to us throughout this project.

We are indeed grateful to Dr. SC Vats, Dr. Rattan Sharma, Dr. Vinay Kumar and other staff members of Vivekananda Institute of Professional Studies (GGS IP University). They are always a source of inspiration for us, and we feel honored because of their faith in us.

We also take this opportunity to extend our gratitude to Dr. OP Rishi, Dr. Jatinder Singh, Dr. Udyan Ghose, Dr. Nitin Malik, Dr. A.D. Lamba for their motivation to execute this project.

We are profoundly thankful to Mr. Deepanshu Gupta for helping us in proofreading and compiling the codes in this manuscript.

It is not possible to complete a book without the support of a publisher. We are thankful to Mr. David Pallai and Ms. Jennifer Blaney of Mercury Learning and Information for their enthusiastic involvement throughout the tenure of this project.

Our heartfelt regards to our parents, siblings and family members who cheered us in good times and encouraged us in bad times.

Lastly, we have always felt inspired by our students. Their questioning minds enriched our knowledge, which we have presented in this book.

INTRODUCTION TO DATA STRUCTURES

In This Chapter

- Introduction
- Types of data structures
- Operations on data structures
- Algorithms
- Approaches for designing an algorithm
- Analyzing an algorithm
- Abstract data types
- Big O notation
- Summary

1.1 Introduction

A data structure is an efficient way of storing and organizing the data elements in the computer memory. Data means a value or a collection of values. Structure refers to a method of organizing the data. The mathematical or logical representation of data in the memory is referred as a data structure. The objective of a data structure is to store, retrieve, and update the data efficiently. A data structure can be referred to as a group of elements grouped under one name. The group of data elements is called members, and they can be of different types. Data structures are used in almost every program and software system. There are various kinds of data structures that are suited for different types of applications. Data structures are the building blocks of a program. For a program to run efficiently, a programmer must choose appropriate data structures. A data structure is a very crucial part of data management. As the name suggests, data management is a task which includes different activities like collection of data, an organization of data into structures, and much more. Some examples where data structures are used include stacks, queues, arrays, binary trees, linked lists, hash tables, and so forth.

A data structure helps us to understand the relationship of one element to another element and organize it within the memory. It is a mathematical or logical representation or organization of data in memory. Data structures are extensively applied in the following areas:

- Compiler Design
- Database Management Systems (DBMS)
- Artificial Intelligence
- Network and Numerical Analysis
- Statistical Analysis Packages
- Graphics
- Operating Systems (OS)
- Simulations

As we see in the previous list, there are many applications in which different data structures are used for their operations. Some data structures sacrifice speed for efficient utilization of memory, while others sacrifice memory utilization and result in faster speed. In today's world programmers aim not just to build a program, but instead to build an effective program. As previously discussed, for a program to be efficient, a programmer must choose appropriate data structures. Hence, data structures are classified into various types. Now, let us discuss and learn about different types of data structures.

Frequently Asked Questions

Q1. Define the term data structure.

Answer.
A data structure is an organization of data in a computer's memory or disk storage. In other words, a logical or mathematical model of a particular organization of data is called a data structure. A data structure in computer science is also a way of storing data in a computer so that it can be used efficiently. An appropriate data structure allows a variety of important operations to be performed using both resources, that is, memory space and execution time, efficiently.

1.2 Types of Data Structures

Data structures are classified into various types.

1.2.1 Linear and Non-Linear Data Structures

A linear data structure is one in which the data elements are stored in a linear, or sequential, order; that is, data is stored in consecutive memory locations. A linear data structure can be represented in two ways; either it is represented by a linear relationship between various elements utilizing consecutive memory locations as in the case of arrays, or it may be represented by a linear relationship between the elements utilizing links from one element to another as in the case of linked lists. Examples of linear data structures include arrays, linked lists, stacks, queues, and so on.

A non-linear data structure is one in which the data is not stored in any sequential order or consecutive memory locations. The data elements in this structure are represented by a hierarchical order. Examples of non-linear data structure include graphs, trees, and so forth.

1.2.2 Static and Dynamic Data Structures

A static data structure is a collection of data in memory which is fixed in size and cannot be changed during runtime. The memory size must be known in advance as the memory cannot be reallocated later in a program. One example is an *array*.

A *dynamic data structure is a collection of data in which memory can be reallocated during execution of a program.* The programmer can add or remove elements according to his/her need. Examples include linked lists, graphs, trees, and so on.

1.2.3 Homogeneous and Non-Homogeneous Data Structures

A *homogeneous data structure is one that contains data elements of the same type,* for example, arrays.

A *non-homogeneous data structure contains data elements of different types,* for example, structures.

1.2.4 Primitive and Non-Primitive Data Structures

Primitive data structures are the fundamental data structures or pre-defined data structures which are supported by a programming language. Examples of primitive data structure types are short, integer, long, float, double, char, pointers, and so forth.

Non-primitive data structures are comparatively more complicated data structures that are created using primitive data structures. Examples of non-primitive data structures are arrays, files, linked lists, stacks, queues, and so on.

Classification of different data structures is shown in Figure 1.1.

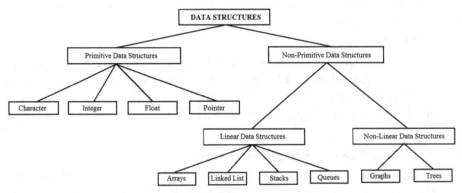

FIGURE 1.1 Classification of different data structures.

We know that C supports various data structures. So, we will now introduce all these data structures, and they will be discussed in detail in the upcoming chapters.

Frequently Asked Questions

Q2. Write the difference between primitive data structures and non-primitive data structures.

Answer.
Primitive data structures – The data structures that are typically directly operated upon by machine-level instructions, that is, the fundamental data types such as int, float, char, and so on, are known as primitive data structures.

Non-primitive data structures – The data structures which are not fundamental are called non-primitive data structures.

Frequently Asked Questions

Q3. Explain the difference between linear and non-linear data structures.

Answer.
The main difference between linear and non-linear data structures lies in the way in which data elements are organized. In the linear data structure, elements are organized sequentially, and therefore they are easy to implement in a computer's memory. In non-linear data structures, a data element can be attached to several other data elements to represent specific relationships existing among them.

1.2.5 Arrays

An array is a collection of homogeneous (similar) types of data elements in contiguous memory. An array is a linear data structure because all elements of an array are stored in linear order. The various elements of the array are referenced by their index value also known as the subscript. In C, an array is declared using the following syntax:

Syntax – <Data type>   array name [size];

The elements are stored in the array as shown in Figure 1.2.

1st element	2nd element	3rd element	4th element	5th element	6th element
array [0]	array [1]	array [2]	array [3]	array [4]	array [5]

FIGURE 1.2 Memory representation of an array.

Arrays are used for storing a large amount of data of similar type. They have various advantages and limitations.

Advantages of using arrays

1. Elements are stored in adjacent memory locations; hence, searching is very fast, as any element can be easily accessed.

2. Arrays do not support dynamic memory allocation, so all the memory management is done by the compiler.

Limitations of using arrays

1. Insertion and deletion of elements in arrays is complicated and very time-consuming, as it requires the shifting of elements.

2. Arrays are static; hence, the size must be known in advance.

3. Elements in the array are stored in consecutive memory locations which may or may not be available.

1.2.6 Queues

A Queue is a linear collection of data elements in which the element inserted first will be the element that is taken out first; that is, a queue is a FIFO (First In First Out) data structure. A queue is a popular linear data structure in which the first element is inserted from one end called the REAR end (also called the tail end), and the deletion of the element takes place from the other end called the FRONT end (also called the head).

Practical Application:

For a simple illustration of a queue, there is a line of people standing at the bus stop and waiting for the bus. Therefore, the first person standing in the line will get into the bus first.

In a computer's memory queues can be implemented using arrays or linked lists. Figure 1.3 shows the array implementation of a queue. Every queue has FRONT and REAR variables which point to the position from where insertion and deletion are done respectively.

FIGURE 1.3 Memory representation of a queue.

1.2.7 Stacks

A Stack is a linear collection of data elements in which insertion and deletion take place only at the top of the stack. A stack is a Last In First Out (LIFO) data structure, because the last element pushed onto the stack will be the first element to be deleted from the stack. Three operations can be performed on the stack, which includes PUSH, POP, and PEEP operations. The PUSH operation inputs an element into the top of the stack, while the POP operation removes an element from the stack. The PEEP operation returns the value of the topmost element in the stack without deleting it from the stack. Every stack has a variable TOP which is associated with it. The TOP pointer stores the address of the topmost element in the stack. The TOP is the position from where insertion and deletion take place.

Practical Application:

A real-life example of a stack is if there is a pile of plates arranged on a table. A person will pick up the first plate from the top of the stack.

In a computer's memory stacks can be implemented using arrays or linked lists. Figure 1.4 shows the array implementation of a stack.

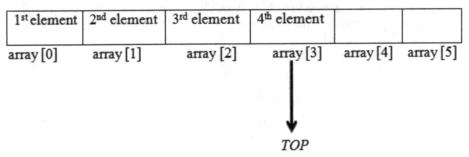

FIGURE 1.4 Memory representation of a stack.

1.2.8 Linked List

The major drawback of the array is that the size or the number of elements must be known in advance. Thus, this drawback gave rise to the new concept of a linked list. *A Linked list is a linear collection of data elements.* These data elements are called nodes, which point to the next node using pointers. *A linked list is a sequence of nodes in which each node contains one or more than one data field and a pointer which points to the next node.* Also, linked lists are dynamic; that is, memory is allocated as and when required.

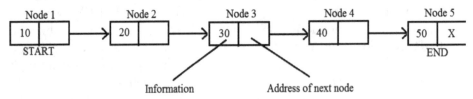

FIGURE 1.5 Memory representation of a linked list.

In the previous figure we have made a linked list in which each node is divided into two slots:

1. The first slot contains the information/data.

2. The second slot contains the address of the next node.

Practical Application:

A simple real-life example is a train; here each coach is connected to its previous and next coach (except the first and last coach).

The address part of the last node stores a special value called NULL, which denotes the end of the linked list. The advantage of a linked list over arrays is that now it is easier to insert and delete data elements, as we don't have to do shifting each time. On the contrary, searching for an element has become difficult. Also, more time is required to search for an element, and it also requires high memory space. Hence, linked lists are used where a collection of data elements is required, and the number of data elements in the collection is not known to us in advance.

Frequently Asked Questions

Q4. Define the term linked list.

Answer.
A linked list or one-way list is a linear collection of data elements called nodes, where pointers give the linear order. It is a popular dynamic data structure. The nodes in the linked list are not stored in consecutive memory locations. For every data item in a node of the linked list, there is an associated pointer that would give the address location of the next node in the linked list.

1.2.9 Trees

A tree is a popular non-linear data structure in which the data elements or the nodes are represented in a hierarchical order. Here, one of the nodes is shown as the root node of the tree, and the remaining nodes are partitioned into two disjointed sets such that each set is a part of a subtree. A tree makes the searching process very easy, and its recursive programming makes a program optimized and easy to understand.

A binary tree is the simplest form of a tree. *A binary tree consists of a root node and two subtrees known as the left subtree and the right subtree, where both subtrees are also binary trees.* Each node in a tree consists of three parts, that is, the extreme left part stores a pointer which points to the left subtree, the middle part will consist of the data element, and the extreme right part stores a pointer which points to the right subtree. The root is the topmost element of the tree. When there are no nodes in a tree, that is, when ROOT = NULL, then it is called an empty tree.

For example, consider a binary tree where R is the root node of the tree. LEFT and RIGHT are the left and right subtrees of R respectively. A is designated as the root node of the tree. Nodes B and C are the left and right child of A respectively. Nodes B, D, E, and G constitute the left subtree of the root. Similarly, nodes C, F, H, and I constitute the right subtree of the root.

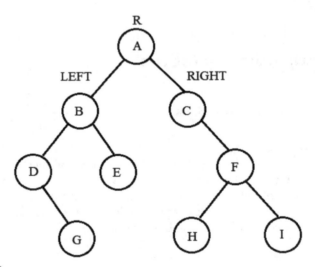

FIGURE 1.6 A binary tree.

Advantages of a tree

1. The searching process is very fast in trees.

2. Insertion and deletion of the elements have become easier as compared to other data structures.

Frequently Asked Questions

Q5. Define binary tree.

Answer.

A binary tree is a hierarchal data structure in which each node has at most two children, that is, a left and right child. In a binary tree, the degree of each node can be at most two. Binary trees are used to implement binary search trees, which are used for efficient searching and sorting. A binary tree is a popular subtype of a k-ary tree, where k is 2.

1.2.10 Graphs

A graph is a general tree with no parent-child relationship. It is a non-linear data structure which consists of vertices, also called nodes, and the edges which connect those vertices to one another. In a graph, any complex relationship can exist. A graph G may be defined as a finite set of V vertices and E edges. Therefore, G = (V, E) where V is the set of vertices and E is the set of edges. Graphs are used in various applications of mathematics and computer science. Unlike a root node in trees, graphs don't have root nodes; rather, the nodes can be connected to any node in the graph. Two nodes are termed as neighbors when they are connected via an edge.

Practical Application:

A real-life example of a graph can be seen in workstations where several computers are joined to one another via network connections.

For example, consider a graph G with six vertices and eight edges. Here, Q and Z are neighbors of P. Similarly, R and T are neighbors of S.

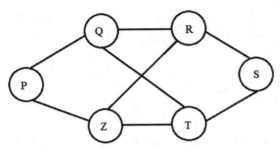

FIGURE 1.7 A graph.

1.3 Operations on Data Structures

Here we will discuss various operations which are performed on data structures.

- **Creation** – It is the process of creating a data structure. Declaration and initialization of the data structure are done here. It is the first operation.

- **Insertion** – It is the process of adding new data elements in the data structure, for example, to add the details of an employee who has recently joined an organization.

- **Deletion** – It is the process of removing a particular data element from the given collection of data elements, for example, to remove the name of an employee who has left the company.

- **Updating** – It is the process of modifying the data elements of a data structure. For example, if the address of a student is changed, then it should be updated.

- **Searching** – It is used to find the location of a particular data element or all the data elements with the help of a given key, for example, to find the names of people who live in New York.

- **Sorting** – It is the process of arranging the data elements in some order, that is, either ascending or descending order. An example is arranging the names of students of a class in alphabetical order.

- **Merging** – It is the process of combining the data elements of two different lists to form a single list of data elements.

- **Traversal** – It is the process of accessing each data element exactly once so that it can be processed. An example is to print the names of all the students of a class.

- **Destruction** – It is the process of deleting the entire data structure. It is the last operation in the data structure.

1.4 Algorithms

An algorithm is a systematic set of instructions combined to solve a complex problem. It is a step-by-finite-step sequence of instructions, each of which has a clear meaning and can be executed in a minimum amount of effort in finite time. In general, an algorithm is a blueprint for writing a program to solve the problem. Once we have a blueprint of the solution, we can easily implement it in any high-level language like C, C++, and so forth. It solves the problem into the finite number of steps. An algorithm written in a programming language is known as a program. A computer is a machine with no brain or intelligence. Therefore, the computer must be instructed to perform a given task in unambiguous steps. Hence, a programmer must define his problem in the form of an algorithm written in English. Thus, such an algorithm should have following features:

1. An algorithm should be simple and concise.

2. It should be efficient and effective.

3. It should be free of ambiguity; that is, the logic must be clear.

Similarly, an algorithm must have following characteristics:

- **Input** – It reads the data of the given problem.

- **Output** – The desired result must be produced.

- **Process/Definiteness** – Each step or instruction must be unambiguous.

- **Effectiveness** – Each step should be accurate and concise. The desired result should be produced within a finite time.

- **Finiteness** – The number of steps should be finite.

1.4.1 Developing an Algorithm

To develop an algorithm, some steps are suggested:

1. Defining or understanding the problem.

2. Identifying the result or output of the problem.

3. Identifying the inputs required by the problem and choosing the best input.

4. Designing the logic from the given inputs to get the desired output.

5. Testing the algorithm for different inputs.

6. Repeating the above steps untill it produces the desired result for all the inputs.

1.5 Approaches for Designing an Algorithm

A complicated algorithm is divided into smaller units which are called modules. Then these modules are further divided into sub-modules. Thus, in this way, a complex algorithm can easily be solved. The process of dividing an algorithm into modules is called modularization. There are two popular approaches for designing an algorithm:

- Top-Down Approach
- Bottom-Up Approach

Now let us understand both approaches.

1. Top-Down Approach – *A top-down approach states that the complex/complicated problem/algorithm should be divided into a smaller number*

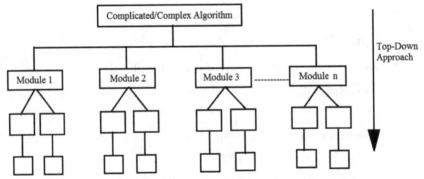

These sub modules can further be divided into one or more sub modules.

FIGURE 1.8 Top-down approach.

of one or more modules. These smaller modules are further divided into one or more sub-modules. This process of decomposition is repeated until we achieve the desired output of module complexity. A top-down approach starts from the topmost module, and the modules are incremented accordingly untill a level is reached where we don't require any more sub-modules, that is, the desired level of complexity is achieved.

2. **Bottom-Up Approach** – A bottom-up algorithm design approach is the opposite of a top-down approach. *In this kind of approach, we first start with designing the basic modules and proceed further toward designing the high-level modules.* The sub-modules are grouped together to form a module of a higher level. Similarly, all high-level modules are grouped to form more high-level modules. Thus, this process of combining the sub-modules is repeated until we obtain the desired output of the algorithm.

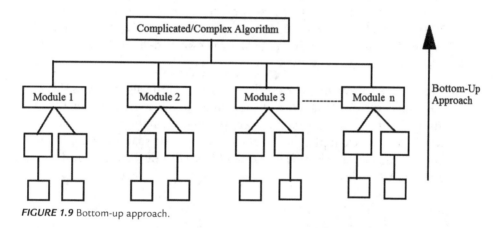

FIGURE 1.9 Bottom-up approach.

1.6 Analyzing an Algorithm

An algorithm can be analyzed by two factors, that is, space and time. We aim to develop an algorithm that makes the best use of both these resources. Analyzing an algorithm measures the efficiency of the algorithm. The efficiency of the algorithm is measured in terms of speed and time complexity. The complexity of an algorithm is a function that measures the space and time used by an algorithm in terms of input size.

Time Complexity – *The time complexity of an algorithm is the amount of time taken by an algorithm to run the program completely. It is the running time of the program.* The time complexity of an algorithm depends upon the input size. The time complexity is commonly represented by using big O notation. For example, the time complexity of a linear search is O(n).

Space Complexity – *The space complexity of an algorithm is the amount of memory space required to run the program completely.* The space complexity of an algorithm depends upon the input size.

Time Complexity is categorized into three types:

1. **Best Case Running Time** – The performance of the algorithm will be best under optimal conditions. For example, the best case for a binary search occurs when the desired element is the middle element of the list. Another example can be of sorting; that is, if the elements are already sorted in a list, then the algorithm will execute in best time.

2. **Average Case Running Time** – It denotes the behavior of an algorithm when the input is randomly drawn from a given collection or distribution. It is an estimate of the running time for "average" input. It is usually assumed that all inputs of a given size are likely to occur with equal probability.

3. **Worst Case Running Time** – The behavior of the algorithm in this case concerns the worst possible case of input instance. The worst case running time of an algorithm is an upper bound on the running time for any input. For example, the worst case for a linear search occurs when the desired element is the last element in the list or the element does not exist in the list.

Frequently Asked Questions

Q6. Define the time complexity.

Answer.
Time complexity is a measure which evaluates the count of the operations performed by a given algorithm as a function of the size of the input. It is the approximation of the number of steps necessary to execute an algorithm. It is commonly represented with asymptotic notation, that is, O(g) notation, also known as big O notation, where g is the function of the size of the input data.

1.6.1 Time-Space Trade-Off

In computer science, time-space trade-off is a way of solving a particular problem either in less time and more memory space or in more time and less memory space. But if we talk in practical terms, designing such an algorithm in which we can save both space and time is a challenging task. So, we can use more than one algorithm to solve a problem. One may require less time, and the other may require less memory space to execute. Therefore, we sacrifice one thing for the other. Hence, there exists a time-space or time-memory trade-off between algorithms. Thus, this time-space trade-off gives the programmer a rational choice from an informed point of view. So, if time is a big concern for a programmer, then he or she might choose a program which takes less or the minimum time to execute. On the other hand, if space is a prime concern for a programmer, then, in that case, he or she might choose a program that takes less memory space to execute at the cost of more time.

1.7 Abstract Data Types

An abstract data type (ADT) is a popular mathematical model of the data objects which define a data type along with various functions that operate on these objects. To understand the meaning of an abstract data type, we will simply break the term into two parts, that is, "data type" and "abstract." The data type of a variable is a collection of values which a variable can take. There are various data types in C that include integer, float, character, long, double, and so on. When we talk about the term "abstract" in the context of data structures, it means apart from detailed specification. It can be considered as a description of the data in a structure with a list of operations to be executed on the data within the structure. Thus, an abstract data type is the specification of a data type that specifies the mathematical and logical model of the data type. For example, when we use stacks and queues, then at that point of time our prime concern is only with the data type and the operations to be performed on those structures. We are not worried about how the data will be stored in the memory. Also, we don't bother about how push() and pop() operations work. We just know that we have two functions available to us, so we have to use them for insertion and deletion operations.

1.8 Big O Notation

The performance of an algorithm, that is, time and space requirements, can be easily compared with other competitive algorithms using asymptotic notations such as the big O notation, the Omega notation, and the Theta notation. The algorithmic complexity can be easily approximated using asymptotic notations by simply ignoring the implementation dependent factors. For instance, we can compare various available sorting algorithms using big O notation or any other asymptotic notation.

Big O notation is one of the popular analysis characterization schemes, since it provides an upper bound on the complexity of an algorithm. In big O, $O(g)$ is representative of the class of all functions that grow no faster than g. Therefore, if $f(n) = O(g(n))$ then $f(n) <= c(g(n))$ for all $n > n_0$ where n_0 represents a threshold and c represents a constant.

An algorithm with $O(1)$ complexity is referred to as a constant computing time algorithm. Similarly, an algorithm with $O(n)$ complexity is referred to as a linear algorithm, $O(n^2)$ for quadratic algorithms, $O(2_n)$ for exponential time algorithms, $O(n^k)$ for polynomial time algorithms, and $O(\log n)$ for logarithmic time algorithms.

An algorithm with complexity of the order of $O(\log_2 n)$ is considered as one of the best algorithms, while an algorithm with complexity of the order of $O(2^n)$ is considered as the worst algorithm. The complexity of computations or the number of iterations required in various types of functions may be compared as follows:

$$O(\log_2 n) < O(n) < O(n \log_2 n) < O(n^2) < O(n^3) < O(2^n)$$

1.9 Summary

- A data structure determines a way of storing and organizing the data elements in the computer memory. Data means a value or a collection of values. Structure refers to a way of organizing the data. The mathematical or logical representation of data in the memory is referred as a data structure.

- Data structures are classified into various types which include linear and non-linear data structures, primitive and non-primitive data structures, static and dynamic data structures, and homogeneous and non-homogeneous data structures.

- A linear data structure is one in which the data elements are stored in a linear or sequential order, that is, data is stored in consecutive memory locations. A non-linear data structure is one in which the data is not stored in any sequential order or consecutive memory locations.

- A static data structure is a collection of data in memory which is fixed in size and cannot be changed during runtime. A dynamic data structure is a collection of data in which memory can be reallocated during execution of a program.

- Primitive data structures are fundamental data structures or predefined data structures which are supported by a programming language. Non-primitive data structures are comparatively more complicated data structures that are created using primitive data structures.

- A homogeneous data structure is one that contains all data elements of the same type. A non-homogeneous data structure contains data elements of different types.

- An array is a collection of *homogeneous* (similar) types of data elements in *contiguous* memory.

- A queue is a linear collection of data elements in which the element inserted first will be the element taken out first, that is, a FIFO data structure. A queue is a linear data structure, in which the first element is inserted from one end called the REAR end and the deletion of the element takes place from the other end called the FRONT end.

- A linked list is a sequence of nodes in which each node contains one or more than one data field and a pointer which points to the next node.

- A stack is a linear collection of data elements in which insertion and deletion take place only at one end called the TOP of the stack. A stack is a Last In First Out (LIFO) data structure, because the last element added to the top of the stack will be the first element to be deleted from the top of the stack.

- A tree is a non-linear data structure in which the data elements or the nodes are represented in a hierarchical order. Here, an initial node is designated as the root node of the tree, and the remaining nodes are partitioned into two disjointed sets such that each set is a part of a subtree.

- A binary tree is the simplest form of a tree. A binary tree consists of a root node and two subtrees known as the left subtree and right subtree, where both the subtrees are also binary trees.

- A graph is a general tree with no parent-child relationship. It is a non-linear data structure which consists of vertices or nodes and the edges which connect those vertices with one another.

- An algorithm is a systematic set of instructions combined to solve a complex problem. It is a step-by-finite-step sequence of instructions, each of which has a clear meaning and can be executed in a minimum amount of effort in finite time.

- The process of dividing an algorithm into modules is called modularization.

- The time complexity of an algorithm is described as the amount of time taken by an algorithm to run the program completely. It is the running time of the program.

- The space complexity of an algorithm is the amount of memory space required to run the program completely.

- An ADT (Abstract Data Type) is a mathematical model of the data objects which define a data type as well as the functions to operate on these objects.

- Big O notation is one of the most popular analysis characterization schemes, since it provides an upper bound on the complexity of an algorithm.

1.10 Exercises

1. What do you understand by a good program?

2. Explain the classification of data structures.

3. What is an algorithm? Discuss the characteristics of an algorithm.

4. What are the various operations that can be performed on the data structures? Explain each of them with an example.

5. Differentiate an array with a linked list.

6. Explain the terms time complexity and space complexity.

7. What do you understand by the complexity of an algorithm?

8. Write a short note on graphs.

9. What is the process of modularization?

10. Differentiate between stacks and queues with examples.

11. What is meant by abstract data types (ADT)? Explain in detail.

12. Discuss the worst case, best case, and average case time complexity of an algorithm.

13. Write a brief note on trees.

14. Explain how you can develop an algorithm to solve a complex problem.

15. Explain time-memory trade-off in detail.

1.11 Multiple Choice Questions

1. Which of the data structures is a FIFO data structure?

   A. Array

   B. Stacks

   C. Queues

   D. Linked List

2. How many maximum children can a binary tree have?

   A. 0

   B. 2

   C. 1

   D. 3

3. Which of the following data structures uses dynamic memory allocation?

   A. Graphs

   B. Linked Lists

   C. Trees

   D. All of these

4. In a queue, deletion is always done from the _____

   A. Front end

   B. Rear end

   C. Middle

   D. None of these

5. Which data structure is used to represent complex relationships between the nodes?

   A. Linked Lists

   B. Trees

   C. Stacks

   D. Graphs

6. Which of the following is an example of a heterogeneous data structure?

   A. Array

   B. Structure

   C. Linked list

   D. None of these

7. In a stack, insertion and deletion takes place from the _____

   A. Bottom

   B. Middle

   C. Top

   D. All of these

8. Which of the following is not part of the Abstract Data Type (ADT) description?

   A. Operations

   B. Data

   C. Both (a) and (b)

   D. None of the above

9. Which of the following data structures allows deletion at both ends of the list but insertion at one end only?

   A. Stack

   B. Input Restricted Dequeue

   C. Output Restricted Dequeue

   D. Priority Queue

10. Which of the following data structures is a linear type?

    A. Trees

    B. Graphs

    C. Queues

    D. None of the above

11. Which one of the following is beneficial when the data is stored and has to be retrieved in reverse order?

    A. Stack

    B. Linked List

    C. Queue

    D. All of the above

12. A binary search tree whose left and right subtree differ in height by 1 at most is a _____

    A. Red Black Tree

    B. M way search tree

    C. AVL Tree

    D. None of the above

13. The operation of processing each element in the list is called _____

    A. Traversal

    B. Merging

    C. Inserting

    D. Sorting

14. Which of the following are the two primary measures of the efficiency of an algorithm?

A. Data & Time

B. Data & Space

C. Time & Space

D. Time & Complexity

15. Which one of the following cases does not exist/occur in complexity theory?

A. Average Case

B. Worst Case

C. Best Case

D. Minimal Case

INTRODUCTION TO THE C LANGUAGE

In This Chapter

- Introduction
- Header files in C
- Main function
- Input and output methods
- Character set used in C
- C tokens
- Data types in C
- Operators in C
- Decision control statements in C
- Looping statements in C
- Break and continue statements
- Functions in C
- Recursion
- Structures in C
- Pointers
- Summary
- Exercises
- Multiple choice questions

2.1 Introduction

C is a high-level programming language which was developed by Denis Ritchie, a scientist of Bell Labs, in the early 1970s. *C is a powerful language, and it is widely used with the UNIX operating system, which is also an extensive and complex operating system.* C is a user-friendly language in which simple English words like `printf`, `scanf`, `if-else`, and so on are used as statements. Initially, C was developed for writing system software, but as we can see nowadays, it has become a common language such that a variety of different software programs are written using C language. C language is often called a middle-level language, as it not only provides different data types or data structures which are needed by a programmer, but it can also access the computer hardware with the help of specially designed functions and declarations. Many programmers are using C language to program all tasks because of its growing popularity. C is a case-sensitive language; that is, it distinguishes between uppercase letters and lowercase letters. Hence, C language is becoming popular because of the following:

- One reason for its popularity is its portability; that is, a program written in C language on one machine or computer can easily be transferred to another machine with minimal modification or with no modifications in it. Hence, it is a platform independent language.

- Programs written in C language are very efficient and fast.

- C supports various other programming languages, so in the future it will be easier for us to understand programs written in C.

- C language is a structured programming language; that is, it makes the user think of a problem regarding blocks or functions.

- C is more powerful and flexible than any other high-level language, as it uses/offers many more functions than any of the other programming languages.

- The most significant advantage of C language is that it is available to anyone and can be used on different types of personal computers.

- Programs written in C are small and efficient.

- C is a general-purpose language.

Frequently Asked Questions

Q1. Write important features of C.

Answer.

1. Flexibility – C is a powerful and flexible language. C is used for projects as an operating system, a word processor, for graphics and spreadsheets, and even as a compiler for other languages. As a result, a large variety of C compilers and accessories are available.

2. Portability – C is a portable language. Portable means that a C program written on one computer system can be run on another system with little or no modification.

3. Compactness – C code should be written in routines called functions. These functions can be reused in other applications or programs. By using pieces of information, we can create useful and reusable code.

2.2 Header Files in C

We all know that when we load a C compiler, some supporting files are stored on the disk. During programming, if we want those files or functions, first we have to include those functions or files in our program to use them. Thus, these files will be loaded from the disk into the memory where these files are called to perform the desired operations. *These files are known as header files.* For example, if we want to use the `printf()` and `scanf()` functions, then both of these functions are defined in a `stdio.h` header file. Also, there are various other functions provided by C compilers which are included in standard header files. Header files can be included by either of the following methods:

```
# include "header file"
# include <header file>
```

The following are some of the standard header files:

1. **`stdio.h`** – It includes standard input and output functions. Examples are `printf(), scanf(), gets(), puts()`, etc.

2. **`conio.h`** – It is used for clearing the screen or holding the screen. Examples are `getch(), clrscr(), getche()`, etc.

3. **string.h** – It includes string handling functions. Examples are strcpy(), strcmp(), strlen(), strcat(), etc.

4. **alloc.h** – It is used for dynamic memory allocation. Examples are malloc(), calloc(), free().

5. **math.h** – It includes all the mathematical functions. Examples are isalpha(), isdigit(), sin(), cos(), etc.

Frequently Asked Questions

Q2. What are header files?

Answer.
In C programming language, header files are a source code that contains standard definitions and data structures that all programmers may use as and when required. These are also called "include files," because the #include statement is used to incorporate them into C programs. Header files use the a.h extension.

2.3 Main Function

The main() function is a part of every C program. *A program cannot execute without the* main() *function.* The main() function is not terminated by any semicolon. C language permits various forms of the main() function:

- main()

- void main()

- int main()

The empty parentheses indicate that the function is without arguments. Also, the keywords void and int before the main() function mean that the function does not return any information and the function returns integer values to the operating system respectively. Remember that when int is used before main(), then the last statement must have a "return 0" statement.

2.4 Input and Output Methods

The most common operations in a C program is to accept the input values from a standard input device and to display the data produced by the program by a standard output device. One way of assigning the values is inputting the values from the user at the beginning of the program, for example, int x = 5. The other way of assigning the values is inputting the values from the user at runtime. Thus, there are various functions in C which are used for assigning the values at runtime. One of the commonly used functions is the scanf() function.

scanf() function – It is used to read any kind of data from the keyboard. The general syntax of the scanf() function is:

Syntax - scanf("specifier/ control string", arguments) ;

The control string or the specifier specifies the type of data that has to be entered from the keyboard. The arguments are the address of the variables which are stored in the memory locations. Each control string starts with a %. Various control strings are as follows:

Control String	Description
%d, %i	Integer values
%u	Unsigned integer values
%e, %f, %g	Floating type values
%c	Character values
%s	String of characters

The scanf() function ignores any blank spaces entered by the user. This function returns the number of inputs which are successfully scanned and stored. The scanf() function is used as follows:

```
int number ;
scanf("%d", &number) ;
```

Now, there is another function which is used for displaying the data entered by the user. This function is the printf() function.

printf() function – It is used to display the data required by the user and print the values of the variables on the screen. The general syntax for printf() function is:

Syntax - printf("specifier/ control string", arguments) ;

The control strings and arguments are discussed previously.

The `printf()` function is used as follows:

```
printf("Hello World!!") ;
```

2.5 Character Set Used in C

The character set allowed in C consists of following characters:

1. **Alphabet** – It includes uppercase as well as lowercase letters of English, i.e., {A, B, C . . ., Z} and {a, b, c . . ., z}.

2. **Digits** – It includes decimal digits, i.e. {0, 1, 2 . . ., 9}.

3. **White Spaces** – It includes spaces, enters, and tabs.

4. **Special Characters** – It consists of special symbols which include {, !, ?, #, <, >, (,), %, ", &, ^, °, <<, >>, [,], +, =, /, -, _, :, ;, }.

2.6 C Tokens

C tokens help us to write a program in C. C supports various types of tokens:

- Keywords
- Identifiers
- Constants
- Variables

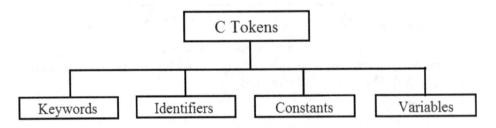

FIGURE 2.1 Various C tokens.

Now, let us discuss all of them.

Keywords – *Keywords in C are the reserved words which have a special meaning*. They are written in lower case. *Keywords cannot be used as* *identifiers*. For example: `auto`, `int`, `float`, `char`, `break`, `switch`, `continue`, `double`, `long`, `long double`, `short`, `unsigned`, `signed`, `while`, `for`, `else`, `void`, and so forth.

Identifiers – *An identifier is a name which is given to a constant, variable, function, or array.* The rules which are used to define identifiers are as follows:

1. An identifier can have letters, digits, or underscores.

2. It should not start with a digit.

3. It can start with an underscore or a letter.

4. An identifier cannot have special symbols.

5. A keyword cannot be used as an identifier.

For example:

Acceptable Identifiers	Unacceptable Identifiers
a345_	au to
c_65	12d
average	n 3_

Constants – *Constants are the fixed values in C that can never be changed.* These are used to define fixed values in a program. For example, the value of pi is always fixed. A constant can be of any basic data types like an integer constant, a character constant, or a float constant.

Integer Constant – It is a constant to which only the integer values are assigned. For example, `const int area = 1000;`

Character Constant – It is a constant to which only the character values are assigned. For example, `const char Malhotra = 'A';`

Float Constant – It is a constant to which only the real or floating type values are assigned. For example, `const float pi = 3.1427;`

Variables – A variable is a name which is used to refer to some memory location. While working with a variable, we refer to the address of the memory where the data is stored. C supports two types of variables, which include character variables and numeric variables.

Numeric Variables – These are used to store the integer or floating type values.

Character Variables – In this variable, single characters are enclosed in single quotes.

Frequently Asked Questions

Q3. Write any five keywords in C language.

Answer.

1. if

2. switch

3. do

4. while

5. for

Frequently Asked Questions

Q4. Which of the following are invalid identifiers and why?

1. static

2. January 2

3. VIPS

4. 2VSIT

Answer.

(i) static is a keyword, and as per convention one should not use a keyword as an identifier, so static is an invalid identifier.

(ii) January 2 is an invalid identifier as an identifier can't have spaces.

(iii) VIPS is a valid identifier.

(iv) 2VSIT is an invalid identifier as the identifier cannot start with a numeral.

2.7 Data Types in C

Data types are the special keywords which define the type of data and the amount of data a variable is holding. Data types are categorized into three categories:

- Basic (Primary) Data Types
- Modified Data Types
- Derived Data Types

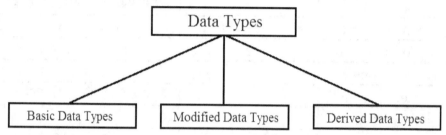

FIGURE 2.2 Categorization of data types.

Basic Data Types

These are primary data types available in C.

Data Type	Bytes (in memory)	Range
Int	2	-32,768 to 32,767
char	1	-128 to 127
double	8	-1.7×10^{-308} to $1.7 \times 10^{+308}$
float	4	-3.4×10^{-38} to $3.4 \times 10^{+38}$

Modified Data Types

Modified data types are those data types which are created by altering the basic data types with the help of some keywords.

- **Integer –** unsignedint (positive values only), signed int (positive as well as negative values), short int, long int, signed long int, unsigned short int, signed short int, unsigned long int.

- **Character** – `unsigned char, signed char.`
- **Double** – `long double`

Further classification is shown in the following table.

Data Type	Bytes (in memory)	Range
unsigned int	2	0 to 65535
signed int	2	-32,768 to 32,767
short int	2	-32,768 to 32,767
long int	4	-2147483648 to 2147483647
unsigned short int	2	0 to 65535
signed short int	2	-32,768 to 32,767
unsigned long int	4	0 to 4294967294
signed long int	4	2147483648 to 2147483647
unsigned char	1	0 – 255
signed char	1	-128 to 127
long double	10	-3.4×10^{-493} to $1.1 \times 10^{+493}$

Derived Data Types

Derived data types are those data types which are created using basic as well as modified data types. These include arrays, structures, unions, enumerations, and so on.

2.8 Operators in C

Operators in C are used to perform some specific operations between the different variables and constants. C supports a variety of operators, which are given as follows:

- Arithmetic Operators
- Logical Operators
- Assignment Operators
- Relational Operators/ Comparison Operators
- Condition Operators/ Ternary Operators
- Bitwise Operators

- Comma Operators

- Unary Operators/ Increment and Decrement Operators

- sizeof Operators

Now, let us discuss all of these operators.

Arithmetic Operators

Arithmetic Operators are those operators which are used in mathematical computation or calculation. The valid arithmetic operators in C are given in the following table

Let x and y be the two variables.

Operator	Operation	Example
+	Addition	x + y
-	Subtraction	x − y
*	Multiplication	x * y
%	Remainder/ Modulus	x % y
/	Division	x / y

Logical Operators

C supports three types of logical operators, which are given as follows:

Operator	Description	Example
!	Logical NOT	!x, !y
&&	Logical AND	x && y
||	Logical OR	x || y

Logical NOT – It is a unary operator. This operator takes a single expression, and it inverts the result such that true becomes false and vice versa. The truth table for logical NOT is given as follows:

x	y	!x	!y
0	1	1	0
1	0	0	1

Logical AND – It is a binary operator. Hence, it takes two inputs or expressions. If both the inputs are true, then the whole expression is true.

If both or even any one of the inputs is false, then the whole expression will be false. The truth table for logical AND is given as follows:

X	Y	X && Y
0	0	0
0	1	0
1	0	0
1	1	1

Logical OR – It is also a binary operator; that is, it also takes two expressions. If both the inputs are false, then the output is false. If a single input or both of the inputs are true, then the output will be true. The truth table for logical OR is given as follows:

X	Y	X || Y
0	0	0
0	1	1
1	0	1
1	1	1

Assignment Operators

Assignment operators are ones which are responsible for assigning values to the variables. These operators are always evaluated from right to left. C supports various assignment operators, which are given in the following table:

Operators	Example
=	x = 5, y = 8
+=	x += y :– x = x + y
–=	x -= y :– x = x – y
*=	x * = y :– x = x * y
%=	x %= y :– x = x % y
/=	x /= y :– x = x / y

Relational Operators

Relational operators are used for comparison between two values or expressions. They are also known as comparison operators. These operators are always evaluated from left to right. The various relational operators used in C are as follows:

Operators	Description	Example
>	Greater than	x > y
<	Less than	x < y
==	Equal to	x == y
>=	Greater than equal to	x >= y
<=	Less than equal to	x <= y
!=	Not equal to	x != y

Conditional Operators

The conditional operator is also known as a ternary operator regarding input; it accepts three operands. The syntax of this operator is as follows:

Syntax – (Expression 1) ?(Expression 2) :(Expression 3) ;

Where, expression 1 is first evaluated. If expression 1 is true, then expression 2 is evaluated and expression 2 will be the answer of this whole expression, else expression 3 is evaluated and expression 3 will be the answer of this whole expression. Conditional Operators can be used to find the larger of two numbers.

Greatest = (x > y) ?x : y ;

Here, if x > y is true, then x is greater than y; that is, (greatest = x) else y is greater than x, that is, (greatest = y).

Bitwise Operators

Bitwise operators are the special operators that are used to perform operations at the bit level. C supports various types of bitwise operators which include the following:

Operators	Description
<<	Right shift
>>	Left shift
&	Bitwise AND
|	Bitwise OR
^	Bitwise XOR

Comma Operator

The comma operator is used to chain together some expressions. First, it evaluates the first expression and discards its value. It then evaluates the second expression, and the calculated result of this expression is returned as the final output. The expressions separated by a comma operator are evaluated in a sequence starting from the left to the right. It has the lowest precedence of all the operators in C. For example, the following statement is given:

$$x = (y = 10 , y - 7) ;$$

Comma Operator

Hence, in the previous example, y has been assigned a value 10. Now y is decremented by 7. So, the value of the expression (y – 7) will be 3 and is assigned to x. Thus, the final value of x = 3.

Unary Operators

A unary operator is one which requires only a single operand to work. C supports two unary operators, which are increment (++) and decrement (--) operators. These operators are used to increase or decrease the value of a variable by one respectively. There are two variants of increment and decrement operators, which are postfix and prefix. In a postfix expression, the operator is applied after the operand. On the other hand, in a prefix expression the operator is applied before the operand.

Operator	Postfix	Prefix
Increment (++)	x++	++x
Decrement (--)	--x	--x

Remember, x++ is not same as ++x; in x++ the value is returned first, and then the value is incremented. In ++x, the value is returned after it is incremented. Similarly, x--is not same as --x. It is true that both these operators increment or decrement the value by 1. For example, b = a ++ is equivalent to

1. b = a,

2. a = a + 1.

Similarly, b = -- a is equivalent to

1. a = a – 1,

2. b = a.

sizeof Operator

The sizeof operator is a unary operator that returns the size of an object, a variable, or a data type in bytes. It is used to determine the amount of memory storage a variable or a data type will take. It is written in the following manner: the keyword `sizeof` is followed by a variable/ expression. A `sizeof` operator has the same precedence as that of unary operators. For example, if we have,

```
int x = 100;
```

Then, answer = `sizeof(x) = 2;`

Therefore, the final answer will be 2 as x is an integer, so it takes 2 bytes of storage space.

Frequently Asked Questions

Q5. What do you mean by the ternary operator?

Answer.

The conditional operator consists of two symbols, the question mark (?) and the colon (:). The syntax for the ternary operator is as follows:

exp1 ? exp2 : exp3

The ternary operator works as follows:

Expression 1 is evaluated first. If the expression is true, then expression 2 is evaluated and its value becomes the value of the expression. If expression 1 is false, expression 3 is evaluated and its value becomes the value of the expression. Note that only one of the expressions is evaluated.

2.9 Decision Control Statements in C

Whenever we talk of a program written in C language, we know that a C program will always execute sequentially, that is, line by line. Initially, the first line will be executed. Then, the second line will execute after the execution of the first line and so on. *Control statements are those that enable a programmer to execute a particular block of code and specify the order in which the various instructions of code are required to be executed.* It determines the flow of control. Control statements define how the control is transferred to other parts of a program. Hence, they are also called decision control statements. A decision control statement is one that helps us to jump from one point of a program to another. A decision control statement is executed in C using the following:

- If statement

- If-else statement

- Nested If-else statement

- Switch Case statement

Now, let us discuss all of them.

If Statement

An If statement is a bidirectional control statement which is used to test the condition and take one of the possible actions. It is the simplest decision control statement and is used very frequently in decision making. The general syntax of an If statement is as follows:

```
if (condition)
   {
     Statement Block of if;      //If condition is true, execute the state-
                                    ments of if.

   }
Statements Block under if;
```

An If statement will check the condition, and if the condition is true then the set of statements under the if block will be executed; otherwise, the set of statements below the if block will be executed. The If block can have one or multiple statements enclosed within curly brackets. Also, the

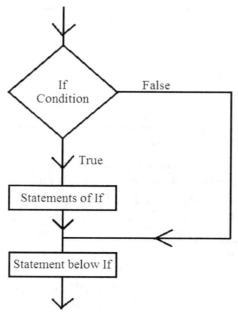

FIGURE 2.3 If statement flow diagram.

else block is optional in a simple if statement because if the condition is false, then the control directly jumps to the next statement. Remember, there is no semicolon after the condition because the condition and the statement should be put as a single statement.

For example:

```
#include <stdio.h>
void main()
{
  int x, y ;
  printf("\n Enter two values: ") ;
  scanf("%d %d", &x, &y) ;
  if (y > x)
    {
      printf("\n %d is greater, y") ;
    }
  getch() ;
}
```

```
Output –
    Enter two values:
    23
    67
    67 is greater
```

If-Else Statement

After discussing the usage of the if statement, we learned that the if statement does nothing when the condition is false. It just passes the control to the next statement. The if-else statement takes care of this aspect. The general syntax of the if-else statement is as follows:

```
if (condition)
    {
       Statements X;          //If condition is true, execute the state-
                              ments of If.

    }
else
    {
       Statements Y;          //If condition is false, execute the statements
                              of else.

    }
```

The If-else statement will check the condition. If the condition is true, then the set of statements X is executed, and the else block is not executed. Otherwise, if the condition is false, then the set of statements Y is executed and the if block is not executed. The If or else blocks can contain one or multiple statements.

For example:

```
#include <stdio.h>
void main()
{
  int x, y ;
  printf("\n Enter two values: ") ;
  scanf("%d %d", &x, &y) ;
```

```
if (y < x)
  {
    printf("\n %d is smaller", y) ;
  }
else
  {
    printf("%d is smaller", x) ;
  }
getch() ;
}
```

Output –

Enter two values:
100
500
100 is smaller

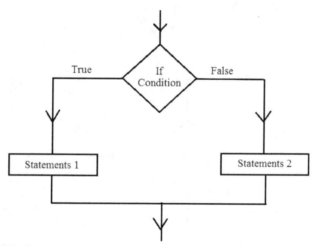

FIGURE 2.4 If-else statement flow diagram.

Nested If-Else Statement

The nested if-else statement is also known as the if-else-if ladder. The if-else-if statement works the same as that of a normal if statement. The general syntax of the if-else-if statement is as follows:

```
if (condition 1)
  {
    Statements 1;              //If condition 1 is true, execute
                                 the statements of If.

  }
else if (condition 2)
  {
    Statements 2;              //If condition 2 is true, execute
                                 the statements of else if.

  }
else
  {
    Statements 3;              //If condition 2 is false, execute the
                                 statements of else.

  }
```

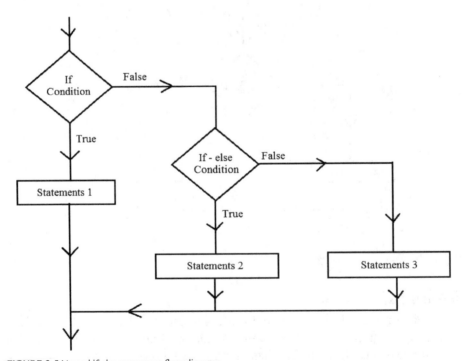

FIGURE 2.5 Nested if-else statement flow diagram.

An if-else-if ladder works in the following manner. First, the if condition is checked. If the condition is true, then the set of statements 1 is executed. If the condition is false, then the else-if condition is checked. If the else-if condition is true, then the set of statements 2 is executed. Otherwise, the set of statements 3 is executed. Remember, after the first if expression, we can have as many else if branches as are needed depending upon the number of expressions to be tested.

For Example:

```
#include <stdio.h>
void main()
{
  int x, y, z ;
  printf("\n Enter three values: ") ;
  scanf("%d %d %d", &x, &y, &z) ;
  if (x > y && x > z)
    {
      printf("\n %d is greater", x) ;
    }
  else if (y > x && y > z)
    {
      printf("%d is greater", y) ;
    }
  else
    {
      printf("%d is greater", z) ;
    }
  getch() ;
}
```

Output –

Enter three values:

10

50

30

50 is greater

SWITCH Statement

As we all know an if statement is used to check the given condition and choose one option depending upon whether the condition is true or false. But if we have several options to choose from, then it will be not a good thing to use if statements for each option as it will become very complex. Hence, to avoid such a problem, a switch statement is used. *The switch statement is a multidirectional conditional control statement. It is a simplified version of an if-else-if statement. It selects one option from the number of options available to us. Thus, it is also known as selector statement.* Its execution is faster than an if-else-if construct. Also, a switch statement is comparatively easy to understand and debug. The general syntax of switch statement is as follows:

```
switch (choice)
{
  case constant 1:
  Statements 1 ;
  break ;

  case constant 2:
  Statements 2 ;
  break ;

  case constant 3:
  Statements 3 ;
  break ;
  .
  .
  .

  case constant n:
  Statements n ;
  break ;

  default:
  Statements D ;
}
```

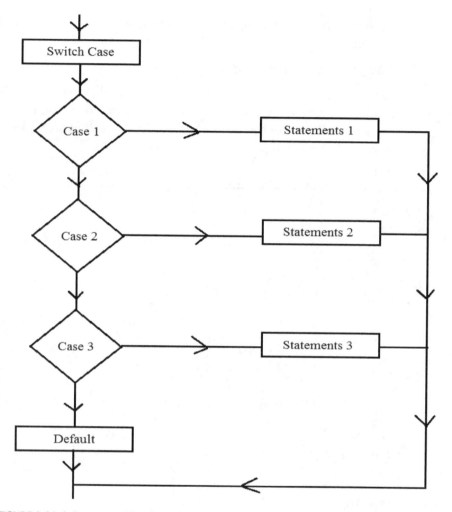

FIGURE 2.6 Switch statement flow diagram.

A switch statement works as follows:

- Initially, the value of the expression is compared with the case constants of the switch construct.

- If the value of the expression and the switch statement match, then its corresponding block is executed until a break is encountered. Once a break is encountered, the control comes out of the switch statement.

- If there is no match in the switch statements, then the set of statements of default is executed.

- All the values of the case constants must be unique.

- There can be only one default statement in the entire switch statement. A default statement is optional; if it is not present and there is no match with any of the case constants, then no action takes place. The control simply jumps out of the switch statement.

For example:

```c
# include<stdio.h>
void main()
{
  int choice ;
  printf("\n Enter your choice: ") ;
  scanf("%d", &ch) ;
  switch(ch)
    {
    case 1 :
    printf("First!!") ;
    break ;
    case 2 :
    printf("Second!!") ;
    break ;
    case 3 :
    printf("Third!!") ;
    break ;

    default :
    printf("wrong choice") ;
    }
  getch() ;
}
```

Output –

Enter your choice: 2
Second

Frequently Asked Questions

Q6. Which one is better—a switch case or an else if ladder?

Answer.

1. The switch permits the execution of more than one alternative, whereas an if statement does not. Various alternatives in an if statement are mutually exclusive, whereas alternatives may or may not be mutually exclusive within a switch statement.

2. A switch can only perform equality tests involving integer type or character type constants; an if statement, on the other hand, allows for more general comparison involving other data types as well.

When there are more than three or four conditions, use the switch case rather than a long nested if statement.

2.10 Looping Statements in C

Looping statements, also known as iterative statements, are the set of instructions which are executed repeatedly until a certain condition or expression becomes false. This kind of repetitive execution of the statements in a program is called a loop. Loops can be categorized into two categories: pre-deterministic loops and deterministic loops. Pre-deterministic loops are ones in which the number of times a loop will execute is known. On the contrary, loops in which it is not known how many times it will execute are called deterministic loops. C supports three types of loops, which include the following:

- While Loop

- Do-while Loop

- For Loop

Now, let us discuss all these loops in detail.

WHILE Loop

A while loop is a loop which is used to repeat a set of one or more instructions/ statements until a particular condition becomes false. In a while loop, the condition is checked before executing the body of the loop or any state-ments in the statements block. Hence, a while loop is also called an entry control loop. A while loop is a deterministic loop, as the number of times it will execute is known to us. The general syntax of while loop is as follows:

```
while (condition)
   {
     block of statements/ body of loop ;
     increment/ decrement ;
   }
```

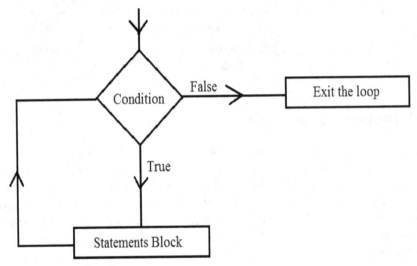

FIGURE 2.7 While loop flow diagram.

A while loop is executed as follows:

1. The condition is tested.

2. If the condition is true, then the statement is executed, and step 1 is repeated.

3. If the condition is false, then the loop is terminated, and the control jumps out to execute the rest of the program.

For Example:

```
# include<stdio.h>
void main()
{
  inti = 1 ;
  while (i < 10)
    {
      printf("\t %d", i) ;
      i = i + 1 ;
    }
  getch() ;
}
```

Output –

   1 2 3 4 5 6 7 8 9

In the above example, i is initialized to 1 and 1 is less than 10, and therefore the condition is true. Hence, the value of i is printed and is incremented by 1. The condition will become false when i becomes 10; thus, at that condition the loop will end.

DO-WHILE Loop

A do-while loop is similar to a while loop. The only difference is that, unlike a while loop in which a condition is checked at the start of the loop, in a do-while loop the condition is checked at the end of the loop. Hence, it is also called an exit control loop. This implies that in a do-while loop the statements must be executed at least once even if the condition is false, because the condition is checked at the end of the loop. The general syntax for a do-while loop is as follows:

```
Do
{
  block of statements/ body of loop ;
  increment/ decrement ;
}  while (condition);
```

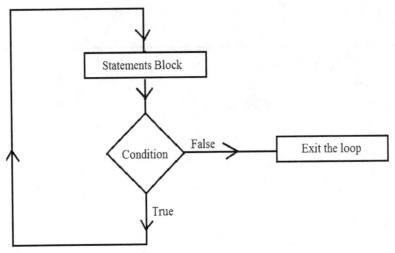

FIGURE 2.8 Do-while loop flow diagram.

The do-while loop continues to execute until the condition evaluates to false. A do-while loop is usually employed in the situations where we require the program to be executed at least once, for instance, menu-driven programs. One of the major disadvantages of using a do-while loop is that a do-while loop will always execute at least once even if the condition is false. Therefore, if the user enters some irrelevant data, it will still execute.

For Example:

```c
# include<stdio.h>
void main()
{
  int i = 0 ;
  do
   {
     printf("\t %d", i) ;
     i = i + 1 ;
   } while (i < 10) ;
  getch() ;
}
```
Output –
    0 1 2 3 4 5 6 7 8 9

In the above code, i is initialized to 0, so the value of i is printed and is incremented by 1. After executing the loop once, now the condition will be checked. Now i = 1 and the condition is true. Therefore, the loop will execute. The condition will become false when i becomes equal to 10. In that case, the loop will be terminated.

FOR Loop

A for loop is a pre-deterministic loop; that is, it is a count-controlled loop such that the programmer knows in advance how many times the for loop is to be executed. In the for loop, the loop variable is always initialized exactly once. The general syntax for the for loop is as follows:

```
for (initialization; condition; increment/decrement)
{
  block of statements/ body of loop ;
}
```

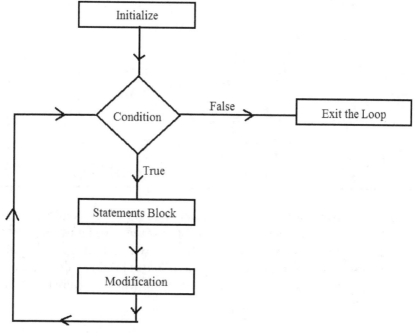

FIGURE 2.9 For loop flow diagram.

In a for loop, the condition is always checked at the top of the loop. Also, with every iteration of the loop, the variable and the condition are checked. If the condition is true, then the statements written within the for loop are executed; otherwise, the control moves out of the loop and the for loop is terminated. As we have seen in the syntax, initialization means to assign a particular value to a variable initially. Second, the condition specifies whether the loop will continue to execute or will terminate. The condition is checked with every iteration of the loop. Iteration means to update the value of a variable either by incrementing it or decrementing it. Also, each section in a for loop is separated by a semicolon. So, it is possible that one of the sections may be empty. For loops are widely used to execute a particular set of statements a limited number of times.

For Example:

```
# include<stdio.h>
void main()
{
  int x  ;
  for (x = 1 ; x <= 10 ; x++)
    {
      printf("\t %d", x) ;
    }
  getch() ;
}
```
Output –
```
    1 2 3 4 5 6 7 8 9 10
```

In the above example, x is a counter variable which is initialized to 1. Now, the condition is checked because 1 is less than 10. Thus, the condition is true, so the value of x is printed. After every iteration, the value of x is incremented and the condition is checked. The condition will become false when i become 11, so at that time the for loop will be terminated and the control will come out of the loop.

2.11 Break and Continue Statements

In C, break statements are used for loops and switch statements. They are used to terminate the execution of the loop. *A break statement causes an intermediate exit from the loop in which the statement appears.* We have already seen its use in the switch statements, as it is used to exit from a switch statement. When a break is encountered the control jumps out of the loop. The break statement is usually used in a situation in which either there is some error or if we don't want to execute the rest of the loop. It has a very simple syntax:

Syntax – `break;`

For example:

```
# include<stdio.h>
void main()
{
  int num = 0 ;
  while(num< 5)
    {
      if(num == 2)
        {
          printf("Hello!!") ;
          break ;
        }
      printf("\n Number = %d", num) ;
      num = num + 1 ;
    }
  getch() ;
}
```

Output –

```
Number = 0
Number = 1
Hello!!
```

In the previous code, when the value of num is equal to two, the break statement is executed and the control jumps out of the while loop following the next statement after the while loop. Hence, the break statement is used to exit from a loop at any point.

As we see a break statement is used to exit a particular loop, and a continue statement is used for doing the next iteration of the loop. Continue statements are also used with loops. Unlike with a break statement, the loop does not terminate when a continue statement is encountered. *A continue statement skips rest of the statements, and the control is transferred to the loop continuation portion of the loop.* Therefore, the execution of the loop resumes with the next iteration. The syntax of the continue statement is as follows:

Syntax –continue ;

For Example –

```
# include<stdio.h>
void main()
{
  int n ;
  for(n =0 ; n <= 8 ; n++)
    {
      if(n == 4)
      continue ;
      printf("\t %d", n) ;
    }
  getch() ;
}
```
Output -
    0 1 2 3 5 6 7 8

In the previous code, as soon as the value of n becomes equal to four, the continue statement is executed and the printf statement is skipped. The control is transferred to the expression, which increments the value of n. Hence, a control statement is the opposite of the break statement.

2.12 Functions in C

As C programmers, we often experience that the size of our program becomes too large and its complexity also increases. So, at that time it is very difficult for a programmer to read the entire code and also to check for any errors in it. Hence, to overcome this problem, *C language enables us to break the entire program into a smaller number of modules or segments. These modules or segments are called functions. Therefore, a function is a predefined block of code designed to perform a particular task.* Functions are used to improve the efficiency of the program. Functions can reduce redundancy and helps to understand the code easily. Each function is designed to perform a particular task. Functions are separated into two categories:

1. **Library Functions** – Library functions are those functions which are predefined in C under various libraries. These are the readymade functions available in C. These readymade functions do not require any coding to execute any operation. These functions can be directly used by just including the related header files, for example,

scanf(), printf(), gets(), puts(), strcpy(), and so on.

2. **User-Defined Functions** – Unlike predefined library functions, these functions can be defined by the programmer or user. We can easily create these types of functions. The general form of a user-defined function is as follows:

```
[return type] <Function name> [parameters/ arguments]
{
  Statements;
  return();
}
```

Where –

a) **Return Type** – Return types are used to identify which kind of value is going to be returned by the functions. Return types are the data types. If a function does not return any value, then the return type is void.

b) Function Name – It identifies the name of a function. The name of the function should not be reserved in the C libraries.

c) Parameters/Arguments – These are the variables or values passed with their data types to the functions for performing various operations.

d) Statements – Statements are the particular steps that are performed by the functions.

There are three things associated with functions, which are as follows:

1. Declaring a Function/ Function Declaration

A function must be declared before it is used. Declaring a function means the compiler must know in advance the number of parameters or arguments and the types of arguments which the function expects to receive and also the data type that the function will return to the calling program. The general form of declaring a function is `[return type] <Function name> [parameters/ arguments]` which has already been discussed.

2. Calling a Function/ Function Call

A function call is that call which transfers the control to the called function to execute the set of statements in that particular block/function. After calling a function and executing it, the control again jumps back to the calling function. There are two types of functions, that is, a calling function and a called function. A calling function is one which calls the function, and the called function is one which is called by the calling function. The general syntax for calling a particular function is – `<function name> (arguments/parameters)`. Arguments may be passed in the form of expressions to the called function.

3. Defining a Function/ Function Definition

After a function is called, then the function must be defined. Defining a function means space is allocated in the memory for that function. The number of arguments and their order must be the same as given in the function declaration. It comprises two parts, that is, the header of the function and the body of the function where `[return type] <Function name> [parameters/ arguments]` is the function header and the set of statements is the function body.

Frequently Asked Questions

Q7. Write down the benefits of using functions in C.

Answer.

1. Modular Programming – It facilitates top-down modular programming. The high-level logic of the overall problem is solved first while the details of each of the lower level functions are addressed later.

2. Reduction of source code – The length of the source program can be reduced by using functions at appropriate places.

3. Easier Debugging – It is easy to locate and isolate a faulty function for investigation.

4. Function Sharing – If a program is divided into smaller subprograms, each subprogram can be written by different team members rather than having the whole team work on a single complex program.

2.12.1 Structure of a Multifunctional Program

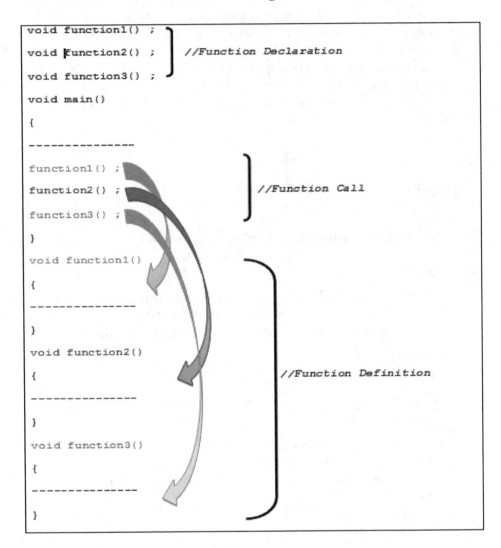

```
void function1() ;  ⎫
void function2() ;  ⎬   //Function Declaration
void function3() ;  ⎭
void main()
{
---------------
function1() ;  ⎫
function2() ;  ⎬   //Function Call
function3() ;  ⎭
}
void function1()
{
---------------
}
void function2()
{
---------------
}                        //Function Definition
void function3()
{
---------------
}
```

2.12.2 Passing Arguments to Functions

There are two ways to pass arguments or parameters to a function. These two ways are as follows:

1. Call by Value

2. Call by Reference

Let us now discuss both in detail.

Call by Value

This is a method in which the values are passed from the calling function to the called function. In this method, the called function creates copies of the actual values of the calling functions argument into its formal parameters. So, in this case, if the called function is supposed to change/modify the actual values of the parameters, then the changes will only be reflected in the called function. These changes will not be reflected in the calling function. This is because the changes which are made to the variables are not the actual variables, but the copies of the actual variables. Hence, this is known as call by value. By default, C programming uses the call by value method to pass the parameters/arguments.

For Example:

```
#include <stdio.h>
void swap(int, int) ;            //Declaration
void main()                      //Main function
{
  int a = 10, b = 20 ;
  swap(a, b) ;                   //Calling function
}
void swap(int a, int b)
{
  int temp ;
  temp = a ;
  a = b ;
  b = temp ;
  printf("\n After swapping a = %d and b = %d", a, b) ;
}
```
Output -

    After swapping a = 20 and b = 10

The major drawback of the call by value technique is that a lot of memory space is consumed since the copy of the variables is created. Also, copying data consumes a lot of time in this technique. On the other hand, the biggest advantage of this technique is that any expressions or variables can be passed as arguments.

Call by Reference

This is a method in which the addresses of the variables are passed from the calling function to the called function. In this method, function arguments are declared as references rather than the normal variables. So, in this case, any changes done by the called function in the arguments will also be reflected in the calling function. An asterisk (*) is placed after the data type in the argument list to indicate that the parameters are passed by call by reference. In this method, no copies of the actual variables are created. Hence the changes are also reflected in the calling function.

For Example:

```
#include <stdio.h>
void swap(int *, int *) ;     //Declaration
void main()                   //Main function
{
  int a = 10, b = 20 ;
  swap(&a, &b) ;              //Calling function
}
void swap(int *a, int *b)
{
  int temp ;
  temp = *a ;
  *a = *b ;
  *b = temp ;
  printf("\n After swapping a = %d and b = %d", a, b) ;
}
```
Output -
    After swapping a = 20 and b = 10

One of the biggest advantages of the call by reference technique is that it provides greater time as well as space complexity, as in this method no copies of data are created. Also, the changes are reflected in the calling function as well. But the biggest drawback of this technique is the use of pointers. The use of pointers should be done very carefully, as the pointers can point anywhere in our systems. So, only those who are experienced in handling pointers should use this technique.

2.13 Recursion

Recursion is a process performed by a function by calling itself a number of times for performing operations. *A recursive function is a function that calls itself and executes the same instruction repeatedly.* Recursive programs are fast and well optimized. Recursion is also an application of stack. Hence, recursion is slower because it must maintain its stack properties.

Recursion makes code small and easy to understand.

For Example:

```
#include<stdio.h>
#include<conio.h>
void main()
{
  int fact, n ;
  int factorial(int) ;
  clrscr() ;
  printf("Enter any number:") ;
  scanf("%d", &n) ;
  fact = factorial(n) ;
  printf("Factorial = %d",fact) ;
  getch() ;
}

int factorial(int x)
{
  int f ;
  if(x == 1 | | x == 0)
  return 1 ;
  else
  if = x * factorial(x - 1) ;
  return f ;
}
```

Output

Enter any number: 6
Factorial = 720

2.14 Structures in C

A structure is a user-defined or custom data type which is used in storing related information, that is, data of different data types. A structure is like an array, but the main difference is that an array contains only information of the same data types. Therefore, *a structure is a collection of one or more different variables or data types grouped under a single name.* Each variable in a structure is known as a member variable. A structure is declared as follows:

Syntax –

```
Struct structure_name
{
  data type variable name 1;
  data type variable name 2;
    .
    .
    .
  Block of statements
};
```

A structure is always declared using the keyword struct followed by the name of the structure. Structure_name is the name of a user-defined data type and will further be used to identify the structure and declare variables/objects of the struct type.

For Example:

```
struct Student
{
  char name[25];
  int age ;
  float height ;
};
```

In the previous example, struct student declares a structure of student having three data fields, that is, name, roll number, and class. There are three elements in the previous structure. Hence, all three data types are accessed separately and are not mixed. Now, let us understand that how structures are used through a program.

```c
#include <stdio.h>
#include <string.h>
struct student
{
  int id;
  char name[20];
  float percentage;
};

int main()
{
  struct student record = {0};//Initializing to null
  record.id=1;//Accessing member variable
  strcpy(record.name, "Ram,");
  record.percentage = 90.5;
  printf(" Id - %d \n", record.id);
  printf(" Name - %s \n", record.name);
  printf(" Percentage - %f \n", record.percentage);
  return 0;
}
```

Output -

Id - 1
Name - Ram
Percentage - 90.500000

2.15 Pointers

A pointer is a special type of variable that is used to store the address of another variable rather than some simple value. Pointers can be used to access the data stored in the memory. Pointers are frequently used with arrays, because pointers are more efficient in handling arrays and data tables.

A pointer is a variable used to store the address of another variable and is used to perform various operations. Pointers give power as well as flexibility to C programmers. Pointers can directly access memory locations and can easily manipulate addresses.

Practical Application:

An example of a pointer is the address of the home of a human being which can be used to easily reach the destination.

Declaration of a pointer - `Data type *variable name;`

For Example:

```
int *ptr ;
int i = 3 ;
ptr = &i ;
```

Therefore, ptr will store the address of the memory location where i is stored.

2.15.1 Arrays and Pointers

The concept of arrays is very much bound to the concept of pointers. Now let us take an example; if we have an array of 10 elements declared as
int array[10] = { 10, 20 ,32, 7, 19, 89, 60, 54, 12, 77 }

The above array will be stored in the memory as shown in the following figure:

arr[0]   arr[1]   arr[2]   arr[3]   arr[4]   arr[5]   arr[6]   arr[7]   arr[8]   arr[9]

10	20	32	7	19	89	60	54	12	77
100	102	104	106	108	110	112	114	116	118

ptr

FIGURE 2.10 Memory representation of arr[].

Here the starting address of the array (100) is the base address of the array. The base address is the address of the first element in the array. Now we will use a pointer variable to store the address of the first element, and ptr will point to the first element of the array.

```
int * ptr ;
ptr = &array[0] ;
```

Similarly, we can store the addresses of other elements. If the pointer variable holds the address of the first element in the array, then the address of the successive elements can be calculated by ptr++.

```
int * ptr ;
ptr = &array[0] ;
ptr++ ;
printf(" The value of second element is %d", *ptr) ;
```

A pointer variable can be prefixed or postfixed with increment or decrement operators. Increment or decrement will depend upon the data type, for example, int - 2 bytes, float - 4 bytes, char - 1 byte, and so on.

Here, data type identifies the type of data that the pointer points to. An asterisk (*) identifies that the variable is going to store and point toward some address. The variable name gives the unique name to the pointer.

Uses of pointers in C:

- Helps in dynamic memory allocation.

- Makes use of arrays and strings more efficiently and optimizes the code.

- Enhances the speed of the execution of code.

- Passes the pointers to functions as arguments.

- Helps in returning the multiple values from a function.

Frequently Asked Questions

Q8. State true or false for the following with reasons.

   (i) A pointer is a variable which stores a value.

   (ii) * is an address operator.

   Answer.
   (i) False, because a pointer is a variable which is used to store the address of another variable.

   (ii) False, * is dereferencing operator.

2.15.2 Drawbacks of Using Pointers

We all know that pointers are very useful in C, but they are also the most dangerous feature of C. If the pointers are not used correctly, they can lead to various problems which are difficult to handle. Some of the drawbacks of pointers are as follows:

1. The improper use of pointers can cause the system to crash.

2. If a pointer is used to read a memory location and if it points to the wrong memory location, then it will be very difficult for the program, as it will produce unexpected results.

3. If the pointers are not used properly, they can point anywhere in the operating system, which can also cause data corruption.

4. Pointers should always be initialized; otherwise, they may contain garbage values which will cause various problems.

5. The debugging process in the case of pointers is a very difficult task.

2.16 Summary

- C is a high-level programming language which was developed by Denis Ritchie, a scientist of Bell Labs, in the early 1970s.

- C is a platform and also supports various other languages like Java and C++. C language is often called middle-level language, as it not only provides different data types or data structures which are needed by a programmer, but it can also access the computer hardware with the help of specially designed functions and declarations.

- During programming, if we want those files or functions, first we have to include those functions or files in our program to use them. Thus, these files will be loaded from the disk to the memory where these files are called to perform the desired operations. Hence, these files are known as header files.

- The `main()` function is a function which is a part of every C program. A program cannot execute without the `main()` function.

- The most common operations in a C program are to accept the input values from a standard input device and to display the data produced by the program by a standard output device.

- Keywords in C are the reserved words which have a special meaning. They are written in lower case. Keywords cannot be used as an identifier. An identifier is a name which is given to a constant, variable, function, or to an array.

- Data types in C are the special keywords which define the type of data and amount of data a variable is holding.

- The four basic data types used in C are `int`, `char`, `float`, and `double`.

- Operators in C are used to perform some specific operations between the different variables and constants.

- Arithmetic operators are those operators which are used in mathematical calculation.

- Assignment operators are used for assigning values to the variables. These operators are always evaluated from right to left.

- Relational operators are used for comparison between two values or expressions. They are also known as comparison operators.

- The conditional operator is also known as a ternary operator, because it takes three operands.

- Bitwise operators are the special operators that are used to perform operations at the bit level.

- The comma operator is used to chain together some expressions.

- The `sizeof` operator is a unary operator that returns the size of a variable or a data type in bytes.

- A unary operator is one which requires only a single operand to work. C supports two unary operators, which are increment (++) and decrement (--) operators. These operators are used to increase or decrease the value of a variable by one respectively.

- Control statements are those that enable a programmer to execute a particular block of code specifying the order in which the various instructions in a program are required to be executed. It determines the flow of control.

- The IF statement is a bidirectional control statement which is used to test the condition and take one of the possible actions.

- Nested if-else statements are also known as if-else-if ladders.

- A switch statement is a multidirectional conditional control statement. It is a simplified version of an if-else-if statement.

- Looping statements, also known as iterative statements, are a set of instructions which are repeatedly executed until a certain condition or expression becomes false.

- A while loop is a loop which is used to repeat a set of one or more instructions/ statements until a particular condition becomes false.

- A do-while loop is similar to a while loop. The only difference is that, unlike a while loop in which a condition is checked at the start of the loop, in a do-while loop the condition is checked at the end of the loop.

- A for loop is a pre-deterministic loop; that is, it is a count-controlled loop such that the program knows in advance how many times the loop is to be executed.

- A break statement causes an intermediate exit from that loop in which the statement appears. A continue statement skips rest of the statements, and the control is transferred to the start of the loop.

- C language enables us to break the entire program into a smaller number of modules or segments. These modules or segments are called functions. Therefore, a function is a predefined block of code designed to perform a particular task.

- Call by value is a method in which the values are passed from the calling function to the called function. In this method, the called function creates copies of the actual values of the calling functions argument into its formal parameters.

- Call by reference is a method in which the addresses of the variables are passed from the calling function to the called function. In this method, function arguments are declared as references rather than the normal variables.

- A structure is a collection of one or more different variables or data types grouped under a single name.

- A pointer is a special type of variable that is used to store the address of another variable.

- An asterisk (*) identifies that the variable is going to store and point toward some address. A variable name gives the unique name to the pointer.

2.17 Exercises

2.17.1 Theory Questions

1. What are the different characteristics of C language which makes it a very popular language?

2. What is the `main()` function?

3. What is the purpose of the `printf()` and `scanf()` functions?

4. What are the different operators used in C? Discuss all of them in detail.

5. What do you mean by header files? Why are header files included in the programs?

6. What are the data types in C? Explain in detail.

7. What do you understand by C tokens? Discuss in detail.

8. Define the term identifiers. What are various rules for identifying an identifier? Give examples.

9. What do you understand by the conditional operator? Explain with the help of an example.

10. What are the decisional control statements in C?

11. Differentiate between while and do-while loops. Give examples.

12. What is the difference between simple if and if-else statements? Explain with the help of an example.

13. Write the syntax of a for loop. Can we skip any part in the for loop or not?

14. What do you mean by structure? Give an example.

15. Explain switch case. What are the various advantages of using a switch case?

16. Define a function. Why are functions needed?

17. What is the difference between a function definition and a function declaration?

18. Discuss the structure of a program having multiple functions.

19. Differentiate between call by value and call by reference. Give suitable examples.

20. What do you mean by pointers? How are they initialized?

21. What are the various drawbacks of using pointers?

22. What do you understand by iterative statements in C? Briefly, discuss all the types.

23. How is a user-defined function different from a predefined function?

24. Give the difference between break and continue statements with suitable examples.

25. Write a short note on arrays and pointers.

26. Differentiate between pre-increment and post-increment operators.

2.17.2 Programming Questions

1. Write a program to print your name on the screen.

2. Write a program that reads five integer values and displays them.

3. Write a C program to add two floating point numbers. Accept the numbers from the user.

4. Write a program to calculate simple interest.

5. Write a program to check whether the given number is even or odd.

6. Write a program to find the largest of three given numbers.

7. Write a menu driven program performing addition, subtraction, multiplication, and division of two numbers using functions.

8. Write a C program to print the following pattern using a for loop:

A. ❁
❁ ❁
❁ ❁ ❁
❁ ❁ ❁ ❁
❁ ❁ ❁ ❁ ❁

B. a
b c
d e f
g h i j

9. Write a program that takes an integer value from the user and prints its corresponding ASCII equivalent.

10. Write a program to find the reverse of a given number using a function.

11. Write a program to check whether a number is divisible by 2 or not using a function.

12. Write a program to add two numbers using pointers.

13. Write a program where both if and else statements are executed in a program.

14. Write a program to perform a call by value and a call by reference using functions.

15. Write a program to find the factorial of a number using a for loop.

16. Write a program to accept a string from the user and to check whether the string is a palindrome or not using a user-defined function.

17. Write a C program to print the numbers from 1 to 10 excluding 5 using a continue statement.

18. Write a program to swap two numbers without using the third variable.

2.18 Multiple Choice Questions

1. A conditional operator is also called a ternary operator as it has _____ operands.

    A. 1

    B. 3

    C. 2

    D. 4

2. Which of the following operator is used to declare a pointer?

    A. >

    B. <

    C. *

    D. &

3. Which of the following is a valid identifier in C?

    A. a_43

    B. cd bd

    C. apple

    D. both (a) and (c)

4. Which operator is used for mathematical computation?

    A. Assignment Operator

    B. Arithmetic Operators

    C. Bitwise Operators

    D. Relational Operators

5. Which of the control strings is associated with floating values?

    A. %f

    B. %g

    C. %e

    D. All of the above

6. A function declaration identifies a function with its:

    A. Arguments

    B. Data type of return value

    C. Name

    D. All of the above

7. Which operator is used for comparison between values?

    A. Logical Operator

    B. Relational Operator

    C. Assignment Operator

    D. Unary Operator

8. In which of the following loops will a block of statements be executed at least once without checking the condition?

    A. For Loop

    B. While Loop

    C. Do-while Loop

    D. All of the above

9. A data structure which is used to store related information together is called a(n) _____.

   A. Structure

   B. Array

   C. Linked List

   D. String

10. *(&variable) is equal to:

   A. &variable

   B. *variable

   C. &(*variable)

   D. Variable

CHAPTER 3

ARRAYS

In This Chapter

3.1 Introduction

We have already studied the basics of programming in data structures and C in the previous chapter in which we aimed to design good programs, where a good program refers to a program which runs correctly and efficiently by occupying less space in the memory, and also takes less time to run and execute. Undoubtedly, a program is said to be efficient when it executes with less memory space and also in minimal time. In this chapter, we will learn about the concept of arrays. An array is a user-defined data type that stores related information together. Arrays are discussed in detail in the following sections.

3.2 Definition of an Array

An array is a collection of homogeneous (similar) types of data elements in contiguous memory. An array is a linear data structure because all elements of the array are stored in linear order. Let us take an example in which we have ten students in a class, and we have been asked to store the marks of all ten students; then we need a data structure known as an array.

36	98	14	74	56	13	7	96	44	82
marks1	marks2	marks3	marks4	marks5	marks6	marks7	marks8	marks9	marks10

FIGURE 3.1. Representation of an array of 10 elements.

In the previous example, the data elements are stored in the successive memory locations and are identified by an index number (also known as the subscript), that is, A_i or $A[i]$. *A subscript is an ordinal number which is used to identify an element of the array.* The elements of an array have the same data type, and each element in an array can be accessed using the same name.

Frequently Asked Questions

Q. What is an array? How can we identify an element in the array?

Answer.
An array is a collection of homogeneous (similar) types of data elements in contiguous memory. An element in an array can be identified by its index number, which is also known as a subscript.

3.3 Array Declaration

We know that all variables must be declared before they are used in the program. Therefore, the same concept also holds with array variables. An array must be declared before it is used. During the declaration of an array, the size of the array has to be specified. Declaring an array involves the following specifications:

- *Data Type* – The data type means the different kinds of values it can store. The data type can be an `integer (int)`, `float`, `char`, or any other valid data type.

- *Array Name* – The name refers to the name of the array which will be used to identify the array.

- *Size* – The size of an array refers to the maximum number of values an array can hold.

Syntax – `data_typearray_name [size] ;`

Example –`int salary [10];`

Data type   array name   size

The previous example declares salary to be an array which has ten elements. In C, the array index starts from zero. The first element of this array will be stored in salary[0], the second element will be stored in salary[1], and so on. Similarly, the last element will be stored in salary[9]. In memory, the array will be shown as in the following figure.

2000	4500	7890	9876	10000	3458	8000	9810	14000	5000
salary[0]	salary[1]	salary[2]	salary[3]	salary[4]	salary[5]	salary[6]	salary[7]	salary[8]	salary[9]

FIGURE 3.2. Memory representation of an array.

Here 0, 1, 2, . . . 9 written in square brackets represent the subscripts which we use to identify a particular element in the array.

3.4 Array Initialization

The initialization of arrays can be done in the following ways:

1. **Initialization at Compile Time** – Initialization of elements of the array at compile time refers to the same way we initialize the normal or ordinary variables at the time of their declaration. When an array is initialized, there is a need to provide a specific value for every element in the array.

The general form of initializing arrays is as follows:

```
data_typearray_name[size] = { list of values } ;
```

An example of initialization of arrays at compile time is as follows:

During the initialization of arrays, we may omit the size of the array. For example,

```
int age[ ] = { 25 , 28, 34 } ;
```

In the previous example, the compiler will automatically allocate memory for all the initialized elements of the array. If the number of values is less than the size provided, then such elements will take zeroes as their assigned values. For example,

```
int marks[10] = { 56, 69, 40, 99, 82, 96, 72 } ;
```

Here the size of the array is 10, but there are only seven elements; hence, the remaining elements will be considered to be zeroes.

56	69	40	99	82	96	72	0	0	0
marks[0]	marks[1]	marks[2]	marks[3]	marks[4]	marks[5]	marks[6]	marks[7]	marks[8]	marks[9]

FIGURE 3.3. Initialization of array marks[10].

2. **Initialization at Runtime** – Initialization of elements of the array at runtime refers to the method of inputting the values from the keyboard. In this method, a while, do-while, or for loop is taken to input the values of the array.

```
#include<stdio.h>
void main()
{
int  i, salary[15] ;
    for( i=0 ; i<15 ; i++ )
    {
scanf("%d", &salary[i]) ;

}//End of for loop

}//End of main
```

FIGURE 3.4. Code for inputting the values.

In the previous code, the index i is at 0, and the values will be input for the index values from 0 to 14, as the array has 15 elements.

3.5   Calculating the Address of Array Elements

The address of the elements in the 1-D array can be calculated very easily, because the array stores all its data elements in contiguous memory locations, storing the base address (address of the first element of the array). Hence, the address of the other data elements can easily be calculated using the base address. The formula to find the address of elements in a 1-D array is as follows:

Address of data element, A[i] = Base Address (BA) + w (i – lower bound)

where A is the array, i is the index of the element for which the address is to be calculated, BA is the base address of the array A, and w is the size of each element (e.g., the size of int is 2 bytes, the size of char is 1 byte, etc.)

Frequently Asked Questions

Q. An array is given intmarks[6] = { 34, 53, 87, 100, 98, 65 }; **calculate the address of marks[3] if the base address is 3000.**

Answer.
It is given that the base address of the array is 3000 and we know that the size of an integer is 2 bytes. Hence we can easily find the address of marks[3].

3000	3002	3004	3006	3008	3010
34	53	87	100	98	65
marks[1]	marks[2]	marks[3]	marks[4]	marks[5]	marks[6]

By putting into the formula –

Address of marks[3] = 3000 + 2 (3 – 1)

$$= 3000 + 2 (2)$$

Address of marks[3] = 3004

3.6   Operations on Arrays

This section discusses various operations that can be performed on arrays. These operations include:

- Traversing an array
- Inserting an element in an array
- Deleting an element in an array

- Searching an element in an array

- Merging of two arrays

- Sorting an array

1. Traversing an Array

Traversing an array means to access every element in an array exactly once so that it can be processed. Examples are printing all the data elements, performing any process on these elements, and so on. Traversing the elements of the array is a very simple process because of the linear structure of the array (all the elements are stored in the contiguous memory locations).

Practical Application:

If there is a line of people standing one after the other, and one boy is distributing advertisement pamphlets one by one to each person standing in the line.

```c
#include<stdio.h>
#include<conio.h>
void main()
{
  int  i, num[5] ;
  for( i=0 ; i<15 ; i++ )
    {
      printf("\n arr[%d] = ", i);
      scanf("%d", &num[i]) ;

    }//End of for loop 1
  printf(" The elements of the array are ") ;
  for( i=0 ; i<5 ; i++ )
    {
      printf("\t%d", arr[i]) ;

    }//End of for loop 2
}//End of main
```

Output

arr[0] = 5

arr[1] = 8

arr[2] = 16

arr[3] = 1

arr[4] = 7

The elements of array are 5   8   16   1   7

In the previous code, the traversing of elements of the array is shown. In the first for loop, all the elements are inputted into the array. Second, all the elements are traversed and printed in the second for loop. Hence, traversing of an array is done.

2. Inserting an Element in an Array

Inserting an element in an array refers to the operation of adding an element to the array. In the case of insertion, we assume that there is enough memory space still available in the array. For example, if we have an array that can hold 20 elements and the array contains only 15 elements, then we have space to accommodate five more elements. However, if the array can hold 15 elements, then we will not be able to insert other elements into the array. Insertion in arrays can be done in three ways:

a. Insertion at the beginning

b. Insertion at a specified position

c. Insertion at the end

Now let us discuss all of these cases in detail.

a. Insertion at the beginning – In this case, the new element to be inserted is inserted at the beginning of the array. To insert an element at the beginning, all the elements stored in the array must move one place forward to vacate the first position in the array. For example, if an array is declared to hold 10 elements and it contains only seven elements, and also if it is given that the new element is to be inserted at the beginning of the array, then all the stored elements must move one place ahead which is shown as follows:

Insert new element 10 at arr[0]

After swapping all the elements and inserting new element 10 into the array, the new array will be:

arr[0]	arr[1]	arr[2]	arr[3]	arr[4]	arr[5]	arr[6]	arr[7]	arr[8]	arr[9]
10	23	15	47	9	33	90	77		

Algorithm for Insertion in the Beginning

We assume *ARR* is an array with *N* elements in it. The maximum elements that can be stored in the array is defined by *SIZE*. We should first check if the array has an empty space available to store any element in it or not, and then we proceed with the insertion process.

```
Step 1: START
Step 2: IF N = SIZE,
            PRINT OVERFLOW
            ELSE
            N = N + 1
Step 3: SET I = N
Step 4: Repeat Step 5 while I>=0
Step 5: SET ARR[I+1] = ARR[I]
            [ END OF LOOP ]
Step 6: SET ARR[0] = New_Element
Step 7: EXIT
```

b. Insertion at a specified position – In this case the new element to be inserted is inserted at specified location/position which is entered by the user. In order to insert a new element in the array, the previously stored elements in the array must move one place forward from their current place until the element at the specified position is reached. For example, if an array is declared to hold 10 elements and it contains only eight elements, and it is also given that the new element is to be inserted at the fifth position of the array, then the stored elements must move one place ahead as shown in the following:

arr[0]	arr[1]	arr[2]	arr[3]	arr[4]	arr[5]	arr[6]	arr[7]	arr[8]	arr[9]
23	15	47	9	33	90	77	100		

Insert new element 30 at arr[4]

After swapping the elements and inserting new element 10 into the middle of the array, the new array will be:

arr[0]	arr[1]	arr[2]	arr[3]	arr[4]	arr[5]	arr[6]	arr[7]	arr[8]	arr[9]
23	15	47	9	30	33	90	77	100	

Practical Application:

It is just like if there are people standing in a line and one person just joins the line from the middle, so now every person has to shift one place backward from the middle so that the person can come in the line; hence it is insertion at the middle.

Algorithm for Insertion at a Specified Position

We assume *ARR* is an array with *N* elements in it. The maximum elements that can be stored in the array is defined by *SIZE*. Let *POS* defined the position at which the new element is to be inserted. We should first check if the array has an empty space available to store any element in it or not, and then we proceed with the insertion process.

```
Step 1: START
Step 2: IF N = SIZE,
            PRINT OVERFLOW
            ELSE
            N = N + 1
Step 3: SET I = N
Step 4: Repeat Step 5 while I>=POS
Step 5: SET ARR[I+1] = ARR[I]
            [ END OF LOOP ]
Step 6: SET ARR[POS] = New_Element
Step 7: EXIT
```

c. **Insertion at the end** – In this case the new element to be inserted is inserted at the end of the array. So, there is no need for swapping the elements in this case. We are just required to check whether there is enough space available in the array or not. For example, if an array is declared to hold 10 elements and it contains only nine elements, then the insertion can take place.

arr[0]	arr[1]	arr[2]	arr[3]	arr[4]	arr[5]	arr[6]	arr[7]	arr[8]	arr[9]
23	15	47	9	30	33	90	77	100	

Insert new element 11 at arr[9]

Now the last element will be inserted at the last position, which is at arr[9] and is vacant. Therefore, the new array after insertion will be:

arr[0]	arr[1]	arr[2]	arr[3]	arr[4]	arr[5]	arr[6]	arr[7]	arr[8]	arr[9]
23	15	47	9	30	33	90	77	100	11

Practical Application:

It is just like a normal line where a person comes and joins the line at the end; hence, there is no need for any shifting in this process.

Algorithm for Insertion at the End

We assume *ARR* is an array with *N* elements in it. The maximum elements that can be stored in the array is defined by *SIZE*. We should first check if the array has an empty space available to store any element in it or not, and then we proceed with the insertion process.

```
Step 1: START
Step 2: IF N = SIZE,
            PRINT OVERFLOW
            ELSE
            N = N + 1
Step 3: SET ARR[N] = New_Element
Step 4: EXIT
```

Write a menu-driven program to implement insertion in a 1-D array discussing all three cases.

```c
#include<stdio.h>
#include<conio.h>
void main()
{
  int  i, n, pos, choice, value, arr[10];
  clrscr();
  printf("Enter the number of elements in array: ") ;
  scanf("%d", &n) ;
  printf("Enter the elements of array ") ;
  //Accepting the elements of array
  for( i=0 ; i<n ; i++ )
    {
      scanf("%d", &arr[i]) ;
    }
```

```c
printf("***MENU***") ;
printf("1. Insertion in beginning ") ;
printf("2. Insertion at specified location ") ;
printf("3. Insertion at end ") ;
printf("Enter your choice: ") ;
scanf("%d", &choice) ;
if(n==10)
  {
    printf("Overflow error ") ;
    exit(0);
  }
else
switch(ch)
  {
    case 1:
    for( i=n-1 ; i>=0 ; i-- )
      {
        arr[i+1] = arr[i] ;
      }
    printf("Enter new value: ") ;
    scanf("%d", &value) ;
    arr[0] =value;
    printf(" After insertion array is ") ;
    for( i=0 ; i<=n ; i++ )
      {
        printf("\t%d", arr[i]) ;

      }
    break ;
    case 2:
    printf("Enter position ") ;
    scanf("%d", &pos) ;
    for( i=n-1 ; i>=p-1 ; i-- )
      {
        arr[i+1] = arr[i] ;
      }
    printf("Enter new value: ") ;
    scanf("%d", &value) ;
    arr[p-1] =value;
    printf(" After insertion array is ") ;
    for( i=0 ; i<=n ; i++ )
```

```
        {
          printf("\t%d", arr[i]) ;


        }
     break ;
     case 3:
     printf("Enter new value: ") ;
     scanf("%d", &value) ;
     arr[n] =value;
     printf(" After insertion array is ") ;
     for( i=0 ; i<=n ; i++ )
       {
          printf("\t%d", arr[i]) ;


        }
     break ;
     default :
     printf("Wrong Choice") ;
     exit(0) ;
    }
  //End of switch case
  getch() ;
} //End of main
```

Output

enter the number of elements

n = 6

arr[0] = 75

arr[1] = 84

arr[2] = 16

arr[3] = 11

arr[4] = 47

arr[5] = 90

```
    ****MENU****
1.      Insertion in beginning
2.      Insertion at specified position
3.      Insertion at end
Enter your choice 1
Enter new value 38
arr[0] = 38
After insertion new array is
38   75   84   16   11 47   90


Enter your choice 2
Enter position 3
Enter new value 65
arr[2] = 65
After insertion new array is
38   75   65   84   16   11   47   90


Enter your choice 3
Enter new value 38
arr[8] = 100
38   75   65   84   16   11   47   90   100
```

3. Deleting an Element in an Array

Deleting an element from an array refers to the operation of the removal of an element from an array. Deletion in an array can be done in three ways:

a. Deletion from the beginning

b. Deletion from a specified position

c. Deletion from the end

Now let us discuss all of these cases in detail.

a. **Deletion from the beginning** – In this case the element to be deleted is deleted from the beginning of the array. In order to delete an element from the beginning, all the elements stored in the array must move one place backward in the array. For example, if an array is declared to hold 10 elements and it contains only seven elements, and it is also given that the element is to be deleted from the beginning of the array, then all the stored elements must move one place back as shown in the following:

arr[0]	arr[1]	arr[2]	arr[3]	arr[4]	arr[5]	arr[6]	arr[7]	arr[8]	arr[9]
23	15	47	9	33	90	77			

Delete 23 from arr[0]

In order to delete the first element, 23, from the array, we must swap all the stored elements backward so that the first element gets deleted as shown. After the deletion of 23 from the array, the new array will be:

arr[0]	arr[1]	arr[2]	arr[3]	arr[4]	arr[5]	arr[6]	arr[7]	arr[8]	arr[9]
15	47	9	30	90	77				

Practical Application:

It is just like if there is a pile of books and a person just picks up the book from the end, so now all the books will be shifted one place forward from where they were placed; hence, this is deletion from the beginning.

Algorithm for Deletion from the Beginning

We assume *ARR* is an array with *N* elements in it.

```
Step 1: START
Step 2: SET I = 0
Step 3: Repeat Step 4 while I<N-1
Step 4: SET ARR[I] = ARR[I+1]
          [END OF LOOP]
Step 5: EXIT
```

b. Deletion from a specified position – In this case the element to be deleted is deleted from the specified location/position in the array which is entered by the user. In order to delete an element from the specified position, the elements stored in the array must move one place backward to their existing place in the array until the element is deleted at the specified position. For example, if an array is declared to hold 10 elements and it only contains eight elements, and it is also given that the element is to be deleted from the specified position which is the fourth position of the array, then the stored elements must move one place back as shown in the following:

arr[0]	arr[1]	arr[2]	arr[3]	arr[4]	arr[5]	arr[6]	arr[7]	arr[8]	arr[9]
43	22	86	7	13	40	60	75		

Delete 7 from arr[3]

In order to delete the fourth element, 7, from the array, we must swap the stored elements backward so that the given element gets deleted as shown. After the deletion of 7 from the array, the new array will be:

arr[0]	arr[1]	arr[2]	arr[3]	arr[4]	arr[5]	arr[6]	arr[7]	arr[8]	arr[9]
43	22	86	13	40	60	75			

Algorithm for Deletion from a Specified Position

We assume *ARR* is an array with *N* elements in it. Let *POS* define the position from which the element is to be deleted.

```
Step 1: START
Step 2: SET I = POS
Step 3: Repeat Step 4 while I<=N-1
Step 4: SET ARR[I+1] = ARR[I]
          [ END OF LOOP ]
Step 5: EXIT
```

c. **Deletion from the end –** In this case the deletion is quite simple. Here we are just required to print all the elements except the last one, as we want to delete the last element. For example, if an array is declared to hold 10 elements and it contains only six elements, and it is also given that the element is to be deleted from the end of the array, then the deletion is shown as follows:

arr[0]	arr[1]	arr[2]	arr[3]	arr[4]	arr[5]	arr[6]	arr[7]	arr[8]	arr[9]
43	22	86	13	40	11				

Delete 11 from arr[5]

After deleting 11 from the array the new array will be:

arr[0]	arr[1]	arr[2]	arr[3]	arr[4]	arr[5]	arr[6]	arr[7]	arr[8]	arr[9]
43	22	86	13	40					

Practical Application:

It is just like if there is a pile of books and a person just picks the first book from the pile; hence, we can say that one book is deleted or removed from the pile, and therefore it is deletion from the end.

Algorithm for Deletion from the End

We assume *ARR* is an array with *N* elements in it.

```
Step 1: START
Step 2: SET N = N-1
Step 3: Repeat Step 4 for I=0 to N
Step 4: Print ARR[I]
            [ END OF LOOP ]
Step 5: EXIT
```

Write a menu-driven program to implement deletion in a 1-D array discussing all three cases.

```c
#include<stdio.h>
#include<conio.h>
void main()
{
  int  i, n, pos, choice, value, arr[10];
  clrscr();
  printf("Enter the number of elements in array: ") ;
  scanf("%d", &n) ;
  printf("Enter the elements of array ") ;
  //Accepting the elements of array
  for( i=0 ; i<n ; i++ )
    {
      scanf("%d", &arr[i]) ;
    }
  printf("***MENU***") ;
  printf("1. Deletion from beginning ") ;
  printf("2. Deletion from specified location ") ;
  printf("3. Deletion from end ") ;
  printf("Enter your choice: ") ;
  scanf("%d", &choice) ;
  if(n==10)
    {
      printf("Overflow error ") ;
      exit(0);
    }
  else
  switch(ch)
    {
```

```c
   case 1:
   for( i=0 ; i<n-1 ; i++ )
     {
       arr[i] = arr[i+1] ;
     }
   printf(" After deletion array is ") ;
   for( i=0 ; i<n-1 ; i++ )
     {
       printf("\t%d", arr[i]) ;
     }
   break ;
   case 2:
   printf("Enter position ") ;
   scanf("%d", &pos) ;
   for( i=p-1 ; i<n-1 ; i++ )
     {
       arr[i] = arr[i+1] ;
     }
   printf(" After deletion array is ") ;
   for( i=0 ; i<n-1 ; i++ )
     {
       printf("\t%d", arr[i]) ;
     }
   break ;
   case 3:
   n = n-1 ;
   printf(" After deletion array is ") ;
   for( i=0 ; i<n ; i++ )
     {
       printf("\t%d", arr[i]) ;

     }
   break ;
   default :
   printf("Wrong Choice") ;
   exit(0) ;
  } //End of switch case
 getch() ;
} //End of main
```

Output

enter the number of elements

n = 7

arr[0] = 25

arr[1] = 81

arr[2] = 66

arr[3] = 21

arr[4] = 43

arr[5] = 20

arr[6] = 39

****MENU****

1.   Deletion from beginning

2.   Deletion from specified position

3.   Deletion from end

Enter your choice 1

After deletion new array is

81   66   21   43   20   39

Enter your choice 2

Enter position 3

After deletion new array is

81   66   43   20   39

Enter your choice 3

After deletion new array is

81 66   43   20

4. Searching for an Element in an Array

Searching for an element in an array means to find whether a particular value exists in an array or not. If that particular value is found, then the searching is said to be successful and the position/location of that particular value is returned. If the value is not found, then searching will be said to be unsuccessful. There are two methods for searching, linear search and binary search. In this chapter we will only discuss linear search in detail, and the binary search technique will be discussed in the upcoming chapters. Now, we will learn how linear search works.

Linear Search

Linear search is a very simple technique used to search a particular value in an array. It is also called a sequential search, as it works by comparing the values to be searched with every element of the array in a sequence until a match is found.

For example, let us take an array of 10 elements which is declared as:

```
int array[10] = { 23, 15, 47, 9, 30, 33, 90, 77,
100, 11 }
```

and search for 90 in the array; then every element of the array will be compared to 90 until 90 is found.

arr[0]	arr[1]	arr[2]	arr[3]	arr[4]	arr[5]	arr[6]	arr[7]	arr[8]	arr[9]
23	15	47	9	30	33	90	77	100	11

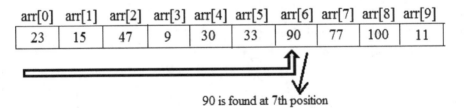

90 is found at 7th position

In this way linear search is used to search for a particular value in the array. The following is the program for a linear search.

Write a program to search an element in an array using the linear search technique.

```
# include <stdio.h>
intlinear_search( intarr[], int n, int value ) ;
void main()
{
  intarr[10], n, i, r, value ;
  clrscr() ;
```

```
   printf("***LINEAR SEARCH***") ;
   printf("\nEnter no of elements") ;
   scanf("%d", &n) ;
   printf("Enter the elements of array") ;
   for( i=0 ; i<n ; i++ )
     {
       printf("\nEnter element %d", i+1) ;
       scanf("%d", &arr[i]) ;
     }
   printf("\nEnter value to search") ;
   scanf("%d", &value) ;
   r = linear_search(arr, n, value) ;
   if(r == -1)
   printf("value not found") ;
   else
   printf("%d value found at %d", value, r+1) ;
   getch() ;
}
intlinear_search( intarr[], int n, int value )
{
  int i;
  for( i=0 ; i<n ; i++ )
    {
      if(arr[i] == value)
      return i ;
    }
  return (-1);
}
```

Output

```
***LINEAR SEARCH***

Enter no of elements  7


Enter elements of array

Enter element 1   15

Enter element 2   65

Enter element 3   87

Enter element 4   99
```

```
        Enter element 5   29
        Enter element 6    6
        Enter element 7   33


        Enter value to search   99
        99 value found at 4ᵗʰ position
```

5. Merging of Two Arrays

The merging of two arrays means copying the elements of the first and second array into the third array. Here we will take two sorted arrays, and the resultant merged array will also be sorted. The concept of merging is explained as follows:

Let us consider two sorted arrays, Array 1 and Array 2, and an Array 3 in which the elements will be placed after sorting.

Array – 1

arr[0]	arr[1]	arr[2]	arr[3]	arr[4]	arr[5]	arr[6]	arr[7]	arr[8]	arr[9]
6	12	18	24	30					

Array – 2

arr[0]	arr[1]	arr[2]	arr[3]	arr[4]	arr[5]	arr[6]	arr[7]	arr[8]	arr[9]
7	14	21	28	35					

Array – 3

arr[0]	arr[1]	arr[2]	arr[3]	arr[4]	arr[5]	arr[6]	arr[7]	arr[8]	arr[9]
6	7	12	14	18	21	24	28	30	35

Array 3 shows how the merged array is formed using the sorted Arrays 1 and 2. Here we compare the elements of the two arrays. First, the first element of Array 1 is compared with the first element of Array 2, and as 6 is less than 7 (6 < 7) therefore 6 will be the first element in the merged array. Now the second element of Array 1 is compared to the first element of Array 2, and as 7 is less than 12 (7 < 12) therefore 7 will be the second element in the merged array.

Now the second element of Array 1 is compared with the second element of Array 2, and as 12 is less than 14 (12 < 14) therefore 12 will be the third element in Array 3. This procedure is repeated until the elements of both Arrays 1 and 2 are placed in the right positions in the merged array, that is, Array 3.

Practical Application:

A real life example of merging would be if there are two different lines and both lines need to be merged according to the height of the people standing in that line, then merging would be done into a new line where the new line would consist of people from both lines in which people would be standing in order according to their heights.

Write a program to merge two sorted arrays.

```c
#include<stdio.h>
#include<conio.h>
void main()
{
  int arr1[5], arr2[5], arr3[10] ;
  int m1, m2, s ;
  int i=0, j=0 , k=0 ;
  clrscr();
  printf("Enter number of elements in array 1: ") ;
  scanf("%d", &m1) ;
  printf("Enter elements of array 1: ") ;
  for( s=0 ; s<m1 ; s++)
    {
      printf("Enter element %d", s ) ;
      scanf("%d", &arr1[s]) ;
    }
  printf("Enter number of elements in array 2: ") ;
  scanf("%d", &m2) ;
  printf("Enter elements of array 2: ") ;
  for( s=0 ; s<m2 ; s++)
    {
      printf("Enter element %d", s) ;
```

```
    scanf("%d", &arr2[s]) ;
  }
while( i<m1 && j<m2)
 {
   if( arr1[i]<arr2[j] )
     {
       arr3[k]=arr[i] ;
       k++ ;
       i++ ;
     }
   else if( arr2[j] < arr1[i] )
     {
       arr3[k] = arr2[j] ;
       j++ ;
       k++ ;
     }
   else
     {
       arr3[k] = arr[i] ;
       k++ ;
       i++ ;
       arr3[k] = arr[j] ;
       k++ ;
       j++ ;
     }
 }// End of while loop
while( i<m1 )
 {
   arr3[k] = arr1[i] ;
   k++ ;
   i++ ;
 }
while( j<m2 )
 {
   arr3[k] = arr2[j] ;
   k++ ;
   j++ ;
 }
printf("After merging new array is: ") ;
for( s=0 ; s<(m1 + m2) ; s++)
```

```
    {
      printf("%d" , arr3[s]) ;
    }
  getch() ;
} // End of main
```

Output

Enter number of elements in array 1:

5

Enter number of elements in array 1:

arr[0] = 6

arr[1] = 12

arr[2] = 18

arr[3] = 24

arr[4] = 30

Enter number of elements in array 2:

5

Enter number of elements in array 2:

arr[0] = 7

arr[1] = 14

arr[2] = 21

arr[3] = 28

arr[4] = 35

After merging new array is:

arr[0] = 6

arr[1] = 7

arr[2] = 12

arr[3] = 14

arr[4] = 18

arr[5] = 21

arr[6] = 24

arr[7] = 28

arr[8] = 30

arr[9] = 35

6. Sorting an Array

Sorting an array means arranging the data elements of a data structure in a specified order either in ascending or descending order. Sorting refers to the process where, for example, in a class of 60 students who have gotten grades on their examination, now the names of the students will be printed according to their grades either in ascending or descending order.

For example – If we have an array of 10 elements declared as

```
int array[10] = { 78, 12, 47, 55, 61, 6, 99, 84,
32, 10 }
```

Then after sorting, the new array will be:

```
array[10] = { 6, 10, 12, 32, 47, 55, 61, 78, 84,
99 }
```

There are various types of sorting techniques which include Selection Sort, Insertion Sort, and Merge Sort; we will learn about selection sort in this chapter, and the other techniques will be discussed in the upcoming chapter.

Selection Sort

Selection Sort is a sorting technique that works by finding the smallest value in the array and placing it in the first position. After that, it then finds the second smallest value and places it in the second position. This process is repeated until the whole array is sorted. It is a very simple technique, and it is also easier to implement than any other sorting technique. Selection Sort is generally used for sorting large records.

Selection Sort Technique

Consider an array with N elements.

Pass 1 – Find the position POS of smallest value in the array of N elements and interchange ARR[POS] with ARR[0]. Thus, A[0] is sorted.

Pass 2 – Find the position POS of smallest value in the array of N-1 elements and interchange ARR[POS] with A[1]. Thus, A[1] is sorted.

.

.

.

Pass N-1 – Find the position POS of the smaller of the elements ARR[N-2] and ARR[N-1] and interchange ARR[POS] with ARR[N-2]. Thus, ARR[0], ARR[1], . . . ARR[N-1] is sorted.

For Example – Sort the given array using selection sort.

arr[0]	arr[1]	arr[2]	arr[3]	arr[4]	arr[5]	arr[6]	arr[7]	arr[8]	arr[9]
16	82	48	34	75	9				

Pass	POS	Array[0]	Array[1]	Array[2]	Array[3]	Array[4]	Array[5]
1	5	9	82	48	34	75	16
2	5	9	16	48	34	75	82
3	3	9	16	34	48	75	82
4	3	9	16	34	48	75	82
5	4	9	16	34	48	75	82
6	5	9	16	34	48	75	82

In this way the selection sort technique works. Below is the program given for selection sort.

Write a program to sort an array using the selection sort technique.

```
# include <stdio.h>
# include <conio.h>
void main()
{
  int i, j, min, pos, arr[10], n, temp;
  clrscr();
```

```
printf("enter no of elements in the array") ;
scanf("%d", &n) ;
printf("\nelements in the array are ") ;
for( i=0 ; i<n ; i++ )
  {
    printf("\nenter element %d", i+1) ;
    scanf("%d", &arr[i]);
  }
printf("Selection Sort") ;
for( i=1 ; i<n ; i++ )
  {
    min = arr[i-1] ;
    pos = i-1;
    for( j=I ; j<n ; j++ )
      {
        if( arr[j] < min )
          {
            min = arr[j] ;
            pos = j ;
          }
      }
    if( pos != i-1 )
      {
        temp = arr[pos] ;
        arr[pos] = arr[i-1] ;
        arr[i-1] = temp ;
      }
  }
printf("after sorting new array is") ;
for( i=0 ; i<n ; i++ )
  {
    printf(" \t%d", arr[i]) ;
  }
getch() ;
}
```

Output

Enter number of elements   5

Enter elements of array

Enter element 1   80

Enter element 2   47

Enter element 3   51

Enter element 4   12

Enter element 5   67

Selection Sort

After sorting new array is

12   47   51   67   80

3.7   2-D Arrays/Two-Dimensional Arrays

We have already discussed 1-D arrays/ one-dimensional arrays and their various types and operations. Now, we will learn about two-dimensional arrays. Unlike one-dimensional arrays, 2-D arrays are organized in the form of grids or tables. They are collection of 1-D arrays. One-dimensional arrays are linearly organized in the memory. A 2-D array consists of two subscripts:

1. first subscript – which denotes the row

2. second subscript – which denotes the column

A 2-D array is represented as shown in the following figure:

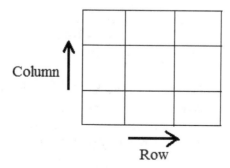

FIGURE 3.5. Representation of a 2-D array.

3.8   Declaration of Two-Dimensional Arrays

As we declared 1-D arrays, similarly we can declare two-dimensional arrays. For declaring two-dimensional arrays we must know the name of the array, the data type of each element, and the size of each dimension (size of rows and columns).

Syntax– `data_type array_name [row_size][column_size] ;`

A two-dimensional array is also called an m X n array, as it contains m X n elements where each element in the array can be accessed by i and j, where `i<=m` and `j<=n` and where i, j, m, n are defined as follows:

i, j = subscripts of array elements,

m = number of rows,

n = number of columns.

For Example – Let us take an array of 3 X 3 elements. Therefore, the array is declared as:

`int marks [3][3] ;`

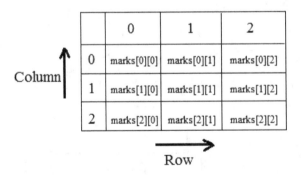

In the previous diagram the array has 3 rows and 3 columns. The first element in the array is denoted by `marks[0][0]`. Similarly, the second element will be denoted by `marks[0][1]`, and so on. Also, data elements in an array can be stored in the memory in two ways:

1. Row Major Order

In row major order the elements of the first row are stored before the elements of the second, third, and n rows. Here the data elements are stored in a row by row basis:

00	01	02	10	11	12	20	21	22				

2. Column Major Order

In column major order the elements of the first column are stored before the elements of the second, third, and n columns. Here the data elements are stored in a column by column basis:

00	10	20	01	11	21	02	12	22				

Now, we will calculate the base address of elements in a 2-D array, as the computer does not store the address of each element. It just stores the address of the first element and calculates the addresses of other elements from the base address of the first element of the array. Hence, the addresses of other elements can be calculated from the given base address.

1. Elements in Row Major Order

$Address(A[i][j]) = Base\ address(BA) + w(\ n(\ i\text{-}1\ ) + (\ j\text{-}1\ )\ )$

2. Elements in Column Major Order

$Address(\ A[i][j]\ ) = Base\ address(BA) + w\ (\ m(\ j\text{-}1\ ) + (\ i\text{-}1\ )\ )$

where w is the size in bytes to store one element.

Frequently Asked Questions

Q. Consider a 25 X 5 two-dimensional array of students which has a base address 500 and the size of each element is 2. Now calculate the address of the element student[15][3] assuming that the elements are stored in

a) Row major order

b) Column major order

Answer.

a) Row major order
Here we are given that w = 2, base address = 500, n = 5, i = 15, j = 3.

Address(A[i][j]) = Base address(BA) + w (n(i-1) + (j-1))

Address(student[15][3]) = 500 + 2 (5(15-1) + (3-1))

= 500 + 2 (5(14) + 2)

= 500 + 2 (72)

= 500 + 144

Address(student[15][3]) = 644

b) Column major order
Here we are given that w = 2, base address = 500, m = 25, i = 15, j = 3

Address(A[i][j]) = Base address(BA) + w (m(j-1) + (i-1))

Address(student[15][3]) = 500 + 2 (25(3-1) + (15-1))

= 500 + 2 (25(2) + 14)

= 500 + 2 (64)

Address(student[15][3]) = 500 + 128 = 628

3.9 Operations on 2-D Arrays

There are various operations that are performed on two-dimensional arrays, which include:

- **Sum** – Let A_{ij} and B_{ij} be the two matrices which are to be added together, storing the result into the third matrix C_{ij}. Two matrices will be added when they are compatible with each other; that is, they should have the same number of rows and columns.

$$C_{ij} = A_{ij} + B_{ij}$$

- **Difference** – Let A_{ij} and B_{ij} be the two matrices which are to be subtracted together, storing the result into third matrix C_{ij}. Two matrices will be subtracted when they are compatible with each other; that is, they should have same number of rows and columns.

$$C_{ij} = A_{ij} - B_{ij}$$

- **Product** – Let A_{ij} and B_{ij} be the two matrices which are to be multiplied together, storing the result into third matrix C_{ij}. Two matrices will be multiplied with each other if the number of columns in the first matrix is equal to number of rows in the second matrix. Therefore, m X n matrix A can be multiplied with a p X q matrix B if n=p.

$$C_{ij} = A_{ik} \ X \ B_{kj} \ for \ k=1 \ to \ n$$

- **Transpose** – The transpose of an m X n matrix A is equal to an n X m matrix B, where

$$B_{ij} = A_{ij}.$$

Write a program to read and display a 3 X 3 array.

```c
#include<stdio.h>
#include<conio.h>
void main()
{
  int array[3][3], i, j ;
  clrscr() ;
  printf("Enter the elements of array ") ;
  for( i=0 ; i<3 ; i++ )
    {
      for( j=0 ; j<3 ; j++ )
        {
          scanf("%d", &array[i][j]) ;
        }
    }
  printf(" The array is : ") ;
  for( i=0 ; i<3 ; i++ )
    {
      printf(" \n ") ;
      for( j=0 ; j<3 ; j++ )
        {
```

```
         printf(" array[%d][%d] = %d", i, j, array[i][j])  ;
      }
   }
 getch() ;
}
```

Output

Enter the elements of array

41

63

78

9

68

12

36

99

10

The array is:

array[0][0] = 41

array[0][1] = 63

array[0][2] = 78

array[1][0] = 9

array[1][1] = 68

array[1][2] = 12

array[2][1] = 36

array[2][2] = 99

array[2][3] = 10

Write a program to find the sum of two matrices.

```c
#include<stdio.h>
#include<conio.h>
void main()
{
  int i, j ;
  int A[3][3], B[3][3], c[3][3] ;
  clrscr() ;
  printf("Enter the elements of A matrix: ") ;
  for( i=0 ; i<3 ; i++ )
    {
      for( j=0 ; j<3 ; j++ )
        {
          scanf("%d", &A[i][j]) ;
        }
    }
  printf("Enter the elements of B matrix: ") ;
  for( i=0 ; i<3 ; i++ )
    {

      for( j=0 ; j<3 ; j++ )
        {
          scanf("%d", &B[i][j]) ;
        }
    }
  for( i=0 ; i<3 ; i++ )
    {
      for( j=0 ; j<3 ; j++ )
        {
          C[i][j] = A[i][j] + B[i][j] ;
        }
    }
  printf("Resultant matrix is : ") ;
  for( i=0 ; i<3 ; i++ )
    {
      for( j=0 ; j<3 ; j++ )
        {
          printf("%d", C[i][j]) ;
        }
    }
} //End of main
```

Output

Enter the elements of A matrix

1 2 3 4 5 6 7 8 9

Enter the elements of B matrix

9 8 7 6 5 4 3 2 1

Resultant matrix is :

10 10 10 10 10 10 10 10 10

Write a program to find the transpose of a 3 X 3 matrix.

```c
#include<stdio.h>
#include<conio.h>
void main()
{
  int i, j ;
  int matrix[3][3], transpose[3][3] ;
  clrscr() ;
  printf("Enter the elements of the matrix: ") ;
  for( i=0 ; i<3 ; i++ )
    {
      for( j=0 ; j<3 ; j++ )
        {
          scanf("%d", &matrix[i][j]) ;
        }
    }
  printf("The elements of matrix are ") ;
  for( i=0 ; i<3 ; i++ )
    {
      printf("\n") ;
      for( j=0 ; j<3 ; j++ )
```

```
          {
            printf("\t %d", matrix[i][j]) ;
          }
      }
   for( i=0 ; i<3 ; i++ )
      {
        for( j=0 ; j<3 ; j++ )
          {
            transpose[i][j] = matrix[j][i] ;
          }
      }
   printf("Elements of transposed matrix are ") ;
   for( i=0 ; i<3 ; i++ )
      {
        printf("\n") ;
        for( j=0 ; j<3 ; j++ )
          {
            printf("\t %d", transpose[i][j]) ;
          }
      }
} //End of main
```

Output

Enter the elements of the matrix

10 30 50 70 90 11 13 15 17

The elements of the matrix are

10 30 50

70 90 11

13 15 17

The elements of transpose matrix are

10 70 13

30 90 11

13 15 17

3.10 Multidimensional Arrays/ N-Dimensional Arrays

A multidimensional array is also known as an n-dimensional array. It is an array of arrays. It has n indices in it which also justifies its name of n-dimensional array. An n-dimensional array is an $m_1 \times m_2 \times m_3 \times \ldots \times m_n$ array as it contains $m_1 \times m_2 \times m_3 \times \ldots \times m_n$ elements. Multidimensional arrays are declared and initialized in the same way as one-dimensional and two-dimensional arrays.

3.11 Calculating the Address of 3-D Arrays

Just like 2-D arrays we can store 3-D arrays in two ways, Row Major Order and Column Major Order.

1. **Elements in Row Major Order**

   Address $([i][j][k])$ = Base Address (BA) + w $(L_3(L_2 (E_1) + E_2) + E_3)$

2. **Elements in Column Major Order**

   Address $([i][j][k])$ = Base Address (BA) + w $((E_3 L_2 + E_2)L_1 + E_1)$

   Where L is length of index, L = Upper bound − Lower bound + 1,

   E is effective address, E = i − Lower bound.

Frequently Asked Questions

Q. Let us take a 3-D array A(4:12, -2:1, 8:14) and calculate the address of A(5, 4, 9) using row major order and column major order where the base address is 500 and w = 4.

Answer.
Length of three dimensions of A −

$L_1 = 12 - 4 + 1 = 9$

$L_2 = 1 - (-2) + 1 = 4$

$L_3 = 14 - 8 = 6$

Therefore, A contains 9 X 4 X 6 = 216 elements

Now, $E_1 = 5 - 4 = 1$

$E_2 = 4 - (-2) = 8$

$E_3 = 9 - 8 = 1$

a) **Row Major Order**

Address $(5, 4, 9 = 500 + 4 (6 (4(1) + 8) + 1)$

$= 500 + 4 (6 (12) + 1)$

$= 500 + 4 (73)$

Address $(5, 4, 9) = 500 + 292 = 792$

b) **Column Major Order**

Address $(5, 4, 9) = 500 + 4 ((1.4 + 8) 9 + 1)$

$= 500 + ((12)9 + 1)$

Address $(5, 4, 9) = 500 + 145 = 645$

Write a program to read and display a 2 X 2 X 2 array.

```
#include<stdio.h>
#include<conio.h>
void main()
{
  int array[2][2][2], i, j, k ;
  clrscr() ;
  printf("Enter the elements of array ") ;
  for( i=0 ; i<2 ; i++ )
    {
      for( j=0 ; j<2 ; j++ )
        {
          for( k=0 ; k<2 ; k++ )
            {
              scanf("%d", &array[i][j][k]) ;
            }
        }
    }
  printf(" The array is : ") ;
  for( i=0 ; i<2 ; i++ )
    {
      printf(" \n ") ;
      for( j=0 ; j<2 ; j++ )
```

```
        {
         printf(" \n ") ;
         for( k=0 ; k<2 ; k++ )
           {
             printf(" array[%d][%d][%d] = %d", i, j, k,
             array[i][j][k] ) ;
           }
        }
     }
  getch() ;
}
```

Output

Enter the elements of array

4

23

9

8

6

2

1

7

The array is :

array[0][0][0] = 4

array[0][0][1] = 23

array[0][1][0] = 9

array[0][1][1] = 8

array[1][0][0] = 6

array[1][0][1] = 2

array[1][1][0] = 1

array[1][1][1] = 7

3.12 Arrays and Pointers

A pointer is a special type of variable that is used to store addresses. Pointers can be used to access and manipulate data stored in the memory. Pointers are very frequently used in arrays, because pointers are more efficient in handling arrays and data tables. A pointer can be referred to as the address of a person's home which can help us easily reach the destination. The concept of arrays is very much bound to the concept of pointers. Now let us take an example: if we have an array of 10 elements declared as

```
int array[10] = { 10, 20 ,32, 7, 19, 89, 60, 54,
12, 77 }
```

The previous array will be stored in the memory as shown in the following figure:

arr[0]	arr[1]	arr[2]	arr[3]	arr[4]	arr[5]	arr[6]	arr[7]	arr[8]	arr[9]
10	20	32	7	19	89	60	54	12	77
100	102	104	106	108	110	112	114	116	118

ptr

FIGURE 3.6. Memory Representation of array[ ].

The starting address of the array (100) is the base address of the array. The base address is the address of the first element in the array. Now we will use a pointer variable to store the address of the first element; in other words, ptr will point to the first element of the array.

```
int * ptr ;

ptr = &array[0] ;
```

We can also store the addresses of other elements. If the pointer variable holds the address of the first element in the array, then the address of the successive elements can be calculated by ptr++.

```
int * ptr ;
ptr = &array[0] ;
ptr++ ;
printf(" The value of second element is %d",*ptr);
```

A pointer variable can be prefixed or postfixed with increment or decrement operators. Increment or decrement will depend upon the data type, for example, `int – 2 bytes, float – 4 bytes, char – 1 byte`, and so on.

3.13 Array of Pointers

An array of pointers is declared as `int * ptr[10]`.

Therefore, from the previous statement an array of 10 pointers is declared where each of the pointers points to a variable. Code for an array of pointers is given as follows:

```c
#include<stdio.h>
void main()
{
  int i, j, k, l, m ;
  int * arr[4] ;
  i = 25
  j = 50
  k = 75
  l = 100
  arr[0] = &i
  arr[1] = &j
  arr[2] = &k
  arr[3] = &l
  for( m=0 ; m<4 ; m++ )
    {
      printf("%u\n", arr[m]) ;
    }
}
```

Output

32012

35260

31010

30058

Note: Here the addresses are random in the memory.

3.14 Arrays and Their Applications

Arrays are very frequently used in C as they have various applications which are very useful. These applications include:

- Arrays are used for sorting the elements in ascending or descending order.

- Arrays are also used to implement various other data structures like stacks, queues, hash tables, etc.

- Arrays are widely used to implement matrices, vectors, and various other kinds of rectangular tables.

- Various other operations can be performed on the arrays which include searching, merging, sorting, etc.

Frequently Asked Questions

Q. List some of the applications of arrays.

Answer.
1. Arrays are very useful in storing the data in contiguous memory locations.
2. Arrays are used for implementing various other data structures such as stacks, queues, etc.
3. Arrays are very useful as we can perform various operations on them.

3.15 Sparse Matrices

A sparse matrix is a matrix with a relatively high proportion of zero entries in it. A sparse matrix is used as it utilizes the memory space efficiently. Storing of null elements in the matrix is a waste of memory, so we adopt a technique to store only not null elements in the sparse matrices.

For Example:

$$\begin{bmatrix} 0 & 0 & 6 & 0 & 0 \\ 1 & 0 & 0 & 0 & 0 \\ 0 & 0 & 0 & 0 & 2 \\ 0 & 5 & 0 & 0 & 0 \end{bmatrix}$$

FIGURE 3.7. Representation of a sparse matrix.

3.16 Types of Sparse Matrices

There are three types of sparse matrices, which are:

1. **Lower-triangular matrix** – In this type of sparse matrix all the elements above the main diagonal must have a zero value, or in other words we can say that all the elements below the main diagonal should contain non-zero elements only. This type of matrix is called a lower-triangular matrix.

$$\begin{bmatrix} 5 & 0 & 0 & 0 \\ 4 & 6 & 0 & 0 \\ -3 & 9 & -5 & 0 \\ 2 & 1 & 7 & 3 \end{bmatrix}$$

FIGURE 3.8. Lower-triangular matrix.

2. **Upper-triangular matrix** – In this type of sparse matrix all the elements above the main diagonal should contain non-zero elements only, or in other words we can say that all the elements below the main diagonal should have a zero value. This type of matrix is called an upper-triangular matrix.

$$\begin{bmatrix} 1 & 2 & 3 & 4 \\ 0 & 6 & -1 & 5 \\ 0 & 0 & -7 & 8 \\ 0 & 0 & 0 & 9 \end{bmatrix}$$

FIGURE 3.9. Upper-triangular matrix.

3. **Tri-diagonal matrix** – In this type, elements with a non-zero value can appear only on the diagonal or adjacent to the diagonal. This type of matrix is a tri-diagonal matrix.

$$\begin{bmatrix} 6 & 2 & 0 & 0 \\ 8 & 9 & -2 & 0 \\ 0 & 5 & -7 & 3 \\ 0 & 0 & 1 & 4 \end{bmatrix}$$

FIGURE 3.10. Tri-diagonal matrix.

3.17 Representation of Sparse Matrices

There are two ways in which the sparse matrices can be represented, which are:

1. **Array Representation/ 3-Tuple Representation** – This representation contains three rows in which the first row represents the number of rows, columns, and non-zero entries/values in the sparse matrix. Elements in the other rows give information about the location and value of non-zero elements.

For example, let us consider a sparse matrix.

$$\begin{bmatrix} 0 & 0 & 0 & 0 & 1 \\ 0 & 0 & 0 & 0 & 0 \\ 0 & 0 & 3 & 0 & 0 \\ 0 & 5 & 0 & 0 & 0 \end{bmatrix}$$

FIGURE 3.11. A sparse matrix.

An array representation of the previous sparse matrix will be:

Row	Column	Non-Zero Value
0	4	1
2	2	3
3	1	5

2. **Linked Representation** – A sparse matrix can also be represented in a linked way. In this representation we store the number of rows, columns, and non-zero entries in a single node, and there is a pointer which points to the next location. Let us consider an example to understand more clearly.

Let us consider a sparse matrix:

$$\begin{bmatrix} 0 & 6 & 0 & 0 & 0 \\ 0 & 0 & 0 & 0 & 0 \\ 0 & 0 & 0 & 8 & 3 \end{bmatrix}$$

Linked representation of the sparse matrix will be as follows:

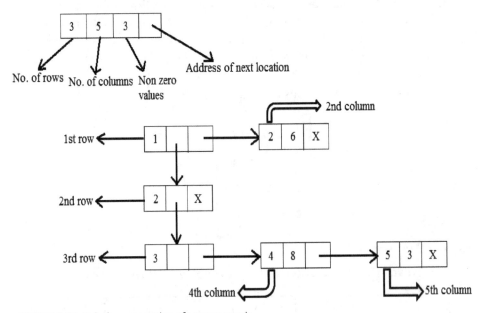

FIGURE 3.12. Linked representation of a sparse matrix.

Frequently Asked Questions

Q. Explain the sparse matrix.

Answer.
A matrix in which the number of zero entries is much higher than the number of non-zero entries is called a sparse matrix. The natural method of representing matrices in memory as two-dimensional arrays may not be suitable for sparse matrices. One may save space by storing only non-zero entries. We can represent a sparse matrix by using a three-tuple method of storage:

1. Row Major Method
2. Column Major Method

3.18 Summary

- An array is a collection of homogeneous (similar) types of data elements in contiguous memory. An array is a linear data structure because all elements of an array are stored in linear order.

- An array must be declared before it is used.

- The initialization of the elements of an array at compile time is done in the same way as when we initialize the normal or ordinary variables at the time of their declaration.

- Initialization of elements of an array at runtime refers to the method of inputting the values from the keyboard.

- The address of the elements in a 1-D array can be calculated very easily, as an array stores all its data elements in contiguous memory locations, storing the base address.

- Traversing an array means to access each and every element in an array exactly once so that it can be processed.

- Insertion of an element in an array refers to the operation of adding an element to the array. It can be done in three ways.

- Deleting an element from an array refers to the operation of the removal of an element from an array. Deletion is also done in three ways.

- Searching an element in an array means to find whether a particular value exists in an array or not. If that particular value is found, then the searching is said to be successful and the position/location of that particular value is returned. If the value is not found, then searching will be said to be unsuccessful.

- A linear search is a very simple technique used to search a particular value in an array.

- The merging of two arrays means copying the elements of the first and second array into the third array.

- Sorting an array means arranging the data elements of a data structure in a specified order either in ascending or descending order.

- Selection Sort is a sorting technique that works by finding the smallest value in the array and placing it in the first position. After that, it then finds the second smallest value and places it in the second position. This process is repeated until whole array is sorted.

- Unlike one-dimensional arrays, 2-D arrays are organized in the form of grids or tables. They are collection of 1-D arrays.

- For declaring two-dimensional arrays, we must know the name of the array, the data type of each element, and the size of each dimension (size of row and column).

- A multidimensional array is also known as an n-dimensional array. It is an array of arrays. It has n indices in it, which also justifies its name of an n-dimensional array.

- A pointer is a special type of variable that is used to store addresses. Pointers can be used to access and manipulate data stored in the memory.

- A sparse matrix is a matrix with a relatively high proportion of zero entries in it. A sparse matrix is used because it utilizes the memory space efficiently.

3.19 Exercises

3.19.1 Theory Questions

1. What do you mean by an array and how is it represented in the memory?

2. What are the various operations that can be performed on arrays? Discuss in detail.

3. Explain the concept of two-dimensional arrays.

4. Briefly explain how arrays are related to the pointers.

5. In how many ways can arrays be initialized? Explain in detail.

6. What do you understand by multidimensional arrays?

7. Consider a one-dimensional array declared as intarr[10], and calculate the address of arr[7] if the base address is 200 and the size of each element is 2.

8. What do you mean by sorting an array? Explain.

9. Write an algorithm to perform the selection sort technique.

10. Explain the process of merging two arrays along with the algorithm.

11. Consider a two-dimensional array declared as intarray[10][10], and calculate the address of the element array[5][6] if the base address = 10000 and the size of each element = 2 assuming the elements are to be stored in column major order.

12. Give some of the applications of the arrays.

13. What do you understand by a linear search? Give the algorithm.

14. Give the advantages of using the selection sort technique for sorting the elements in an array.

15. What are sparse matrices? Also explain its types.

16. Consider a three-dimensional array A(2:6, -1:7, 9:10), and calculate the address of A(9, 6, 8) using row major order and column major order where the base address is 2000 and w = 4.

17. Explain the linked representation of sparse matrices in detail.

18. Write the formulae for calculating the addresses of elements in row major and column major order in 2-D and 3-D arrays.

3.19.2 Programming Questions

1. Write a program to traverse an entire array.

2. Write a program to perform insertion at a specified position in a one-dimensional array.

3. Write a program to multiply two matrices.

4. Write a program which reads a matrix and displays the

   a) Sum of its rows' elements

   b) Sum of its columns' elements

   c) Sum of its diagonal's elements

5. Write a program to show the concept of an array of pointers.

6. Write a program to perform the deletion of an element from the beginning.

7. Write a menu-driven program to perform various insertions and deletions in an array using the switch case.

8. Write a program to read and display a square matrix.

9. Write a program which reads an array of 50 integers. Display all the pairs of elements whose sum is 25.

10. Write a program to convert a normal matrix into a sparse matrix.

11. Write a program to read an array of 10 integers and then find the smallest and largest numbers in the array.

12. Write a program to add two sparse matrices.

3.19.3 Multiple Choice Questions

1. If an array is declared as intarray[20][20], then how many elements can it store?

   A. 20

   B. 40

   C. 400

   D. None of these

2. The elements of an array are always stored in _____ memory locations.

   A. Random

   B. Sequential

   C. Both

   D. None of these

3. What will be the output of the given program?

```
#include<stdio.h>
main()
{
  int  arr[5] = {5, 1, 15, 20, 25} ;
  int a, b, c ;
   a = ++arr[1] ;
   b =  arr [1]++ ;
   c =   arr[i++] ;
  printf("%d, %d, %d", a, b, c) ;
  return 0 ;
}
```

   A. 1, 2, 5

   B. 2, 1, 15

   C. 3, 2, 15

   D. 2, 3, 20

4. What will be the output of the following program after execution?
   void main()

   ```
   {
   int array[5] = {2, 4, 6, 8, 10} ;
   printf("%d", array[6]) ;
   }
   ```

   A. 0

   B. 10

   C. Garbage value

   D. None of these

5. If an array is declared as int array[], then the nth element can be accessed by:

   A. array[n]

   B. *(array + n)

   C. *(n + array)

   D. None of these

   E. All of these

6. Array[5] = 19 initializes the _____ element of the array with value 19.

   A. 4th

   B. 5th

   C. 6th

   D. 7th

7. By default, the first subscript of the array is _____

   A. 2

   B. 1

   C. -1

   D. 0

8. A multi-dimensional array, in simple terms, is an

   A. array of arrays

   B. array of pointers

   C. array of addresses

9. A loop is used to access all the elements of an array.

   A. False

   B. True

   C. None of the above

10. Declaring an array means specifying the _____, _____, and _____.

   A. Data type, name, size

   B. Data elements, name, data type

   C. Name, size, address

   D. All of the above

LINKED LISTS

In This Chapter

- Introduction
- Definition of a linked list
- Memory allocation in a linked list
- Types of linked lists
- Header linked lists
- Applications of linked lists
- Polynomial representation
- Summary
- Exercises

4.1 Introduction

We have already learned that an array is a collection of data elements stored in contiguous memory locations. Also, we studied that arrays were static in nature; that is, the size of the array must be specified when declaring an array, which limits the number of elements to be stored in the array. For example, if we have an array declared as intarray[15], then the array can contain a maximum of 15 elements and not more than that. This method of allocating memory is good when the exact number of elements is known, but if we are not sure of the number of elements then there will be a problem, as in data structures our aim is to make programs efficient by consuming less memory space along with minimal time. To overcome this problem, we will use linked lists.

4.2 Definition of a Linked List

A linked list is a linear collection of data elements. These data elements are called nodes, and they point to the next node by means of pointers. A linked list is a data structure which can be used to implement other data structures such as stacks, queues, trees, and so on. *A linked list is a sequence of nodes in which each node contains one or more than one data field and a pointer which points to the next node.* Also, linked lists are dynamic in nature; that is, memory is allocated as and when required. There is no need to know the exact size or exact number of elements as in the case of arrays. The following is an example of a simple linked list which contains five nodes:

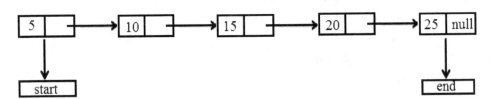

FIGURE 4.1 A linked list.

In the previous figure, we have made a linked list in which each node is divided into two parts:

1. *The first part contains the information/data.*

2. *The second part contains the address of the next node.*

The last node will not have any next node connected to it, so it will store a special value called NULL. Usually NULL is defined by -1. Therefore, the NULL pointer represents the end of the linked list. Also, there is another special pointer START that stores the address of the first node of the linked list. Therefore, the START pointer represents the beginning of the linked list. If START = NULL then it means that the linked list is empty. A linked list, since each node points to another node which is of the same type, is known as a self-referential data type or a self-referential structure.

The self-referential structure in a linked list is as follows:

```
struct node
{
  int info ;
  struct node *next ;
} ;
```

Practical Application:

- A simple real-life example is how each coach on a train is connected to its previous and next coach (except the first and last). In terms of programming, consider the coach body as a node and the connectors as links to the previous and next nodes.

- The brain is also a good example of a linked list. In the initial stages of learning something by heart, the natural process is to link one item to another item. It's a subconscious act. Also, when we forget something and try to remember, then our brain follows associations and tries to link one memory with another and so on until we finally recall the lost memory.

Frequently Asked Questions

Q1. Define linked list.

Answer.
A linked list is a linear collection of data elements, called nodes, where the linear order is given by means of pointers. It is a dynamic data structure. For every data item in a linked list, there is an associated pointer that gives the memory location of the next data item in the linked list. The data items in the linked list are not in consecutive memory locations.

Frequently Asked Questions

Q2. List the advantages and disadvantages of a linked list.

Answer.

Advantages of linked lists

1. Linked lists are dynamic data structures; that is, they can grow or shrink during the execution of the program.

2. Linked lists have efficient memory utilization. Memory is allocated whenever it is required, and it is de-allocated whenever it is no longer needed.

3. Insertion and deletion are easier and efficient.

4. Many complex applications can be easily carried out with linked lists.

Disadvantages of linked lists

1. They consume more space because every node requires an additional pointer to store the address of the next node.

2. Searching a particular element in the list is difficult and time consuming.

4.3 Memory Allocation in a Linked List

The process or concept of linked lists supports dynamic memory allocation. Now, what is meant by dynamic memory allocation? The answer to this simple question is that the process of allocating memory during the execution of the program or the process of allocating memory to the variables at the runtime is called dynamic memory allocation. Until now we have studied arrays in which we used to declare the size of the array initially such as array[50]. This statement after execution allocates the memory for 50 integers. But there can be a problem if we use only 30% of the memory and the rest of the allocated memory is either wasted or is not used. Therefore, to overcome this problem of wastage of memory space or in other words to utilize the memory efficiently, dynamic memory allocation is used which allows us to allocate/reserve the memory that is actually required. Hence, it will overcome the problem of wastage of memory space as in the case of arrays. Dynamic memory allocation is best when we are not aware of the memory requirements in advance. C language provides some functions which are used to dynamically allocate memory, as shown in the following table:

Function	Use of the Function	Syntax
malloc()	Allocates the requested memory space and returns a pointer at the first byte of allocated memory space.	ptr = (cast-type *) malloc(byte-size) ;
calloc()	Allocates memory space for elements of an array, initializes to zero returning a pointer to the memory.	ptr = (cast-type *) calloc(n, elem-size) ;
free()	Deallocates the previously allocated memory space.	free(ptr) ;
realloc()	Alters the size of memory allocated previously.	ptr = realloc (ptr, newsize) ;

4.4 Types of Linked Lists

There are different types of linked lists which we will be discussed in this section. These include:

1. Singly Linked List

2. Circular Linked List

3. Doubly Linked List

4. Header Linked List

Now we will discuss all of them in detail.

4.4.1 Singly Linked List

A Singly Linked List is the simplest type of linked list in which each node contains some information/data and only one pointer which points to the next node in the linked list. The traversal of data elements in a singly linked list can be done only in one way.

FIGURE 4.2 Singly linked list.

4.4.2 Operations on a Singly Linked List

Various operations can be performed on a singly linked list, which include:

- Traversing a linked list
- Searching for a given value in a linked list
- Inserting a new node in a linked list
- Deleting a node from a linked list
- Concatenation of two linked lists
- Sorting a linked list
- Reversing a linked list

Let us now discuss all these operations in detail.

a) Traversing a linked list

Traversing a linked list means accessing all the nodes of the linked list exactly once. A linked list will always contain a START pointer, which stores the address of the first node of the linked list and which also represents the beginning of the linked list, and a NULL pointer which represents the end of the linked list. For traversing a linked list, we will use another pointer variable PTR which will point to the node which is currently being accessed. The algorithm for traversing a linked list is shown as follows:

Algorithm for traversing a linked list

```
Step 1: Set PTR = START
Step 2: Repeat Steps 3 & 4 while PTR != NULL
Step 3: Print PTR -> INFO
Step 4: Set PTR = PTR -> NEXT
            [End of Loop]
Step 5: Exit
```

b) Searching for a given value in a linked list

Searching for a value in a linked list means to find a particular element/value in the linked list. As we discussed earlier, a node in a linked list contains two parts; one part is the information part and the other is the address part. Hence, searching refers to the process of finding whether or not the given value exists in the information part of any node. If the value is present, then the address of that particular value is returned and the search is said to be successful; otherwise, the search is unsuccessful. A linked list will always contain a START pointer which stores the address of the first node of the linked list and also represents the beginning of the linked list, and a NULL pointer which represents the end of the linked list. There is another variable PTR which will point to the current node being accessed. SEARCH_VAL is the value to be searched in the linked list and POS is the position/address of the node at which the value is found. The algorithm for searching a value in a linked list is given as follows:

Algorithm to search a value in a linked list

```
Step 1: Set PTR = START
Step 2: Repeat Step 3 while PTR != NULL
Step 3: IF SEARCH_VAL = PTR -> INFO
            Set POS = PTR
            Print Successful Search!!
            Go to Step 5
            [End of If]
            ELSE
            Set PTR = PTR -> NEXT
            [End of Loop]
Step 4: Print Unsuccessful Search!!
Step 5: Exit
```

For example, if we have a linked list and we are searching for 15 in the list, then the steps are shown as follows:

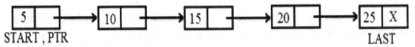

The value to be searched is 15 but here ptr->info = 5, therefore 15 != 5, hence we will move to the next node

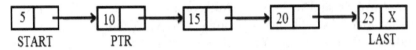

Now ptr -> info = 10, therefore 15 != 10, hence we will move to the next node

Here, ptr -> info = 15, therefore 15 = 15, so POS = PTR. POS will store the address of 15. Hence, search is successful

FIGURE 4.3 An example of searching a linked list.

c) Inserting a new node in a linked list

Here, we will learn how a new node is inserted in an existing linked list. We will discuss three cases in the insertion process which include:

1. New node is inserted at beginning of the linked list.

2. New node is inserted at end of the linked list.

3. New node is inserted after the given node in a linked list.

Let us now discuss all of these cases in detail.

1. Inserting a new node in the beginning of a linked list

In the case of inserting a new node in the beginning of a linked list, we will first check the overflow condition, which is whether the memory is available for a new node. If the memory is not available, then an overflow message is displayed; otherwise, the memory is allocated for the new node. Now, we will initialize the node with its info part, and its address part will contain the address of the first node of the list which is the START pointer. Hence, the new node is added as the first node in the list and the START pointer will point to the first node of the list. Now to understand better let us take an example. Consider a linked list as shown in the following figure with five nodes; a new node will be inserted in the beginning of the linked list.

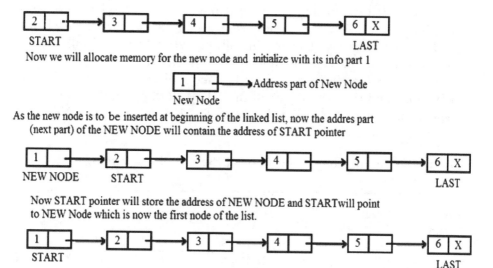

FIGURE 4.4 Inserting a new node at the beginning of a linked list.

From the previous example, it is clear how a new node will be inserted in an already existing linked list. Let us now understand the its algorithm:

Algorithm for inserting a new node in the beginning of a linked list

```
Step 1: START
Step 2: IF PTR = NULL
            Print OVERFLOW
            Go to Step 8
            [End of If]
Step 3: Set NEW NODE = PTR
Step 4: Set PTR = PTR -> NEXT
Step 5: Set NEW NODE -> INFO = VALUE
Step 6: Set NEW NODE -> NEXT = START
Step 7: Set START = NEW NODE
Step 8: EXIT
```

2. Inserting a new node at the end of a linked list

To insert the new node at the end of the linked list, we will first check the overflow condition, which is whether the memory is available for a new node. If the memory is not available, then an overflow message is displayed; otherwise, the memory is allocated for the new node. Then a PTR variable is made which will initially point to START and will be used to traverse the linked list until it reaches the last node. When it reaches the last node, the NEXT part of the last node will store the address of the new node and the NEXT part of the NEW NODE will contain NULL which will denote the end of the linked list. Let us understand this with the help of an algorithm:

Algorithm for inserting a new node at the end of a linked list

```
Step 1: START
Step 2: IF PTR = NULL
            Print OVERFLOW
            Go to Step 10
            [End of If]
Step 3: Set NEW NODE = PTR
Step 4: Set PTR = PTR -> NEXT
Step 5: Set NEW NODE -> INFO = VALUE
Step 6: Set NEW NODE -> NEXT = NULL
Step 7: Set PTR = START
Step 8: Repeat Step 8 while PTR -> NEXT != NULL
            Set PTR = PTR -> NEXT
            [End of Loop]
Step 9: Set PTR -> NEXT = NEW NODE
Step 10: EXIT
```

From the previous algorithm we understand how to insert a new node at the end of already existing linked list. Now we will study further with the help of an example. Consider a linked list as shown in the following figure with four nodes, and a new node will be inserted at the end of the linked list:

Now we will allocate memory for the new node and initialize with its info part

As the NEW NODE is to be inserted at the end of the linked list, so we will use another pointer variable PTR which will initially point to the START.

Now in the next step PTR variable will be moved till the last node until it has found a NULL. And finally it reaches the last node.

After reaching to the last node now we will store the address of the NEW NODE in the address part(next part) of PTR so that it starts pointing to the NEW NODE.

Finally, NEW NODE is inserted at the end of the linked list.

FIGURE 4.5 Inserting a new node at the end of a linked list.

3. Inserting a new node after a node in a linked list

In this case, a new node is inserted after a given node in a linked list. As in the other cases, we will again check the overflow condition. If the memory for the new node is available, it will be allocated; otherwise, an overflow message is printed. Then a PTR variable is made which will initially point to START, and the PTR variable is used to traverse the linked list until it reaches the value/node after which the new node is to be inserted. When it reaches that node/value, then the NEXT part of that node will store the address of the new node and the NEXT part of the NEW NODE will store the address of its next node in the linked list. Let us understand this with the help of an example. Consider a linked list with four nodes, and a new node is to be inserted after the given node:

Now we will allocate memory for the new node and initialize with its info part 1

Two variables PTR and PREV are used which initially point to the START such that PTR, PREV, START all point to the first node.

Now, PTR and PREV are moved till info part of PREV is equal to value of node after which NEW NODE is to be inserted. PREV will always point to the node before PTR.

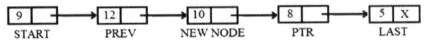

Hence, NEW NODE is to inserted after 12. Also address part of PREV will now store the address of NEW NODE. Similarly, address part of NEW NODE will store the address of PTR.

FIGURE 4.6 Inserting a new node after a given node in a linked list.

From the previous example, we learned how a node can be inserted after a given node. Now we will understand this with the help of an algorithm.

Algorithm for inserting a new node after a given node in a linked list

```
Step 1: START
Step 2: IF PTR = NULL
            Print OVERFLOW
            Go to Step 10
            [End of If]
Step 3: Set NEW NODE = PTR
Step 4: Set PTR = PTR -> NEXT
```

```
Step 5: Set NEW NODE -> INFO = VALUE
Step 6: Set PTR = START
Step 7: Set PREV = PTR
Step 8: Repeat Step 8 while PREV -> INFO != GIVEN_VAL
            Set PREV = PTR
            Set PTR = PTR -> NEXT
            [End of Loop]
Step 9: Set PREV -> NEXT = NEW NODE
Step 10: Set NEW NODE -> NEXT = PTR
Step 11: EXIT
```

d) Deleting a node from a linked list

In this section, we will learn how a node is deleted from an already existing linked list. We will discuss three cases in the deletion process which include:

1. Node is deleted from the beginning of the linked list.

2. Node is deleted from the end of the linked list.

3. Node is deleted after a given node from the linked list.

Let us now discuss all of these cases in detail.

1. Deleting a node from the beginning of the linked list

In the case of deleting a node from the beginning of a linked list, we will first check the underflow condition, which occurs when we try to delete a node from a linked list which is empty. This situation exists when the **START** pointer is equal to **NULL**. If the condition is true, then the underflow message is printed on the screen; otherwise, the node is deleted from the linked list. Consider a linked list as shown in the following figure with five nodes; the node will be deleted from the beginning of the linked list.

From the previous example, it is clear how a node is deleted from an already existing linked list. Let us now understand its algorithm:

Algorithm for deleting a node from the beginning of a linked list

```
Step 1: START
Step 2: IF START = NULL
            Print UNDERFLOW
            [End Of If]
Step 3: Set PTR = START
Step 4: Set START = START -> NEXT
Step 5: FREE PTR
Step 6: EXIT
```

We will make another pointer variable PTR which will initially point to the START.

Now, as the first node is to be deleted so we will move START pointer to the next node which is at 9.

Finally we will free the first node of the linked list. Hence, new linked list will be –

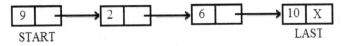

FIGURE 4.7 Deleting a node from the beginning of a linked list.

In the previous algorithm, first we check for the underflow condition, that is, whether there are any nodes present in the linked list or not. If there are no nodes, then an underflow message will be printed; otherwise, we move to Step 3 where we are initializing initializing PTR to START, that is, PTR will now store the address of the first node. In the next step START is moved to the second node, as now START will store the address of the second node. Hence, the first node is deleted and the memory which was occupied by the PTR (initially the first node of the list) is free.

2. Deleting a node from the end of the linked list

In the case of deleting a node from the end of the linked list, we will first check the underflow condition. This situation exists when the START pointer is equal to NULL. Hence, if the condition is true then the underflow message is printed on the screen; otherwise, the node is deleted from the linked list. Consider a linked list as shown in the following figure with five nodes; the node will be deleted from the end of the linked list.

We will make another pointer variable PTR which will initially point to the START.

We will make another pointer variable PREV which will always point to the node just before the node pointed by PTR. Move PTR till the next part of the PTR = NULL.

Finally set the next part of PREV is equal to NULL. Also LAST will now point to PREV and the last node is deleted.

FIGURE 4.8 Deleting a node from the end of a linked list.

Let us now understand the algorithm of deleting a node from the end of a linked list.

Algorithm for deleting a node from the end of a linked list

```
Step 1: START
Step 2: IF START = NULL
            Print UNDERFLOW
            [End Of If]
Step 3: Set PTR = START
Step 4: Repeat while PTR -> NEXT != NULL
            Set PREV = PTR
            Set PTR = PTR -> NEXT
            [End of Loop]
Step 5: Set PREV -> NEXT = NULL
Step 6: FREE PTR
Step 7: EXIT
```

In the previous algorithm, we again check for the underflow condition. If the condition is true then the underflow message is printed; otherwise, PTR is initialized to the START pointer, that is, PTR is pointing to the first node of the list. In the loop we have taken another pointer variable PREV which will always point to one node before the PTR node. After reaching the second to last and last node of the list, we will set the next part of PREV to NULL. Therefore, the last node is deleted, and the memory which was occupied by the PTR node is now free.

3. Deleting a node after a given node from the linked list

In the case of deleting a node after a given node from the linked list, we will again check the underflow condition as we checked in both the other cases. This situation exists when the START pointer is equal to NULL. Hence, if the condition is true then the underflow message is printed; otherwise, the node is deleted from the linked list. Consider a linked list as shown in the following figure with five nodes initially; the node will be deleted after a given node from the linked list.

We will make another pointer variable PTR which will initially point to the START.

Two other pointer varaibles PTR and PREV are used which will initially point to START such that PTR, PREV, START all point to the first node.

Now PTR and PREV are moved such that PREV points to the node containing the value after which the node is to be deleted and PTR points to the node which is to be deleted.

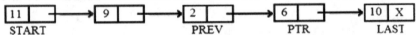

Now we know that node containing 6 is to be deleted from the linked list. So, we set the NEXT part of PREV to NEXT part of PTR such that PREV will now point to LAST node.

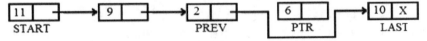

Now PTR is deleted and new list after deletion is given below -

FIGURE 4.9 Deleting a node after a given node from the linked list.

Now let us understand the previous case with the help of an algorithm.

Algorithm for deleting a node after a given node from the linked list

```
Step 1: START
Step 2: IF START = NULL
            Print UNDERFLOW
            [End Of If]
Step 3: Set PTR = START
Step 4: Set PREV = START
Step 5: Repeat while PREV  -> INFO != GIVEN_VAL
            Set PREV = PTR
            Set PTR = PTR -> NEXT
            [End of Loop]
Step 6: Set PREV -> NEXT = PTR -> NEXT
Step 7: FREE PTR
Step 8: EXIT
```

In the previous algorithm, we are first checking for the underflow condition. If the condition is true then the underflow message is printed; otherwise, PTR is initialized to the START pointer, that is, PTR is pointing to the first node of the list. In the loop we have taken another pointer variable PREV which will always point one node before the PTR node. After reaching the node containing the given value which is to be deleted, we will set the next pointer of the node containing the given value to the address contained in the next part of the succeeding node. Therefore, the node is deleted and the memory which was being occupied by the PTR is now free.

e) Concatenation of two linked lists

A concatenated linked list is created by the process of concatenating two different-sized linked lists into one linked list. Let us understand the concept of concatenation with the help of a C function:

```c
void concatenate(struct node *head1, struct node *head2)
{
  struct node *ptr;
  ptr = head1;
  while(ptr→next!= NULL)
    {
      ptr = ptr→next;
    }
  ptr→next = head2 ;
}
```

f) Sorting a linked list

Sorting is the process of arranging the data elements in a sequence, either in ascending order or in descending order. In this we are arranging the information of the linked list in a sequence. Let us understand it with the help of a C function:

```c
void sorting()
{
  int new;
  struct node *ptr, *temp;
  ptr = start;
  while(ptr→next!= NULL)
    {
      temp = ptr→next;
      while(temp!=NULL)
        {
          if(ptr→info > temp→info)
            {
              temp = ptr→info;
              ptr→info = temp→info;
              temp→info = new;
            }
          temp = temp→next;
        }
      ptr = ptr→next;
    }
}
```

g) Reversing a linked list

In the process of reversing a linear linked list, we will take three pointer variables, that is, PREV, PTR, and NEW, which will hold the addresses of the previous node, current node, and the next node respectively in the linked list. We will begin with the address of the first node which is held in another pointer variable START which is assigned to PTR, and PREV is assigned to NULL. Now, let us understand it with the help of a C function:

```
void reverse_list()
{
 ptr = start;
 prev = NULL;
 while(ptr != NULL)
   {
    new = ptr→next;
    ptr→next = prev;
    prev = ptr;
    ptr = new;
   }
}
```

Write a menu-driven program for singly linked lists performing insertion and deletion of all cases.

```
# include <stdio.h>
# include <conio.h>
# include <alloc.h>
struct node          // Self Referential Structure
{
 int data ;
 struct node * next ;
}* start ;
void add_at_beg();
void add_after(int item);
void add_before(int item);
void add_at_end();
void delete_at_beg();
void delete_at_mid();
void delete_at_end();
void main()
{
 int choice, item;
 start= NULL:
 clrscr();
 do
   {
    printf(" SINGLY LINKED LISTS");
    printf("\n\t\t MENU");
```

```
printf(" \n 1 : addition at beginning");
printf(" \n 2 : addition after given node");
printf(" \n 3 : addition before given node");
printf(" \n 4 : addition at end");
printf(" \n 5 : deletion at beginning");
printf(" \n 6 : deletion at middle");
printf(" \n 7 : deletion at end");
printf(" \n 8 :Exit");
printf(" \n Enter your choice: ");
scanf("%d", &choice);
switch(choice)
  {
    case 1:              // Case 1 is for addition
                         //     at beginning

    add_at_beg();
    break;

    case 2:              // Case 2 is for addition
                         //     after a given node
    printf(" \n enter item");
    scanf(" %d", &item);
    add_after(item);
    break;

    case 3:              // Case 3 is for addition
                         //     before a given node
    printf(" \n enter item");
    scanf(" %d", &item);
    add_before(item);
    break;

    case 4:
    add_at_end();        // Case 4 is for addition
                         //     at end

    break;

    case 5:
    delete_at_beg();     // Case 5 is for deletion
                         //     at beginning
    break;
```

```
        case 6:
        printf(" \n enter item\n");
        scanf(" %d",&item);    // Case 6 is for deletion
                               at middle
        delete_at_mid(item);
        break:

        case7:
        delete_at_end();        // Case 7 is for deletion
                                at end

        case 8:
          exit(0);

        default:
        printf("wrong choice");
        break;
     }
   }
 while(ch!=  0);
 getch();
}

void_add_at_beg()
{
  struct node *ptr = (struct node *) malloc (size of
  (struct node));     //memory is allocated for ptr
  printf(" enter value of node");
  scanf("%d", &ptr→data);
  ptr→next = start;
  start= ptr;
  printf("Successful Insertion!!");
  getch();
  return;
}

void add_after(int item)
{
  struct node *ptr = (struct node *) malloc (size of
  ( structnode));
  struct node *loc ;
```

```
  loc = start;
  printf(" enter new node");
  scanf("%d", &ptr→data);
  if(start==NULL)
    {
      printf(" list is empty , create a new list");
      ptr→next = start;
      start= ptr;
      return;
    }
  while(loc != NULL)
    {
      if(loc→data==item)
        {
          ptr→next = loc→next;
          loc→next = ptr;
          printf(" data is entered");
          return;
        }
      else
        {
          loc = loc→next;
        }
    }
}

void_add_before(int item)
{
  struct node *ptr = (struct node *) malloc ( size of
  (struct node));
  struct node *loc, *old;
  old = start;
  loc= start→next;
  printf(" enter new node value ");
  scanf("%d", &ptr→data);
  if(start==NULL)
    {
      printf(" list is empty ,create 1st  node");
      ptr→next =start;
      start= ptr;
    }
```

```
   while(loc!= NULL)
    {
      if(loc→data==item)
        {
          ptr→next = loc;
          old→next = ptr;
          printf(" data is entered before item");
          return;
        }
      else
        {
          old=loc;
          loc = loc→next;
        }
    }
}

void add_at_end()
{
  struct node*ptr = (struct node *) malloc (size of
  ( struct node));
  struct node*loc ;
  loc = start;
  printf(" enter new node");
  scanf("%d", &ptr→data);
  if(start==NULL)
    {
      printf(" list is empty , create new node");
      ptr→next = start;
      start= ptr;
    }
  while(loc→next!= NULL)
    {
      loc = loc→next;
    }
  ptr→next = NULL;
  loc→next = ptr;
  printf(" data is entered at the end");
  return;
}
```

```c
void delete_at_beg()
{
 struct node *ptr;
 if(start == NULL)
   {
     printf(" list is empty , create new");
     ptr→next = start;
     start = ptr;
     return;
   }
   else
   {
     ptr = start;
     start = start→next;
   }
  printf(" %d data is deleted",p→data);
  free(ptr);
}

void delete_at_mid(int item)
{
  struct node*ptr ,*loc *old;
  if(start==NULL)
   {
     printf(" list is empty , create 1st  node ");
     ptr→next = start;
     start= ptr;
   }
   else
    {
      old = start;
      loc = start→next;
      while(loc!=NULL)
        {
          if(loc→data == item)
            {
              ptr = loc;
```

```
                old→next=loc→next;
                free(ptr);
                return;
              }
            else
              {
                old = loc;
                loc = loc→next;
              }
            printf("item not found");
          }
      }
}

void delete_at_end()
{
  struct node *ptr,*loc;
  if(start == NULL)
    {
      printf(" list is empty , create 1st node ");
      ptr→next = start;
      start = ptr;
    }
  else
    {
      loc = start;
      ptr = start→next;
      while(ptr→next!=NULL)
        {
          loc = ptr;
          ptr = ptr→next;
        }
      loc→next= NULL;
      free(ptr);
    }
}
```

Output –

SINGLY LINKED LIST

MENU

1: Addition at beginning

2: Addition after given node

3: Addition before given node

4: Addition at end

5: Deletion at beginning

6: Deletion at middle

7: Deletion at end

8: Exit

Enter your choice: 1

Enter value for node

15

Successful Insertion!!

After discussing the singly linked list, we will now learn about another type of linked list, the circular linked list.

4.4.3 Circular Linked Lists

Circular linked lists are a type of singly linked list in which the address part of the last node will store the address of the first node, unlike in singly linked lists in which the address part of the last node stores a unique value, NULL. While traversing a circular linked list we can begin from any node and we traverse the list in any direction, because a circular linked list does not have a first or last node. The memory declarations for representing a circular linked list are the same as for a linear linked list.

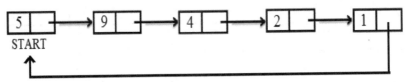

FIGURE 4.10 Circular linked list.

4.4.4 Operations on a Circular Linked List

Various operations can be performed on a circular linked list, which include:

a. Inserting a new node in a circular linked list

b. Deleting a node from a circular linked list

Let us now discuss both these cases in detail.

a) Inserting a new node in a circular linked list

Here, we will learn how a new node is inserted in an existing linked list. We will discuss two cases in the insertion process which include:

1. New node is inserted at the beginning of the circular linked list.

2. New node is inserted at the end of the circular linked list.

3. New node is inserted after a given node (same as that for a singly linked list).

1. Inserting a new node in the beginning of a circular linked list

In the case of inserting a new node in the beginning of a circular linked list, we will first check the overflow condition, that is, whether the memory is available for a new node. If the memory is not available then an overflow message is printed; otherwise, the memory is allocated for the new node. Now we will initialize the node with its info part, and its address part will contain the address of the first node of the list which is the START pointer. Hence, the new node is added as the first node in the list, and the START pointer will point to the first node of the list. Now let us take an example. Consider a linked list as shown in the following figure with four nodes; a new node is to be inserted in the beginning of the circular linked list.

Now memory is allocated for the new node and we initialize its info part with 6

We will take another pointer variable PTR which will initially point to the START.

Now PTR is moved so that it points to the last node.

As the new node is to be inserted in the beginning of the list so now PTR will store the address of new node and new node will store the the address of START.

Now the new node is inserted at the beginning so START will point to the first node of the list i.e. new node.

FIGURE 4.11 Inserting a new node in the beginning of a circular linked list.

Now let us understand the previous case with the help of an algorithm.

Algorithm for inserting a new node in the beginning of a circular linked list

```
Step 1: START
Step 2: IF TEMP = NULL
             Print OVERFLOW
             [End Of If]
Step 3: Set NEW NODE = TEMP
Step 4: Set NEW NODE -> INFO = VAL
```

```
Step 5: Set PTR = START
Step 6: Repeat while PTR  -> NEXT != START
            Set PTR = PTR -> NEXT
            [End of Loop]
Step 7: Set NEW NODE -> NEXT = START
Step 8: Set PTR -> NEXT = NEW NODE
Step 9: Set START = NEW NODE
Step 10: EXIT
```

2. Inserting a new node at the end of a circular linked list

In this case, we will first check the overflow condition, that is, whether the memory is available for a new node. If the memory is not available, then an overflow message is printed; otherwise, the memory is allocated for the new node. Then a PTR variable is made which will initially point to START, and the PTR variable will be used to traverse the linked list until it reaches the last node. When it reaches the last node, the NEXT part of the last node will store the address of the new node and the NEXT part of the NEW NODE will contain the address of the first node of the linked list which is denoted by START. Let us understand it with the help of an algorithm:

Algorithm for inserting a new node at the end of a circular linked list

```
Step 1: START
Step 2: IF TEMP = NULL
            Print OVERFLOW
            [End Of If]
Step 3: Set NEW NODE = TEMP
Step 4: Set NEW NODE -> INFO = VAL
Step 5: Set NEW NODE -> NEXT = START
Step 6: Set PTR = START
Step 7: Repeat while PTR  -> NEXT != START
            Set PTR = PTR -> NEXT
            [End of Loop]
Step 8: Set PTR -> NEXT = NEW NODE
Step 9: EXIT
```

Let us take an example to understand it. Consider a linked list as shown in the following figure with four nodes; a new node is to be inserted at the end of the circular linked list.

FIGURE 4.12 Inserting a new node at the end of a circular linked list.

b) Deleting a node from a circular linked list

In this section, we will learn how a node is deleted from an already existing circular linked list. We will discuss two cases in the deletion process which include:

1. Node is deleted from the beginning of the circular linked list.

2. Node is deleted from the end of the circular linked list.

3. Node is deleted after a given node (same as that for a singly linked list).

1. Deleting a node from the beginning of a circular linked list

In the case of deleting a node from the beginning of a linked list, we will first check the underflow condition which occurs when we try to delete a node from the linked list which is empty. This situation exists when the START pointer is equal to NULL. Hence, if the condition is true then an underflow message is displayed; otherwise, the node is deleted from the linked list. Consider a linked list as shown in the following figure with four nodes; the first node will be deleted from the linked list.

We will make another pointer variable PTR which will initially point to START

Now PTR is moved till it points to the last node.

Now the Next part of PTR will store the address of the second node of the list and first node is freed. So the second node now becomes the first node of the list.

FIGURE 4.13 Deleting a node from the beginning of a circular linked list.

From the previous example, it is clear how a node will be deleted from an already existing linked list. Let us now understand its algorithm:

Algorithm for deleting a node from the beginning of a circular linked list

```
Step 1: START
Step 2: IF START = NULL
            Print UNDERFLOW
            [End Of If]
Step 3: Set PTR = START
Step 4: Repeat while PTR -> NEXT != START
            Set PTR = PTR -> NEXT
            [End of Loop]
Step 5: Set PTR -> NEXT = START -> NEXT
Step 6: FREE START
Step 7: Set START = START -> NEXT
Step 8: EXIT
```

The previous algorithm shows how a node is deleted from the beginning of the linked list. First, we check with the underflow condition. Now a pointer variable PTR is used which will traverse the entire list until it reaches the last node of the list. Now, we change the next part of PTR to store the address of the second node of the list. Hence, the memory that occupied the first node is freed. Finally, the second node now becomes the first node of the linked list.

2. Deleting a node from the end of a circular linked list

In this case, we will first check the underflow condition, which is when we try to delete a node from the linked list which is empty. This situation occurs when the START pointer is equal to NULL. Hence, if the condition is true then an underflow message is printed; otherwise, the node is deleted from the linked list. Consider a linked list as shown in the following figure with four nodes; the last node will be deleted from the linked list.

We will take two pointer variables PTR and PREV which will initially point to START.

Now PTR is moved till it reaches the last node. PREV will always point to the node preceding PTR.

Now the Next part of PREV will store the address of START and the memory allocated by PTR is freed. So PREV is now the last node of the list.

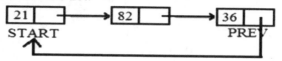

FIGURE 4.14 Deleting a node from the end of a circular linked list.

Let us now understand its algorithm:

Algorithm for deleting a node from the end of a circular linked list

```
Step 1: START
Step 2: IF START = NULL
            Print UNDERFLOW
            [End Of If]
Step 3: Set PTR = START
Step 4: Repeat while PTR -> NEXT != START
            Set PREV = PTR
            Set PTR = PTR -> NEXT
            [End of Loop]
Step 5: Set PREV -> NEXT = START
Step 6: FREE PTR
Step 7: EXIT
```

The previous algorithm shows how a node is deleted from the end of the linked list. First, we are checking with the underflow condition. Now a pointer variable PTR is used to traverse the entire list until it reaches the last node of the list. In the while loop we will use another pointer variable PREV which will always point to the node preceding PTR. When we reach the last node and its preceding node, that is, the second to last node, we will now change the next part of PREV to store the address of START. Hence, the memory occupied by the last node is freed. Finally, the second to last node now becomes the last node of the linked list. In this way, deletion of a node from the end is done in a circular linked list.

Write a menu-driven program for circular linked lists performing insertion and deletion of all the cases.

```
# include <stdio.h>
# include <conio.h>
# include <alloc.h>
struct node          //Self Referential Structure
{
  int data ;
  struct node * next ;
}* start ;
void add_at_beg();
void add_after(int item);
void add_before(int item);
void add_at_end();
void delete_at_beg();
void delete_at_mid();
void delete_at_end();
void main()
{
  int choice, item;
  start = NULL:
  clrscr();
  do
    {
      printf(" CIRCULAR LINKED LISTS");
      printf("\n\t MENU");
      printf(" \n 1 : addition at beginning");
      printf(" \n 2 : addition after given node");
```

```
printf(" \n 3 : addition before given node");
printf(" \n 4 : addition at end");
printf(" \n 5 : deletion at beginning");
printf(" \n 6 : deletion at middle");
printf(" \n 7 : deletion at end");
printf(" \n 8 : Exit");
scanf("%d", &choice);
switch(choice)
  {
    case 1:      //Case 1 is for addition at beginning
    add_at_beg();
    break;

    case 2:      //Case 2 is for addition after given
                   node
    printf(" \n enter item");
    scanf(" %d", &item);
    add_after(item);
    break;

    case 3:       //Case 3 is for addition before given
                    node
    printf(" \n enter item");
    scanf(" %d", &item);
    add_before(item);
    break;

    case 4:
    add_at_end(); //Case 4 is for addition at end-
    break;

    case 5:
    delete_at_beg(); //Case 5 is for deletion at beg-
                          inning
    break;
    case 6:
    printf(" \n enter item\n");
    scanf(" %d", &item);  //Case 6 is for deletion at
                            middle

    delete_at_mid(item);
    break:
```

```
        case7:
        delete_at_end();   //Case 7 is for deletion at end

        case 8:
        exit(0);

        default:
        printf("wrong choice");
        break;
      }
   }
  while(ch!=  0);
  getch();
}

void_add_at_beg()
{
  struct node *temp;
  struct node *ptr = (struct  node  *)  malloc (size of
  (struct node));
  printf(" enter value of node");
  scanf("%d", &ptr→data);
  temp = start;
  while(temp→next != start)
    {
      temp = temp→next;
    }
  ptr→next = start;
  start= ptr;
  temp→next = start;
  printf("Successful Insertion!!");
  getch();
  return;
}

void add_after(int item)
{
  struct node *ptr = (struct  node  *)  malloc (size of
  (struct node));
  struct node *loc ;
  loc = start;
```

```
   printf(" enter new node");
   scanf("%d", &ptr→data);
   if(start==NULL)
     {
       printf(" list is empty , create a new list");
       ptr→next = start;
       start= ptr;
       return;
     }
   while(loc != NULL)
     {
       if(loc→data==item)
         {
           ptr→next = loc→next;
           loc→next = ptr;
           printf(" data is entered");
           return;
         }
       else
         {
           loc = loc→next;
         }
     }
}

void add_before(int item)
{
  struct node *ptr = (struct node *) malloc ( size of
  (struct node));
  struct node *loc, *old;
  old = start;
  loc= start→next;
  printf(" enter new node value ");
  scanf("%d", &ptr→data);
  if(start==NULL)
    {
      printf(" list is empty ,create 1st  node");
      ptr→next =start;
      start= ptr;
    }
  while(loc!= NULL)
```

```
   {
     if(loc→data==item)
       {
         ptr→next = loc;
         old→next = ptr;
         printf(" data is entered before item");
         return;
       }
     else
       {
         old=loc;
         loc = loc→next;
       }
   }
}

void add_at_end()
{
  struct node *ptr = (struct node *) malloc (size of
  ( struct node));
  struct node *temp ;
  temp = start;
  printf(" enter new node");
  scanf("%d", &ptr→data);
  if(start == NULL)
    {
      printf(" list is empty , create new node");
      ptr→next = start;
      start= ptr;
    }
  while(temp→next != start)
    {
      temp = temp→next;
      temp→next = ptr;
      ptr→next = start;
      printf(" data is entered at the end");
      return;
    }
}
void delete_at_beg()
{
   struct node *ptr, *temp;
```

```
   if(start == NULL)
    {
      printf(" list is empty , create new");
      ptr→next = start;
      start = ptr;
      return;
    }
  temp = start;
  while(temp→next != start);
  temp = temp→next;
  ptr = start;
  start = ptr→next;
  temp→next = start;
  printf(" %d data is deleted", ptr→data);
  free(ptr);
}

void delete_at_mid(int item)
{
  struct node*ptr ,*loc *old;
  if(start==NULL)
    {
      printf(" list is empty , create 1st  node ");
      ptr→next = start;
      start= ptr;
    }
  else
    {
      old = start;
      loc = start→next;
      while(loc!=NULL)
        {
          if(loc→data == item)
            {
              ptr = loc;
              old→next=loc→next;
              free(ptr);
              return;
            }
          else
            {
```

```
            old = loc;
            loc = loc→next;
          }
        printf("item not found");
      }
    }
}

void delete_at_end()
{
  struct node *ptr, *temp;
  if(start == NULL)
    {
      printf(" list is empty , create 1st node ");
      ptr→next = start;
      start = ptr;
    }
  temp = start;
  ptr = start→nex t;
  while(temp→next != start)
    {
      ptr = temp;
      temp = temp→next;
    }
  ptr→next =start;
  free(temp);
}
```

Output –

CIRCULAR LINKED LIST

MENU

1. Addition at beginning

2. Addition after given node

3. Addition before given node

4. Addition at end

5. Deletion at beginning

6. Deletion at middle

7. Deletion at end

8. Exit

Enter your choice: 1
Enter value for node
34
Successful Insertion!!

4.4.5 Doubly Linked List

A doubly linked list is also called a two-way linked list; it is a special type of linked list which can point to the next node as well as the previous node in the sequence. In a doubly linked list each node is divided into three parts:

1. The first part is called the previous pointer, which contains the address of the previous node in the list.

2. The second part is called the information part, which contains the information of the node.

3. The third part is called the next pointer, which contains the address of the succeeding node in the list.

START   LAST

FIGURE 4.15 Doubly linked list.

The structure of a doubly linked list is given as follows:

```
struct node
{
  struct node * prev ;
  int info ;
  struct node * next ;
} ;
```

The first node of the linked list will contain a NULL value in the previous pointer to indicate that there is no element preceding in the list and, similarly, the last node will also contain a NULL value in the next pointer field to indicate that there is no element succeeding it in the list. Doubly linked lists can be traversed in both directions.

4.4.6 Operations on a Doubly Linked List

Various operations can be performed on a circular linked list, which include:

- Inserting a New Node in a Doubly Linked List

- Deleting a Node from a Doubly Linked List

Let us now discuss both these operations in detail.

a) Inserting a New Node in a Doubly Linked List

In this section, we will learn how a new node is inserted into an already existing doubly linked list. We will consider four cases for the insertion process in a doubly linked list.

1. New Node is inserted at the beginning.

2. New Node is inserted at the end.

3. New Node is inserted after a given node.

4. New Node is inserted before a given node.

1. Inserting a new node in the beginning of a doubly linked list

In this case of inserting a new node in the beginning of a doubly linked list, we will first check with the overflow condition, that is, whether the memory is available for a new node. If the memory is not available, then an overflow message is displayed; otherwise, the memory is allocated for the new node. Now, we will initialize the node with its info part, and its address part will contain the address of the first node of the list, which is the START pointer. Hence, the new node is added as the first node in the list, and the START pointer will point to the first node of the list. Now to understand better let us take an example. Consider a linked list as shown in following figure with four nodes; a new node will be inserted in the beginning of the linked list.

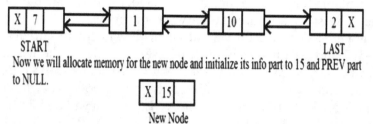

Now we will allocate memory for the new node and initialize its info part to 15 and PREV part to NULL.

New Node

As the new node is to be inserted at the beginning of the linked list, so the address part (next part) of the new node will contain the address of the START pointer. Similarly, the prev part of the START will store the address of the new node. Now the New Node becomes the first node of the list.

FIGURE 4.16 Inserting a new node in the beginning of a doubly linked list.

From the above example, it is clear how a new node will be inserted in an already existing doubly linked list. Let us now understand its algorithm:

Algorithm for inserting a new node in the beginning of a doubly linked list

```
Step 1: START
Step 2: IF PTR = NULL
            Print OVERFLOW
            Go to Step 9
            [End of If]
Step 3: Set NEW NODE = PTR
Step 4: Set NEW NODE -> INFO = VALUE
Step 5: Set NEW NODE -> PREV = NULL
Step 6: Set NEW NODE -> NEXT = START
Step 7: Set START -> PREV = NEW NODE
Step 8: Set START = NEW NODE
Step 9: EXIT
```

2. Inserting a new node at the end of a doubly linked list

In the case of inserting the new node at the end of the linked list, we will first check the overflow condition, which is whether the memory is available for a new node. If the memory is not available then an overflow message is printed; otherwise, the memory is allocated for the new node. Then a PTR variable is made which will initially point to START, and a PTR variable will be used to traverse the list until it reaches the last node. When it reaches the last node, the NEXT part of the last node will store the address of the new node, and the NEXT part of the NEW NODE will contain NULL, which will denote the end of the linked list. The PREV part of the NEW NODE will store the address of the node pointed to by PTR. Let us understand it with the help of an algorithm:

Algorithm for inserting a new node at the end of a linked list

```
Step 1: START
Step 2: IF PTR = NULL
            Print OVERFLOW
            [End of If]
Step 3: Set NEW NODE = PTR
Step 4: Set PTR = PTR -> NEXT
Step 5: Set NEW NODE -> INFO = VALUE
Step 6: Set NEW NODE -> NEXT = NULL
Step 7: Set PTR = START
Step 8: Repeat while PTR -> NEXT != NULL
            Set PTR = PTR -> NEXT
            [End of Loop]
Step 9: Set PTR -> NEXT = NEW NODE
Step 10: Set NEW NODE -> PREV = PTR
Step 11: EXIT
```

Hence, from the previous algorithm we understood how to insert a new node at the end of a doubly linked list. Now, we will study this further with the help of an example. Consider a linked list as shown in the following figure with four nodes; a new node will be inserted at the end of the doubly linked list:

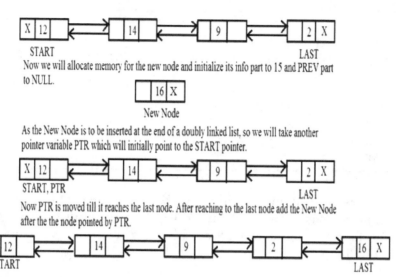

FIGURE 4.17 Inserting a new node at the end of a doubly linked list.

3. Inserting a new node after a given node in a doubly linked list

In this case, a new node is inserted after a given node in a doubly linked list. As in the other cases, we will again check the overflow condition in it. If the memory for the new node is available, then it will be allocated; otherwise, an overflow message is displayed. Then a PTR variable is made which will initially point to START, and the PTR variable is used to traverse the linked list until its value becomes equal to the value after which the new node is to be inserted. When it reaches that node/value, then the NEXT part of that node will store the address of the new node, and the PREV part of the NEW NODE will store the address of the preceding node. Let us understand it with the help of the following algorithm:

Algorithm for inserting a new node after a given node in a linked list

```
Step 1: START
Step 2: IF PTR = NULL
             Print OVERFLOW
             Go to Step 10
             [End of If]
Step 3: Set NEW NODE = PTR
Step 4: Set NEW NODE -> INFO = VALUE
```

```
Step 5: Set PTR = START
Step 6: Repeat while PTR -> INFO != GIVEN_VAL
            Set PTR = PTR -> NEXT
            [End of Loop]
Step 7: Set NEW NODE -> NEXT = PTR -> NEXT
Step 8: Set NEW NODE -> PREV = PTR
Step 9: Set PTR -> NEXT = NEW NODE
Step 10: EXIT
```

Now, we will understand more about the same with the help of an example. Consider a doubly linked list as shown in the following figure with four nodes; a new node will be inserted after a given node in the linked list:

FIGURE 4.18 Inserting a new node at the end of a doubly linked list.

4. Inserting a new node before a given node in a doubly linked list

In this case, a new node is inserted before a given node in a doubly linked list. As in the other cases, we will again check the overflow condition in it. If the memory for the new node is available, then it will be allocated; otherwise, an overflow message is displayed. Then a PTR variable is made which will initially point to START, and the PTR variable is used to traverse the linked list until its value becomes equal to the value before which the new node is to be inserted. When it reaches that node/value, then the PREV part of that node will store the address of the NEW NODE, and the NEXT part of the NEW NODE will store the address of the succeeding node. Now to understand better let us take an example. Consider a linked list as shown in the following figure with four nodes; a new node will be inserted before a given node in the linked list.

FIGURE 4.19 Inserting a new node before a given node in a doubly linked list.

From the previous example, it is clear how a new node will be inserted in an already existing doubly linked list. Let us now understand its algorithm:

Algorithm for inserting a new node before a given node in a doubly linked list

```
Step 1: START
Step 2: IF PTR = NULL
            Print OVERFLOW
            Go to Step 10
            [End of If]
Step 3: Set NEW NODE = PTR
Step 4: Set NEW NODE -> INFO = VALUE
Step 5: Set PTR = START
Step 6: Repeat while PTR -> INFO != GIVEN_VAL
            Set PTR = PTR -> NEXT
            [End of Loop]
Step 7: Set NEW NODE -> NEXT = PTR
Step 8: Set NEW NODE -> PREV = PTR -> PREV
Step 9: Set PTR -> PREV = NEW NODE
Step 10: EXIT
```

b) Deleting a Node from a Doubly Linked List

In this section, we will learn how a node is deleted from an already existing doubly linked list. We will consider four cases for the deletion process in a doubly linked list.

1. Node is deleted from the beginning of the linked list.

2. Node is deleted from the end of the linked list.

3. Node is deleted after a given node from the linked list.

4. Node is deleted before a given node from the linked list.

Now let us discuss all the previous cases in detail.

1. Deleting a node from the beginning of the doubly linked list

In the case of deleting a node from the beginning of the doubly linked list, we will first check the underflow condition, which occurs when we try to delete a node from the linked list which is empty. This situation exists when the START pointer is equal to NULL. Hence, if the condition is true, then the underflow message is displayed; otherwise, the node is deleted from the linked list. Consider a linked list as shown in the following figure with five nodes; the node will be deleted from the beginning of the linked list.

Here we will free the memory occupied by the first node of the list. Also the PREV part of the second node will contain NULL. Hence now the second node becomes the first node of the list.

FIGURE 4.20 Deleting a node from the beginning of the doubly linked list.

Let us understand this with the help of an algorithm:

Algorithm for deleting a node from the beginning of a doubly linked list

```
Step 1: START
Step 2: IF START = NULL
            Print UNDERFLOW
            [End Of If]
Step 3: Set PTR = START
Step 4: Set START = START -> NEXT
Step 5: Set START -> PREV = NULL
Step 6: FREE PTR
Step 7: EXIT
```

In the previous algorithm, first we are checking for the underflow condition, which is whether there are any nodes present in the linked list or not. If there are no nodes then an underflow message will be printed; otherwise, we move to Step 3 where we are initialling PTR to START, that is, PTR will now store the address of the first node. In the next step START is moved to the second node, as now START will store the address of the second node. Also, the PREV part of the second node will now contain a value NULL. Hence, the first node is deleted and the memory which was being occupied by the PTR is free (initially the first node of the list).

2. Deleting a node from the end of the doubly linked list

In the case of deleting a node from the end of the linked list, we will first check the underflow condition. This situation exists when the START pointer is equal to NULL. Hence, if the condition is true then underflow message is printed on the screen; otherwise, the node is deleted from the linked list. Consider a linked list as shown in the following figure with five nodes; the node will be deleted from the end of the linked list.

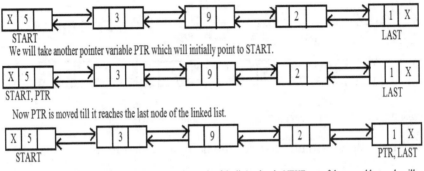

We will take another pointer variable PTR which will initially point to START.

Now PTR is moved till it reaches the last node of the linked list.

Here we will free the memory occupied by PTR (last node of the list). Also the NEXT part of the second last node will contain NULL. Hence, the second last node now becomes the last node of the list.

FIGURE 4.21 Deleting a node from the end of the doubly linked list.

From the previous example, it is clear how a node will be deleted from an already existing doubly linked list. Let us now understand its algorithm:

Algorithm for deleting a node from the end in a doubly linked list

```
Step 1: START
Step 2: IF START = NULL
            Print UNDERFLOW
            [End Of If]
Step 3: Set PTR = START
Step 4: Repeat while PTR -> NEXT != NULL
            Set PTR = PTR -> NEXT
            [End of Loop]
Step 5: Set PTR -> PREV -> NEXT= NULL
Step 6: FREE PTR
Step 7: EXIT
```

In the previous algorithm, again we are checking for the underflow condition. If the condition is true then the underflow message is printed; otherwise, PTR is initialized to the START pointer, that is, PTR is pointing to the first node of the list. In the loop PTR is traversed until it reaches the last node of the list. After reaching the last node of the list, we can also access the second to last node by taking the address from the PREV part of the last node. Therefore, the last node is deleted, and the memory is now free which was being occupied by the PTR.

3. Deleting a node after a given node from the doubly linked list

In the case of deleting a node after a given node from the linked list, we will again check the underflow condition as we checked in both the other cases. This situation exists when the START pointer is equal to NULL. Hence, if the condition is true then the underflow message is displayed; otherwise, the node is deleted from the linked list. Consider a linked list as shown in the following figure with five nodes; the node will be deleted after a given node from the linked list.

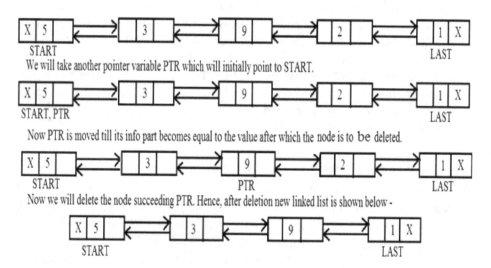

FIGURE 4.22 Deleting a node after a given node from the doubly linked list.

Now let us understand the previous case with the help of an algorithm.

Algorithm for deleting a node after a given node from the linked list

```
Step 1: START
Step 2: IF START = NULL
            Print UNDERFLOW
            [End Of If]
Step 3: Set PTR = START
Step 4: Repeat while PTR  -> INFO != GIVEN_VAL
            Set PTR = PTR -> NEXT
            [End of Loop]
Step 5: Set TEMP = PTR -> NEXT
Step 6: Set PTR -> NEXT = TEMP -> NEXT
Step 7: Set LAST -> PREV = PTR
Step 8: FREE TEMP
Step 9: EXIT
```

In the previous algorithm, first we are checking for the underflow condition. If the condition is true then the underflow message is printed; otherwise, PTR is initialized to the START pointer, that is, PTR is pointing to the first node of the list. In the loop PTR is moved until its info part becomes equal to the node after which the node is to be deleted. After reaching that node of the list, we can also access the succeeding node by taking the address from the NEXT part of that node. Therefore, the node is deleted and the memory is now free which was being occupied by the TEMP.

4. Deleting a node before a given node from the doubly linked list

In the case of deleting a node before a given node from the linked list, we will again check the underflow condition as we checked in both the other cases. This situation occurs when the START pointer is equal to NULL. Hence, if the condition is true then the underflow message is printed; otherwise, the node is deleted from the linked list. Consider a linked list as shown in the following figure with five nodes; the node will be deleted before a given node from the linked list.

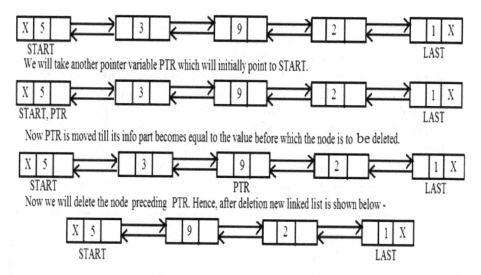

We will take another pointer variable PTR which will initially point to START.

Now PTR is moved till its info part becomes equal to the value before which the node is to be deleted.

Now we will delete the node preceding PTR. Hence, after deletion new linked list is shown below -

FIGURE 4.23 Deleting a node before a given node from the doubly linked list.

From the previous example, it is clear how a node will be deleted from an already existing doubly linked list. Let us now understand its algorithm:

Algorithm for deleting a node before a given node in a doubly linked list

```
Step 1: START
Step 2: IF START = NULL
            Print UNDERFLOW
            [End Of If]
Step 3: Set PTR = START
Step 4: Repeat while PTR  -> INFO != GIVEN_VAL
            Set PTR = PTR -> NEXT
            [End of Loop]
Step 5: Set TEMP = PTR -> PREV
Step 6: Set TEMP -> PREV -> NEXT = PTR
Step 7: Set PTR -> PREV = TEMP -> PREV
Step 8: FREE TEMP
Step 9: EXIT
```

In the above algorithm, first we are checking for the underflow condition. If the condition is true then the underflow message is printed; otherwise, PTR is initialized to the START pointer, that is, PTR is pointing to the first node of the list. In the loop PTR is moved until its info part becomes equal to the node before which the node is to be deleted. After reaching that node of the list, we can also access the preceding node by taking the address from the PREV part of that node. Therefore, the node is deleted and the memory is now free which was being occupied by the TEMP.

Write a menu-driven program for doubly linked lists performing insertion and deletion of all cases.

```c
# include <stdio.h>
# include <conio.h>
# include <alloc.h>
struct node //Self Referential Structure
{
  struct node *prev ;
  int data ;
  struct node *next ;
}* start ;
void add_at_beg() ;
void add_after(int item);
void add_before(int item);
void add_at_end();
void delete_at_beg();
void delete_at_mid();
void delete_at_end();
void main()
{
  int choice, item;
  start= NULL:
  clrscr();
  do
    {
      printf(" DOUBLY LINKED LISTS");
      printf("\n\t MENU");
      printf(" \n 1 : addition at beginning");
      printf(" \n 2 : addition after given node");
      printf(" \n 3 : addition before given node");
      printf(" \n 4 : addition at end");
```

```c
printf(" \n 5 : deletion at beginning");
printf(" \n 6 : deletion at middle");
printf(" \n 7 : deletion at end");
printf(" \nEnter your choice: ");
scanf("%d", &choice);
switch(choice)
  {
    case 1:
                        //Case 1 is for addition at beg-
                          inning
    add_at_beg();
    break;

    case 2:
                        //Case 2 is for addition after
                          given node
    printf("\n enter item");
    scanf(" %d", &item);
    add_after(item);
    break;

    case 3:
                        //Case 3 is for addition before
                          given node
    printf(" \n enter item");
    scanf(" %d", &item);
    add_before(item);
    break;

    case 4:
    add_at_end();       //Case 4 is for addition at end
    break;

    case 5:
    delete_at_beg();  //Case 5 is for deletion at
                          beginning
    break;

    case 6:
                        //Case 6 is for deletion at
                          middle
    printf(" \n enter item\n");
    scanf(" %d", &item);
```

```c
        delete_at_mid(item);
        break:

        case7:
        delete_at_end();   //Case 7 is for deletion at end

        case 8:
        exit(0);

        default:
        printf("wrong choice");
        break;
      }
  }
 while(ch!=  0);
 getch();
}

void_add_at_beg()
{
  struct  node  *ptr  =  (struct  node*)  malloc  (size  of
( struct node));
  printf(" enter new node");
  scanf("%d", &ptr→data);
  if(start == NULL)
    {
      printf(" list is empty , create new");
      ptr→next = NULL;
      ptr→prev= NULL;
      start= ptr;
      return;
    }
  else
    {
      ptr→next = start;
      start→prev = ptr;
      ptr→prev = NULL;
      start = ptr;
      return;
    }
```

```
    printf("data is entered");
  }

 void add_after(int item)
 {
  struct node *ptr = (struct node*) malloc (size of
  ( struct node));
  struct node*loc ;
  loc = start;
  printf(" enter new node");
  scanf("%d", &ptr→data);
  if(start == NULL)
    {
      printf(" list is empty , create new");
      ptr→next = NULL;
      ptr→prev= NULL;
      start = ptr;
      return;
    }
  while(loc!= NULL)
    {
      if(loc→data==item)
        {
          loc→next→prev = ptr;
          ptr→next = loc→next;
          loc→next = ptr;
          ptr→prev = loc;
          return;
        }
      else
        {
          loc = loc→next;
        }
    }
  printf(" data is entered");
}

 void_add_before(int item)
 {
  struct node *ptr = (struct node *) malloc ( size of
  (struct node));
```

```
  struct node *loc;
  loc = start;
  printf(" enter new node");
  scanf("%d", &ptr→data);
  if(start == NULL)
    {
     printf(" list is empty , create new");
     ptr→next = NULL;
     ptr→prev= NULL;
     start = ptr;
     return;
    }
  while(loc!= NULL)
    {
     if(loc→data==item)
       {
         loc→prev→next = ptr;
         ptr→prev= loc→prev;
         loc→prev = ptr;
         ptr→next = loc;
         return;
       }
     else
       {
         loc = loc→next;
       }
    }
 printf(" data is entered before item");
}

void add_at_end()
{
 struct node *ptr = (struct node*) malloc (size of
 (struct node));
 struct node *loc ;
 loc = start;
 printf(" enter new node");
 scanf("%d", &ptr→data);
 if(start == NULL)
   {
     printf(" list is empty , create new");
```

```
      ptr→next = NULL;
      ptr→prev = NULL;
      start = ptr;
      return;
    }
  while(loc!= NULL)
    {
      if(loc→data==item)
        {
          loc→next = ptr;
          ptr→prev = loc;
          ptr→next= NULL;
          return;
        }
      else
        {
          loc = loc→next;
        }
    }
printf(" data is entered at the end");
}

void delete_at_beg()
{
  struct node *ptr;
  struct node *loc ;
  if(start == NULL)
    {
      printf(" list is empty , create new");
      ptr→prev = NULL;
      ptr→next = NULL;
      start = ptr;
      return;
    }
  else
    {
      ptr = start;
      start = start→next;
      start→prev = NULL;
      printf(" data is deleted");
      free(ptr);
```

```c
    }
}

void delete_at_mid(int item)
{
  struct node *ptr ,*loc ;
  loc = start;
  printf(" enter new node");
  scanf("%d", &ptr→data);
  if(start==NULL)
    {
      printf(" list is empty , create new");
      ptr→next = NULL;
      ptr→prev= NULL;
      start = ptr;
      return;
    }
  while(loc!= NULL)
    {
      if(loc→data==item)
        {
          ptr = loc;
          loc→prev→next= loc→next;
          loc→next→prev= loc→prev;
          printf("data is deeted");
          free(ptr);
          return;
        }
      else
        {
          loc = loc→next;
        }
    }
}

void delete_at_end()
{
  struct node *ptr ,*loc ;
  loc = start;
  printf(" enter new node");
  scanf("%d", &ptr→data);
```

```
    if(start==NULL)
     {
       printf(" list is empty , create new");
       ptr→next = NULL;
       ptr→prev= NULL;
       start = ptr;
       return;
     }
    while(loc→next != NULL)
     {
       loc = loc→next;
     }
    ptr = loc;
    loc→prev→next=NULL;
    printf("item is deleted");
    free(ptr);
}
```

Output –
　　DOUBLY LINKED LIST
　　　　MENU

1. Addition at beginning

2. Addition after given node

3. Addition before given node

4. Addition at end

5. Deletion at beginning

6. Deletion at middle

7. Deletion at end

8. Exit

Enter your choice: 1

Enter value for node

56

Now let us discuss header linked lists.

4.5 Header Linked Lists

Header linked lists are a special type of linked list which always contain a special node, called the header node, at the beginning. This header node usually contains vital information about the linked list, like the total number of nodes in the list, whether the list is sorted or not, and so on. There are two types of header linked lists, which include:

1. **Grounded Header Linked List** – This linked list stores a unique value NULL in the address field (next part) of the last node of the list.

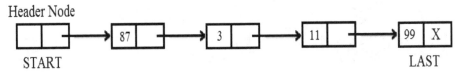

FIGURE 4.24 Deleting a node before a given node from the doubly linked list.

2. **Circular Header Linked List** – This linked list stores the address of the header node in the address field (next part) of the last node of the list.

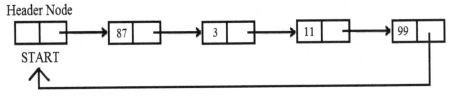

FIGURE 4.25 Circular header linked list.

Frequently Asked Questions

Q3. What are the uses of a header node in a linked list?

Answer.
The header node is a node of a linked list which may or may not have the same data structure of that of a typical node. The only common thing between a typical node and a header node is that they both have a pointer pointing to a typical node. Such a node can be used to store some extra pointers.

Write a program to implement a header linked list.

```c
# include <stdio.h>
# include<conio.h>
# include <alloc.h>
struct node
{
  int data;
  struct node *next;
} *start = NULL;
struct node *create_header (struct node *);
struct node *display (struct node *);
int main()
{
  int choice;
  clrscr();
  while(choice != 3)
    {
      printf("HEADER LINKED LIST");
      printf("\n\t\tMENU");
      printf("\n 1 : Create list");
      printf("\n 2 : Display ");
      printf("\n 3 : Exit ");
      printf("\n  enter your choice: ");
      scanf("%d", & choice);
      switch(choice)
        {
          case 1 :
          start = create_header(start);
          printf("\n HEADER LIST CREATED");
          break;

          case 2:
          start = display (start);
          break;

          case 3:
          exit(0);
        }
      getch();
      return 0;
    }
}
```

```c
struct node *create_header (struct node * start)
{
 struct node * new, *ptr;
 int number;
 printf("\n enter data: ");
 scanf("%d", &number);
 while (number == 0)
   {
     new = (struct node*) malloc (sizeof (struct node));
     new ->data =  number;
     new->next = NULL;
     if (start->next == NULL)
       {
         start = (struct node*) malloc (sizeof (struct
         node));
         start->next = new;
       }
   else
       {
         ptr = start;
         while (ptr->next != NULL)
           {
             ptr = ptr->next;
             ptr->next = new;
           }
         printf("\ n enter the data:");
         scanf("%d" , & number);
       }
     return start;
   }
}
struct node *display(struct node *start)
{
  struct node *ptr;
  ptr = start;
  while (ptr!= NULL)
  printf("%d", ptr->data);
  ptr = ptr-> next;
  return start;
}
```

Output –
　　HEADER LINKED LIST
　　　　MENU
　　1: Create list
　　2: Display
　　3: Exit
　　Enter your choice: 1
　　Enter data: 75

Write a program to implement a circular header linked list.

```
# include <stdio.h>
# include <conio.h>
# include <alloc.h>
struct hnode//Self Referential Structure
{
  int data;
  hnode *next;
}* start;
void create()
{
  hnode→start = new hnode();   //Creating a header linked
                                      list
  start→data = 0;
  start→ next = start;
  return 0;
}
void begin();
void insert();
void display();
void delete(int);
void main()
{
  int choice, item;
  clrscr();
  create();
  do
    {
    printf(" CIRCULAR HEADER LIST");
    printf("\n MENU");
    printf(" \n 1: INSERT ");
```

```
      printf(" \n 2 : DELETE");
      printf(" \n 3 : DISPLAY");
      printf(" \n 4 : EXIT");
      printf("\n Enter your choice:");
      scanf("%d", &choice);
      switch (choice)
        {
          case 1:
          insert();            //Case 1 is for Insertion
          break;
          case 2:
            {
              printf(" \n enter item you want to delete: ");
              scanf(" %d", &item);  //Case 2 is for Deletion
              del (item);
              break;
            }
          case 3:
          display();            //Case 3 is for Display
          break;
          case 4:
          exit(0);
          default :
          printf ("wrong choice");
          break;
        }
    }
  while(choice !=  0);
  getch();
}
void display()
{
  hnode *ptr = new hnode;
  if(start→next = start)
    {
      printf("\n list is empty");
      return;
    }
  else
    {
```

```
        printf (" \n current information is :", start→data);
        for (ptr = start→next ; ptr != start; ptr = ptr→next)
          {
            printf("data is:", ptr→data);
          }
        return;
      }
  }

void insert()
{
  hnode *ptr = new hnode;
  hnode *old, *loc;
  printf("\nEnter Data");
  scanf("%d", &ptr→data);
  old = start;
  loc = start→next;
  while(loc!= start)
    {
      if (loc→data > = ptr→data)
        {
          ptr→next = old→next;
          old→next = ptr;
          (start→data)++;
          return;
        }
      else
        {
          old = loc ;
          loc = loc→ next;
        }
    }
  ptr→next = start;
  old→next = ptr;
  (start→next)++;
  return;
}

void delete()
{
  hnode *ptr, *old, *loc;
  if (start→next ==NULL)
```

```
     {
       printf("\n list is empty");
       if (start→next== start)
         {
           printf(" \n cannot delete");
           return;
         }
       old = start;
       loc = start→next;
       while ( loc!= start&& item>ptr→data)
         {
           if(loc→data==item)
             {
               old→next = loc→next;
               printf("\n deleted item is:", loc→data);
               (start→data)--;
               return;
             }
           else
             {
               old = loc;
               loc = loc→next;
             }
         }
       printf("\n item is  not in list\n");
     }
}

void display()
{
  hnode *ptr = new hnode;
  if(start→next = start)
    {
      printf("\n list is empty");
      return;
    }
  else
    {
      printf (" \n current information is :", start→data);
      for (ptr = start→next ; ptr != start; ptr = ptr→next)
```

```
          {
              printf("data is:", ptr→data);
          }
          return;
      }
  }
```

Output –
    CIRCULAR HEADER LINKED LIST
          MENU
    1: INSERT
    2: DELETE
    3: DISPLAY
    4: EXIT
    Enter your choice: 1
    Enter Data
    78

4.6 Applications of Linked Lists

Linked lists have various applications, but one of the most important applications of linked lists is polynomial representation; linked lists can be used to represent polynomials and there are different operations that can be performed on them. Now let us see how polynomials can be represented in the memory using linked lists.

4.7 Polynomial Representation

Consider a polynomial $10x^2 + 6x + 9$. In this polynomial, every individual term consists of two parts: first, a coefficient, and second, a power. Here, the coefficients of the expression are 10, 6, and 9, and 2, 1, and 0 are the respective powers of the coefficients. Now, every individual term can be represented using a node of the linked list. The following figure shows how a polynomial expression can be represented using a linked list:

Exponent Power

FIGURE 26: Linked representation of a polynomial

4.8 Summary

- A linked list is a sequence of nodes in which each node contains one or more than one data field and a pointer which points to the next node.

- The process of allocating memory during the execution of the program or the process of allocating memory to the variables at runtime is called dynamic memory allocation.

- A singly linked list is the simplest type of linked list, in which each node contains some information/data and only one pointer which points to the next node in the linked list.

- Traversing a linked list means accessing all the nodes of the linked list exactly once.

- Searching for a value in a linked list means to find a particular element/value in the linked list.

- A circular linked list is also a type of singly linked list in which the address part of the last node will store the address of the first node.

- A doubly linked list is also called a two-way linked list; it is a special type of linked list which can point to the next node as well as the previous node in the sequence.

- A header linked list is a special type of linked list which always contains a special node, called the header node, at the beginning. This header node usually contains vital information about the linked list like the total number of nodes in the list, whether the list is sorted or not, and so forth.

- One of the most important applications of linked lists is polynomial representation, because linked lists can be used to represent polynomials and there are different operations that can be performed on them.

4.9 Exercises

4.9.1 Theory Questions

1. What is a linked list? How it is different from an array?

2. How many types of linked lists are there? Explain in detail.

3. What is the difference between singly and doubly linked lists?

4. List the various advantages of linked lists over arrays.

5. What is a circular linked list? What are the advantages of a circular linked list over a linked list?

6. Define a header linked list and explain its utility.

7. Give the linked representation of the following polynomial: $10x^2y - 6x + 7$

8. Specify the use of a header node in a header linked list.

9. List the various operations that can be performed in the linked lists.

4.9.2 Programming Questions

1. Write an algorithm/program to insert a node at a desired position in a circular linked list.

2. Write a program to insert and delete the node at the beginning in a doubly linked list.

3. Write an algorithm to reverse a singly linked list.

4. Write a program to delete a node from a header linked list.

5. Write an algorithm to concatenate two linked lists.

6. Write a program to implement a circular header linked list.

7. Write a program to count the non-zero values in a header linked list.

8. Write a program that inserts a node in the linked list before a given node.

9. Write an algorithm to search for an element from a given linear linked list.

10. Write a program that inserts a node in a doubly linked list after a given node.

4.9.3 Multiple Choice Questions

1. Linked lists are best suited for:

    A. Data structure

    B. Size of structure and data are constantly changing

    C. Size of structure and data are fixed

    D. None of these

2. Each node in a linked list must contain at least _____ fields.

   A. Four fields

   B. Three fields

   C. One field

   D. Two fields

3. Which type of linked list stores the address of the header node in the address field of the last node?

   A. Doubly linked list

   B. Circular header linked list

   C. Singly linked list

   D. Header linked list

4. The situation in a linked list when START = NULL is:

   A. Overflow

   B. Underflow

   C. Both

   D. None of these

5. Linked lists can be implemented in what type of data structures?

   A. Queues

   B. Trees

   C. Stacks

   D. All of these

6. Which type of linked list contains a pointer to the next as well as the previous nodes?

   A. Doubly linked list

   B. Singly linked list

   C. Circular linked list

   D. Header linked list

7. The first node in the linked list is called the _____.

    A. End

    B. Middle

    C. Start

    D. Begin

8. A linked list cannot grow and shrink during compile time.

    A. False

    B. It might grow

    C. True

    D. None of the above

9. Data elements in the linked list are known as _____.

    A. Nodes

    B. Pointers

    C. Lists

    D. All of the above

10. What does NULL represent in the linked list?

    A. Start of list

    B. End of list

    C. None of the above

QUEUES

In This Chapter

- Introduction
- Definition of a queue
- Implementation of a queue
- Operations on queues
- Types of queues
- Applications of queues
- Summary
- Exercises

5.1 Introduction

A queue is an important data structure which is widely used in many computer applications. A queue can be visualized with many examples from our day-to-day life with which we are already familiar. A very simple illustration of queue is a line of people standing outside to enter a movie theater. The first person standing in the line will enter the movie theater first. Similarly, there are many daily life examples in which we can see the queue being implemented. Hence, we observe that whenever we talk about a queue, we see that that the element at the first position will be served first. Thus, a queue can be described as a FIFO (first in, first out) data structure; that is, the element which is inserted first will be the first one to be taken out. Now, let us discuss more about queues in detail.

5.2 Definition of a Queue

A queue is a linear collection of data elements in which the element inserted first will be the element taken out first (i.e., a queue is a FIFO data structure). A queue is an abstract data structure, somewhat similar to stacks. Unlike stacks, a queue is open from both ends. *A queue is a linear data structure, in which the first element is inserted from one end called the REAR end (also called the tail end), and the deletion of the element takes place from the other end called the FRONT end (also called the head).* One end is always used to insert data and the other end is used to remove data.

Queues can be implemented by using arrays or linked lists. We will discuss the implementation of queues using arrays and linked lists in this section.

Practical Application:

- A real-life example of a queue is people moving on an escalator. The people who got on the escalator first will be the first ones to step off of it.

- Another illustration of a queue is a line of people standing at the bus stop waiting for the bus. Therefore, the first person standing in the line will get into the bus first.

5.3 Implementation of a Queue

Queues can be represented by two data structures:

1. Representation of queue using arrays.

2. Representation of queue using linked lists.

Now, let us discuss both of them in detail.

5.3.1 Implementation of Queues Using Arrays

Queues can be easily implemented using arrays. Initially the front end (head) and the rear end (tail) of the queue point at the first position or location of the array. As we insert new elements into the queue, the rear keeps on incrementing, always pointing to the position where the next element will be inserted, while the front remains at the first position. The representation of a queue using an array is shown as follows:

FIGURE 5.1. Array representation of a queue.

5.3.2 Implementation of Queues Using Linked Lists

We have already studied how a queue is implemented using an array. Now let us discuss the same using linked lists. We already know that in linked lists, dynamic memory allocation takes place, that is, the memory is allocated at runtime. But in the case of arrays, memory is allocated at the start of the program. This we have already discussed in the chapter about linked lists. If we are aware of the maximum size of the queue in advance, then implementation of a queue using arrays will be efficient. But if the size is not known in advance, then we will use the concept of a linked list, in which dynamic memory allocation takes place. As we all know a linked list has two parts, in which the first part contains the information of the node and the second part stores the address of the next element in the linked list. Similarly, we can also implement a linked queue. Now, the START pointer in the linked list will become the FRONT pointer in a linked queue and the end of the queue will be denoted by REAR. All insertion operations will be done at the rear end only. Similarly, all deletion operations will be done at the front end only.

FIGURE 5.4. A linked queue.

5.3.2.1 Insertion in Linked Queues

Insertion is the process of adding new elements in the already existing queue. The new elements in the queue will always be inserted from the rear end. Initially, *we will check whether FRONT = NULL.* If the condition is true, then the queue is empty; otherwise, the new memory is allocated for the new node. We will understand it further with the help of an algorithm:

Algorithm for inserting a new element in a linked queue

```
Step 1: START
Step 2: Set NEW NODE -> INFO = VAL
        IF FRONT = NULL
        Set FRONT = REAR = NEW NODE
        Set FRONT -> NEXT = REAR -> NEXT = NEW NODE
        ELSE
        Set REAR -> NEXT = NEW NODE
        Set NEW NODE -> NEXT = NULL
        Set REAR  = NEW NODE
        [End of If]
Step 3: EXIT
```

In the previous algorithm, first we are allocating the memory for the new node. Then we are initializing it with the information to be stored in it. Next, we are checking if the new node is the first node of the queue or not. If new node is the first node of the queue, then we are storing NULL in the address part of the new node. In this case, the new node is tagged as FRONT as well as REAR. However, if the new node is not the first node of the queue, then in that case it is inserted at the REAR end of the queue.

For Example – Consider a linked queue with five elements; a new element is to be inserted in the queue.

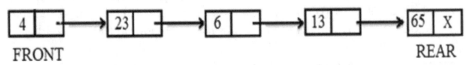

FRONT   REAR

FIGURE 5.5. Linked queue before insertion.

After inserting the new element in the queue, the updated queue becomes as shown in the following figure:

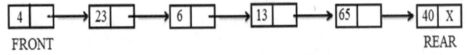

FRONT   REAR

FIGURE 5.6. Linked queue after insertion.

5.3.2.2 Deletion in Linked Queues

Deletion is the process of removing elements from the already existing queue. The elements from the queue will always be deleted from the front end. Initially, we will check with the underflow condition, that is, whether FRONT = NULL. If the condition is true, then the queue is empty, which means we cannot delete any elements from it. Therefore, in that case an underflow error message is displayed on the screen. We will understand it further with the help of an algorithm:

Algorithm for deleting an element from a queue

```
Step 1: START
Step 2: IF FRONT = NULL
            Print UNDERFLOW ERROR
            [End of If]
Step 3: Set TEMP = FRONT
Step 4: Set FRONT = FRONT -> NEXT
Step 5: FREE TEMP
Step 6: EXIT
```

In the previous algorithm, we first check with the underflow condition, that is, whether the queue is empty or not. If the condition is true, then an underflow error message will be displayed; otherwise, we will use a pointer variable TEMP which will point to the FRONT. In the next step, FRONT is now pointing to the second node in the queue. Finally, the first node is deleted from the queue.

For Example – Consider a linked queue with five elements; an element is to be deleted from the queue.

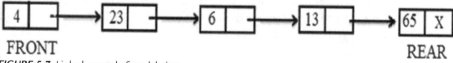

FRONT   REAR

FIGURE 5.7. Linked queue before deletion.

After deleting an element from the queue, the updated queue becomes as shown in the following figure:

FRONT   REAR

FIGURE 5.7. Linked queue after deletion.

Write a menu-driven program implementing a linked queue performing insertion and deletion operations.

```c
# include<stdio.h>
# include<conio.h>
struct node
{
 int info ;
 struct node *next ;
}
*front = NULL, *rear = NULL ;
void insertion(int val) ;
void deletion() ;
void display() ;
void main()
{
 int val, choice ;
 while(1)
   {
    clrscr() ;
    printf("\n***MENU***") ;
    printf("\n1. INSERTION IN QUEUE") ;
    printf("\n2. DELETION IN QUEUE") ;
    printf("\n3. DISPLAY") ;
    printf("\n4. EXIT") ;
    printf("\nenter your choice: ") ;
    scanf("%d", &choice) ;
    switch(choice)
      {
       case 1 :
       printf("enter value to insert: ") ;
       scanf("%d", &val) ;
       insertion(queue, val) ;
       break ;

       case 2 :
       deletion(queue, val) ;
       break ;

       case 3 :
       display(queue) ;
```

```
            break ;

            case 4 :
            printf("!!Exit!!") ;
            exit(0) ;

            default :
            printf("wrong choice") ;
        }
    }
}

void insertion(int val)
{
  struct node *Newnode ;
  //Case 1 is for inserting an element in the linked queue
  Newnode = (struct node*)malloc(sizeof(struct node)) ;
  Newnode -> info = val ;
  Newnode -> next = NULL ;
  if(front == NULL)
    {
      front = rear = Newnode
    }
  else
    {
      rear -> next = Newnode ;
      rear = Newnode ;
    }
  printf("Success!!") ;
  getch() ;
}

void deletion()
{
  struct node *temp ;
  //Case 2 is for deleting an element from the linked
  queue
  if(front == NULL)
    {
      printf("\nEmpty queue") ;
```

```
    }
  else
   {
    temp = front ;
    front = front -> next ;
    printf("deleted value is %d", n) ;
    free(temp) ;
   }
  getch() ;
}

void display()
{
  struct node *ptr ;
  //Case 3 is for displaying the elements in the linked
  queue
  if(front == NULL)
   {
    printf("\nEmpty queue") ;
   }
  ptr = front ;
  while(ptr -> next != NULL)
   {
    printf("%d", ptr -> info) ;
    ptr = ptr -> next ;
   }
  printf("%d->NULL", ptr -> info) ;
  getch() ;
}
```

Output –

```
    ***MENU***

  1: INSERTION IN QUEUE

  2: DELETION IN QUEUE

  3: DISPLAY

  4: EXIT
```

```
Enter your choice: 1
Enter value to insert: 183
Success!!
```

Frequently Asked Questions

Q. Define queues; in what ways can a queue be implemented?

Answer.

A queue is a linear data structure, in which the first element is inserted from one end called the REAR end (also called the tail end) and the deletion of the element takes place from the other end called the FRONT end (also called the head). Each type of queue can be implemented in two ways:

1.   Array Representation (Static Representation)

2.   Linked List Representation (Dynamic Representation)

5.4 Operations on Queues

The two basic operations that can be performed on queues are as follows:

5.4.1 Insertion

Insertion is the process of adding new elements in the queue. However, before inserting any new element in the queue, we must always check for the overflow condition, which occurs when we try to insert an element in a queue which is already full. An overflow condition can be checked as follows: If REAR = MAX – 1, where MAX is the size of the queue. Hence, if the overflow condition is true, then an overflow message is displayed on the screen; otherwise, the element is inserted into the queue. Insertion is always done at the rear end. Insertion is also known as En-queue.

For Example – Let us take a queue which has five elements in it. Suppose we want to insert another element, 50, in it; then REAR will be incremented by 1. Thus, a new element is inserted at the position pointed to by REAR. Now, let us see how insertion is done in the queue in the following figure:

After inserting 50 in it, the new queue will be:

FIGURE 5.2. Queue after inserting a new element.

Algorithm for inserting a new element in a queue

```
Step 1: START
Step 2: IF REAR = MAX - 1
            Print OVERFLOW ERROR
            [End of If]
Step 3: IF FRONT = -1 && REAR = -1
            Set FRONT = 0
            Set REAR = 0
            ELSE
            REAR = REAR + 1
            [End of If]
Step 4: Set QUE[REAR] = ITEM
Step 5: EXIT
```

In the previous algorithm, first we check for the overflow condition. In Step 2, we are checking to see whether the queue is empty or not. If the queue is empty then both FRONT and REAR are set to zero; otherwise, REAR is incremented to the next position in the queue. Finally, the new element is stored in the queue at the position pointed to by REAR.

5.4.2 Deletion

Deletion is the process of removing elements from the queue. However, before deleting any element from the queue, we must always check for the underflow condition, which occurs when we try to delete an element from the queue which is empty. An underflow condition can be checked as follows: If FRONT > REAR or FRONT = -1. Hence, if the underflow condition is true, then an underflow message is displayed on the screen; otherwise, the element is deleted from the queue. Deletion is always done at the front end. Deletion is also known as De-queue.

For Example – Let us take a queue which has five elements in it. Suppose we want to delete an element, 7, from a queue; then FRONT will be incremented by 1. Thus, the new element is deleted from the position pointed to by FRONT. Now, let us see how deletion is done in the queue in the following figure:

After deleting 7 from it, the new queue will be:

FIGURE 5.3. Queue after deleting an element.

Algorithm for deleting an element from a queue

```
Step 1: START
Step 2: IF FRONT > REAR or FRONT = -1
          Print UNDERFLOW ERROR
          [End of If]
Step 3: Set ITEM = QUE[FRONT]
Step 4: Set FRONT = FRONT + 1
Step 5: EXIT
```

In the previous algorithm, first we check for the underflow condition, that is, whether the queue is empty or not. If the queue is empty then no deletion takes place; otherwise, FRONT is incremented to the next position in the queue. Finally, the element is deleted from the queue.

Write a menu-driven program for a linear queue performing insertion and deletion operations.

```c
# include<stdio.h>
# include<conio.h>
# define SIZE 10
void insertion(int queue[], int n) ;
void deletion(int queue[], int n) ;
void display(int queue[]) ;
int front = -1, rear = -1 ;
void main()
{
  int queue[SIZE], n, ch ;
  while(1)
    {
      clrscr() ;
      printf("\n***MENU***") ;
      printf("\n1. INSERTION IN QUEUE") ;
      printf("\n2. DELETION IN QUEUE") ;
      printf("\n3. DISPLAY") ;
      printf("\n4. EXIT") ;
      printf("\nenter your choice: ") ;
      scanf("%d", &ch) ;
      switch(ch)
        {
```

```
        case 1 :
        printf("enter value to insert: ") ;
        scanf("%d", &n) ;
        insertion(queue, n) ;
        break ;

        case 2 :
        deletion(queue, n) ;
        break ;

        case 3 :
        display(queue) ;
        break ;

        case 4 :
        printf("!!Exit!!") ;
        exit(0) ;

        default :
        printf("wrong choice") ;
      }
    }
}

void insertion(int queue[], int n)
{
  //Case 1 is for inserting an element in the queue
  if(front == 0 || rear == SIZE-1
    {
      printf("\noverflow error") ;
    }
  else
    {
      rear = rear + 1 ;
      queue[rear] = n ;
      printf("Success!!") ;
      getch() ;
    }
}
```

```
void deletion(int queue[], int n)
{
  int i ;   //Case 2 is for deleting an element from the
            queue
  if(front == -1 && rear == -1)
    {
      printf("\nunderflow error") ;
    }
  else
    {
      for(i = front ; i<rear ; i++)
        {
          queue[i] = queue[i+1] ;
        }
      rear -- ;
      printf("deleted value is %d", n) ;
    }
  getch();
}

void display(int queue[])
{
  int i ;
  //Case 3 is for displaying the elements of the queue
  front = front + 1 ;
  for(i = rear ; i > front ; i--)
    {
      printf("\n%d", queue[i]) ;
    }
  getch() ;
}
```

Output –

MENU

1: INSERTION IN QUEUE

2: DELETION IN QUEUE

3: DISPLAY

4: EXIT

```
Enter your choice: 1
Enter value to insert: 56
Success!!
```

5.5 Types of Queues

This section discusses various types of queues which include:

1. Circular Queue

2. Priority Queue

3. De-Queue (Double-ended queue)

Let us discuss all of them one by one in detail.

5.5.1 Circular Queue

A circular queue is a special type of queue which is implemented in a circular fashion rather than in a straight line. A circular queue is a linear data structure in which the operations are performed based on the FIFO (First In First Out) principle and the last position is connected to the first position to make a circle. It is also called a "ring buffer."

5.5.1.1 Limitation of Linear Queues

In linear queues, we studied how insertion and deletion takes place. We discussed that while inserting a new element in the queue, it is only done at the rear end. Similarly, while deleting an element from the queue, it is only done at the front end. Now let us consider a queue of 10 elements given as follows:

arr[0]	arr[1]	arr[2]	arr[3]	arr[4]	arr[5]	arr[6]	arr[7]	arr[8]	arr[9]
36	98	14	74	56	13	7	96	44	82

Front   Rear

The queue is now full, so we cannot insert any more elements in it. If we delete three elements from the queue, now the queue will be:

arr[0]	arr[1]	arr[2]	arr[3]	arr[4]	arr[5]	arr[6]	arr[7]	arr[8]	arr[9]
			74	56	13	7	96	44	82

Front   Rear

Thus, we can see that even after the deletion of three elements from the queue, the queue is still full, as REAR = MAX – 1. We still cannot insert any new elements in it as there is no space to store new elements. Therefore, this is a major drawback of the linear queue.

To overcome this problem we can shift all the elements to the left so that the new elements can be inserted from the rear end, but shifting all the elements of the queue can be a very time-consuming procedure, as the practical queues are very large in size. Another solution to this problem is a circular queue. First of all let us see how a circular queue looks, as in the following figure:

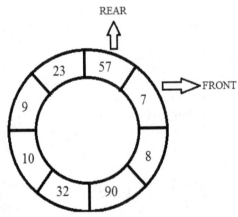

FIGURE 5.8. A circular queue.

In a circular queue, the elements are stored in a circular form such that the first element is next to the last element in the queue as shown in the figure. A circular queue will be full when FRONT = 0 and REAR = MAX – 1 or FRONT = REAR + 1. In that case an overflow error message will be displayed on the screen. Similarly, a circular queue will be empty when both FRONT and REAR are equal to zero. In that case, an underflow error message will be displayed on the screen. Now, let us study both insertion and deletion operations on the circular queue.

Practical Application:

A circular queue is used in operating systems for scheduling different processes.

Frequently Asked Questions

Q. What is a circular queue? List the advantages of a circular queue over a simple queue.

Answer.
A circular queue is a particular kind of queue where new items are added to the rear end of the queue and items are read off from the front end of the queue, so there is constant stream of data flowing in and out of the queue. A circular queue is also known as a "circular buffer." It is a structure that allows data to be passed from one process to another, making the most efficient use of memory. The only difference between a linear queue and circular queue is that in a linear queue when the rear points to the last position in the array, we cannot insert data even if we have deleted some elements. But in a circular queue we can insert elements as long as there is free space available. The main advantage of a circular queue as compared to a linear queue is that it avoids the wastage of space.

5.5.1.2 Inserting an Element in a Circular Queue

While inserting a new element in the already existing queue, we will first check for the overflow condition, which occurs when we are trying to insert an element in the queue which is already full as previously discussed. The position of the new element to be inserted can be calculated by using the following formula:

REAR = (REAR + 1) % MAX, where MAX is equal to the size of the queue.

For Example – Let us consider a circular queue with 3 elements in it. Suppose we want to insert an element 56 in it. Let us see how insertion is done in the circular queue.

Step 1: Initially the queue contains 3 elements. FRONT denotes the beginning of the circular queue and REAR denotes the end of the circular queue.

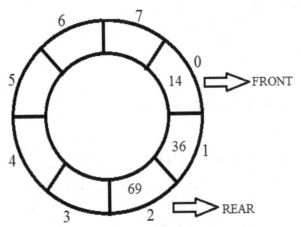

FIGURE 5.9. Initial circular queue without insertion.

Step 2: Now, the new element is to be inserted in the queue. Hence, REAR = REAR + 1, that is, REAR will be incremented by 1 so that it points to the next location in the queue.

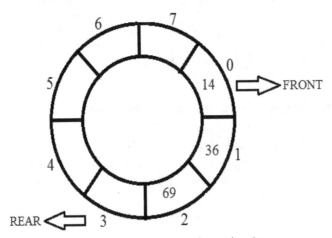

FIGURE 5.10. REAR is incremented by 1 so that it points to the next location.

Step 3: Finally, in this step the new element is inserted at the location pointed to by REAR. Hence, after insertion the queue is shown as in the following figure:

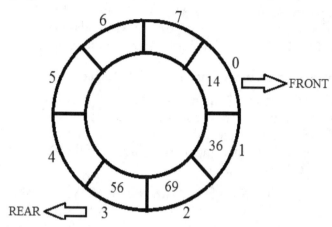

FIGURE 5.11. Final queue after inserting a new element.

Algorithm for inserting an element in a circular queue

Here QUEUE is an array with N elements. FRONT and REAR point to the front and rear elements of the queue. ITEM is the value to be inserted.

```
Step 1:  START
Step 2:  IF (FRONT = 0 && REAR = MAX - 1) OR (FRONT =
         REAR + 1)
              Print OVERFLOW ERROR
Step 3:  ELSE
              IF (FRONT = -1)
              Set FRONT = 0
              Set REAR = 0
Step 4:  ELSE
              IF (REAR = MAX - 1)
              Set REAR = 0
              ELSE
              REAR = REAR + 1
              [End of If]
              [End of If]
Step 5:  Set CQUEUE[REAR] = ITEM
Step 6:  EXIT
```

In the previous algorithm, first we check with the overflow condition. Second, we check if the queue is empty or not. If the queue is empty then FRONT and REAR are set to zero. In Step 4, if REAR has reached its maximum capacity, then we set REAR = 0; otherwise, REAR is incremented by 1 so that it points to the next position where the new element is to be inserted. Finally, the new element is inserted in the queue.

5.5.1.3 Deleting an Element from a Circular Queue

While deleting an element from the already existing queue, we will first check for the underflow condition, which occurs when we are trying to delete an element from the queue which is empty. After deleting an element from the circular queue, the position of the FRONT end can be calculated by the formula:

FRONT = (FRONT +1) % MAX, where MAX is equal to the size of the queue.

For Example – Let us consider a circular queue with 7 elements in it. Suppose we want to delete an element 45 from it. Let us see how deletion is done in the circular queue.

Step 1: Initially the queue contains 7 elements. FRONT denotes the beginning of the circular queue and REAR denotes the end of the circular queue.

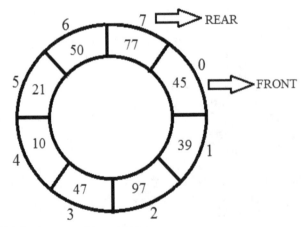

FIGURE 5.12. Initial circular queue without deletion.

Step 2: Now, the element is to be deleted from the queue. Hence, FRONT = FRONT + 1, that is, FRONT will be incremented by 1 so that it points to the next location in the queue. Also, the value is deleted from the queue. Thus, the queue after deletion is shown as follows:

FIGURE 5.13. Final queue after deleting an element.

Algorithm for deleting an element from a circular queue

Here CQUEUE is an array with N elements. FRONT and REAR point to the front and rear elements of the queue. ITEM is the value to be deleted.

```
Step 1: START
Step 2: IF (FRONT = -1)
            Print UNDERFLOW ERROR
Step 3: ELSE
            Set ITEM = CQUEUE[FRONT]
Step 4: IF (FRONT = REAR)
            Set FRONT = -1
            Set REAR = -1
Step 5: ELSE IF (FRONT = MAX - 1)
            Set FRONT = 0
            ELSE
            FRONT = FRONT + 1
            [End of If]
            [End of If]
Step 6: EXIT
```

In the previous algorithm, we first check with the underflow condition. Second, we store the element to be deleted in ITEM. Third, we check to see if the queue is empty or not after deletion. Also, if FRONT has reached its maximum capacity, then we set FRONT = 0; otherwise, FRONT is incremented by 1 so that it points to the next position. Finally, the element is deleted from the queue.

Write a menu-driven program for a linear queue performing insertion and deletion operations.

```c
# include <stdio.h>
# define  MAX 10
int cqueue[MAX], front = -1, rear = -1 ;
int item ;
void main()
{
  int choice ;
  clrscr() ;
  while(1)
    {
      printf("\n MENU OF CIRCULAR QUEUE") ;
      printf("\n 1. Insertion in Circular Queue") ;
      printf("\n 2. Deletion in Circular Queue") ;
      printf("\n 3. Display") ;
      printf("\n 4. Exit");
      printf("\n enter your choice") ;
      scanf("%d", &choice);
      switch(choice)
        {
          case 1 :
          printf(" \n enter item") ;
          //Case 1 is for inserting an element in the cir-
          cular queue
          scanf("%d", &item) ;
          if((front == 0 && rear == MAX - 1) || (front ==
          rear + 1))
            {
              printf("\ncircular queue overflow") ;
              getch() ;
              exit(0) ;
            }
```

```
    if((front == -1) && (rear == -1))
     {
       front = 0 ;
       rear = 0 ;
     }
    else
     {
       rear = (rear + 1) % MAX ;
       cqueue[rear] = item ;
       printf("success") ;
     }
   getch() ;
   break ;

   case 2 :
   if(front == -1 && rear == -1)
   //Case 2 is for deleting an element from the cir-
   cular queue
     {
       printf("\n circular queue underflow") ;
       getch() ;
       exit(0) ;
     }
   else if (front == rear)
     {
       front = rear = -1 ;
       item = cqueue[front] ;
     }
   else
     {
       item = cqueue[front] ;
       front = (front + 1) % MAX ;
       printf("deleted value is %d", item) ;
     }
   getch() ;
   break ;

   case 3 :
   int i ;
   //Case 3 is for displaying the elements of the
   circular queue
```

```
        front = front + 1 ;
        for(i = front ; i <= rear; i++)
          {
            printf("%d\n", cqueue[i]) ;
          }
        break ;

        case 4 :
        exit(0) ;

        default :
        printf("wrong choice") ;
        exit(0) ;
      }
  }
}
```

Output –

MENU OF CIRCULAR QUEUE

1: Insertion in Circular Queue

2: Deletion in Circular Queue

3: Display

4: Exit

Enter your choice

1

Enter item

18

Success!!

5.5.2 Priority Queue

A priority queue is another variant of a queue in which elements are processed on the basis of assigned priority. Each element in a priority queue is assigned a special value called the priority of the element. The elements in the priority queue are processed on the basis of the following rules:

1. An element with higher priority is processed first and then the element with lower priority is processed.

2. If the two elements have the same priority, then the elements are processed on the First Come First Served basis. The priority of the element is selected by its value called the implicit priority, and the priority number given with each element is called the explicit priority.

A priority queue is like a modified queue or stack data structure, but where additionally each element has a "priority" associated with it. In a priority queue, insertion and deletion operations are also done according to the assigned priority. If we want to delete an element from the priority queue, then the element with the highest priority is processed first and is deleted. The case is the same with insertion. The priority given to the elements in the queue is based on several factors. Priority queues are commonly used in operating systems for executing higher priority processes first. The priority assigned to these processes may be based on the time taken by the CPU to execute these processes completely.

Practical Application:

In an operating system, if there arefour processes to be executed where the first process needs 3 ns to complete, the second process needs 5 ns to complete, the third process needs 9 ns to complete, and the fourth needs 8 ns to complete, then the first process will be given the highest priority and will be the first to be executed among all the processes.

Now the priority queues are further divided into two types which are:

1. **Ascending Priority Queue** – In this type of priority queue, elements can be inserted in any order, but at the time of deletion of elements from the queue, the smallest element is searched and deleted first.

2. Descending Priority Queue – In this type of priority queue, elements can be inserted in any order. But at the time of deletion of elements from the queue, the largest element is searched and deleted first.

Frequently Asked Questions

Q. Define Priority Queue.

Answer.

A priority queue is a collection of elements such that each element has been assigned a priority and such that the order in which elements are deleted and processed comes from the following rules:

a. An element of higher priority is processed before any element of lower priority.

b. Two elements with same priority are processed according to the order in which they were added to the queue.

The array elements in a priority queue can have the following structure:

```
struct data
{
      int item ;
      int priority ;
      int order ;
} ;
```

5.5.2.1 Implementation of a Priority Queue

A priority queue can be implemented in two ways:

1. Array Representation of a Priority Queue

2. Linked Representation of a Priority Queue

Let us now discuss both these implementations in detail.

a. Implementation of a priority queue using arrays

While implementing a priority queue using arrays, the following points must be considered:

- Maintain a separate queue for each level of priority or priority number.

- Each queue will appear in its own circular array and must have its own pairs of pointers, that is, FRONT AND REAR.

- If each queue is allocated the same amount of memory, then a 2D array can be used instead of a linear array.

For example – FRONT [K] and REAR [K] are the pointers containing the front and rear values of row "K" of the queue, where K is the priority number. Suppose we want to insert an element with priority K, then we will add the element at the REAR end of row K; K is the row as well as the priority number of that element. If we add F with priority number 4, then the queue will be given as shown in the following:

FRONT	REAR
2	2
1	3
0	0
5	1
4	4

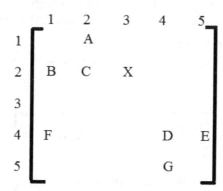

FIGURE 5.14. Priority queue after inserting a new element.

b. Implementation of a priority queue using linked lists

A priority queue can be implemented using a linked list. While implementing the priority queue using a linked list, every node will have three parts:

a. Information part

b. Priority number of the element

c. Address of the next element

An element with higher priority will precede the element having lower priority. Also, priority number and priority are opposite to each other, that is, an element having a lower priority number means it has higher priority. For example, if there are two elements X and Y with priority numbers 2 and 7 respectively, then X will be processed first because it has higher priority.

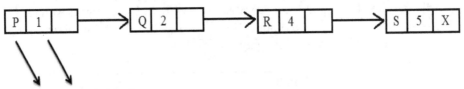

Element Priority Number

FIGURE 5.15. A linked priority queue.

5.5.2.2 Insertion in a Linked Priority Queue

While inserting a new element in a linked priority queue, first we will traverse the entire queue until we find a node which has lower priority than the new element. Thus, the new element is inserted before the element with the lower priority. Also, if there is an element in the queue which has same priority as that of the new element, then in that case the new element is inserted after that element.

For Example – Consider a priority queue with four elements given as follows:

FIGURE 5.16. Linked priority queue before insertion.

Now, a new element with information A and priority number 3 is to be inserted; hence, the element will be inserted before R that has priority number 4, which is lower than that of the new element. The priority queue after inserting a new element is shown as follows:

FIGURE 5.17. Linked priority queue after inserting a new element.

5.5.2.3 Deletion in a Linked Priority Queue

Deleting an element from a linked priority queue is a very simple process. In that case, the first node from the priority queue is deleted and the information of that node is processed first.

For Example – Consider a priority queue with five elements given as follows:

FIGURE 5.18. Linked priority queue before deletion.

Now, the first node from the queue is deleted. So, the priority queue after deletion is shown as follows:

FIGURE 5.19. Linked priority queue after deleting the first node.

Write a menu-driven program for a priority queue performing insertion and deletion operations.

```c
# include <stdio.h>
# include <conio.h>
# define MAX 5
void insert_by_priority(int) ;
void delete_by_priority(int) ;
void create() ;
void check(int) ;
void display_pqueue() ;
int p_queue[MAX] ;
int front, rear ;
void main()
{
```

```c
int n, choice ;
printf("\n***MENU***") ;
printf("\n1 - Insert an element into priority queue") ;
printf("\n2 - Delete an element from priority queue") ;
printf("\n3 - Display priority  queue") ;
printf("\n4 - Exit");
create() ;
while (1)
  {
    printf("\nEnter your choice: ") ;
    scanf("%d", &choice) ;
    switch (choice)
      {
        case 1 :
        printf("\nEnter value to insert: ") ;
        scanf("%d", &n) ;
        insert_by_priority(n) ;
        break ;

        case 2 :
        printf("\nEnter value to delete : ") ;
        scanf("%d", &n) ;
        delete_by_priority(n) ;
        break ;

        case 3 :
        display_pqueue() ;
        break ;

        case 4 :
        exit(0) ;

        default :
        printf("\nChoice is incorrect ") ;
      }
  }
}

void create()
{
  front = rear = -1;
```

```
    //Function to create an empty priority queue
}

 void insert_by_priority(int data)
{
 if (rear >= MAX - 1)
 //Function to insert value into priority queue
  {
    printf("\nQueue overflow") ;
    return ;
  }
 if ((front == -1) && (rear == -1))
  {
    front ++ ;
    rear ++ ;
    p_queue[rear] = data ;
    return ;
  }
 else
 check(data) ;
 rear ++ ;
}

void check(int data)
{
 int i, j ;
 //Function to check priority and place element

 for (i = 0 ; i <= rear ; i++)
  {
    if (data >= p_queue[i])
      {
        for (j = rear + 1 ; j > i ; j--)
          {
            p_queue[j] = p_queue[j - 1] ;
          }
        p_queue[i] = data ;
        return ;
      }
  }
 p_queue[i] = data ;
}
```

```c
void delete_by_priority(int data)
{
 int i ;
 // Function to delete an element from queue
 if ((front==-1) && (rear==-1))
   {
     printf("\nQueue is empty") ;
     return ;
   }
 for (i = 0; i <= rear; i++)
   {
     if (data == p_queue[i])
       {
         for (; i < rear; i++)
           {
             p_queue[i] = p_queue[i + 1] ;
           }
         p_queue[i] = -99 ;
         rear -- ;
         if (rear == -1)
         front = -1 ;
         return ;
       }
   }
 printf("\n%d not found in queue to delete", data) ;
}

void display_pqueue()
{
 if((front == -1)&&(rear == -1))
 // Function to display queue elements
   {
     printf("\nQueue is empty") ;
     return ;
   }
 for (; front <= rear ; front++)
   {
     printf(" %d ", p_queue[front]) ;
   }
```

```
    front = 0 ;
}
```

Output –

    MENU

    1 – Insert an element into priority queue

    2 – Delete an element from priority queue

    3 – Display priority queue

    4 – Exit

    Enter your choice 1

    Enter value to insert

    54

5.5.3 De-queues (Double-Ended Queues)

A double-ended queue (de-queue, pronounced "deck") is a special type of data structure in which insertion and deletion of elements is done at either end, that is, either at the front end or at the rear end of the queue. It is often called a head-tail linked list because elements are added or removed from either the head (front) end or tail (end). De-queues are implemented using circular arrays in the computer's memory. The LEFT and RIGHT two pointers are maintained in the de-queue, which point to either end of the queue.

FIGURE 5.20. A double-ended queue.

Practical Application:

A real life example of a de-queue is that in a train station, the entry and exit of passengers can take place from both sides.

There are two types of double-ended queues, which include:

1. Input Restricted De-Queue – In this, the deletion operation can be performed at both ends (i.e., both front and rear end) while the insertion operation can be performed only at one end (i.e., rear end).

FIGURE 5.21. An input restricted double-ended queue.

2. Output Restricted De-Queue – In this, the insertion operation can be performed at both ends while the deletion operation can be performed only at one end (i.e., front end).

FIGURE 5.22. An output restricted double-ended queue.

Write a menu-driven program for a double-ended queue performing insertion and deletion operations.

```c
#include<stdio.h>
#include<conio.h>
#include<stdlib.h>
# define size[5]
int deque[size] ;
int front = -1, rear = -1 ;
void display() ;
void insert_front() ;
void insert_rear() ;
void delete_front() ;
void delete_rear() ;
int choice, item ;
void main()
{
  clrscr() ;
  while(1)
    {
      printf("\n Menu") ;
      printf("\n 1. Insert from Front") ;
      printf("\n 2. Insert from Rear") ;
      printf("\n 3. Delete from Front") ;
      printf("\n 4. Delete from Rear") ;
      printf("\n 5. Display") ;
      printf("\n 6. Exit") ;
      printf("\nEnter your choice: ") ;
      scanf("%d", &choice) ;
      switch(choice)
        {
          case 1:
          insert_front() ;
          getch() ;
          break ;

          case 2:
          insert_rear() ;
          getch() ;
          break ;

          case 3:
          delete_front() ;
```

```
            getch() ;
            break ;

            case 4:
            delete_rear() ;
            getch() ;
            break ;

            case 5:
            display() ;
            getch() ;
            break ;

            case 6:
            exit(0) ;

            default:
            printf("\n Invalid Choice") ;
            getch() ;
            break ;
        }
    }
}

void insert_front()
{
  if(front==0)
  //Case 1 is for inserting an element in the queue from
  //front end
    {
      printf("\n Queue is Full") ;
    }
  else
  front = front - 1 ;
  printf("\n Enter a no") ;
  scanf("%d", &item) ;
  deque[front] = item ;
}

void insert_rear()
{
  if(rear == max)
```

```
    //Case 2 is for inserting an element in the queue from
    //rear end
      {
        printf("\n Queue is Full") ;
      }
    else
    rear = rear + 1 ;
    printf("\n Enter a no") ;
    scanf("%d", &item) ;
    deque[rear] = item ;
}

void delete_front()
{
  if(front == max)
  //Case 3 is for deleting an element in the queue from
  //front end
    {
      printf("\n Queue is Empty") ;
    }
  else
  item = deque[front] ;
  front = front + 1 ;
  printf("\n No. deleted is %d", item) ;
}

void delete_rear()
{
  if(rear == 0)
  //Case 4 is for deleting an element in the queue from
  //rear end
    {
      printf("\n Queue is Empty") ;
    }
  else
  item = deque[rear] ;
  rear = rear - 1 ;
  printf("\n No. deleted is %d", item) ;
}

void display()
```

```
{
  int i ;
  printf("\n The Queue is:") ;
  //Case 5 is for displaying the elements of the queue
  for(i = front ; i <= rear ; i++)
    {
      printf("%d \n ", deque[i]) ;
    }
}
```

Output –

   MENU

   1. Insert from Front

   2. Insert from Rear

   3. Delete from Front

   4. Delete from Rear

   5. Display

   6. Exit

   Enter your choice:

   1

   Enter a no

   25

5.6 Applications of Queues

- In real life, call center phone systems use queues to hold people calling them in an order until a service representative is free.

- The handling of interruptions in real-time systems uses the concept of queues. The interruptions are handled in the same order as they arrive, that is, First Come First Served.

- The round-robin technique for processor scheduling is implemented using queues.

- Queues are often used as buffers on portable CD players, MP3 players, and in iPod playlists.

5.7 Summary

- A queue is a linear collection of data elements in which the element inserted first will be the element taken out first (i.e., a queue is a FIFO data structure).

- A queue is a linear data structure in which the first element is inserted from one end called the REAR end, and the deletion of the element takes place from the other end called the FRONT end.

- The implementation of queues can be done in two ways, which are implementation through arrays and implementation through linked lists.

- Insertion and deletion are the two basic operations which are performed on the queues.

- A circular queue is a linear data structure in which the operations are performed based on a FIFO (First in First Out) principle and the first index comes after the last index.

- A priority queue is a queue in which elements are processed on the basis of assigned priority. Each element in a priority queue is assigned a special value called priority of the element.

- When a priority queue is implemented using linked lists, then every node of the list will have three parts, that is, a data part, priority number of the element, and the address of the next element.

- A double-ended queue is a special type of data structure in which insertion and deletion of elements is done at either end, that is, either at the front end or at the rear end of the queue.

- An input restricted de-queue is a queue in which deletion can be done at both ends, but insertion is done only at the rear end.

- An output restricted de-queue is a queue in which insertion can be done at both ends, but deletion is done only at the front end.

- There various applications of queues.

5.8 Exercises

5.8.1 Theory Questions

1. What is a linear queue? Give its real life example.

2. What is a circular queue and how it is different from a linear queue?

3. Define priority queues.

4. Discuss various operations which can be performed on the queues.

5. Define queues and in what ways a queue can be implemented. What do you understand by double-ended queues? Discuss the different types of de-queues in detail.

6. Give some of the applications of queues.

7. Why are queues known as First-In-First-Out structures?

8. Explain the concept of a linked queue and also discuss how insertion and deletion takes place in it.

5.8.2 Programming Questions

1. Write a program to create a linear queue containing nine elements.

2. Write an algorithm to implement a priority queue.

3. Write a code for insertion and deletion in a queue.

4. Give an algorithm for insertion of an element in a circular queue. Write a program to implement a queue which allows insertion and deletion at both ends.

5. Write an algorithm that reverses the elements of a queue.

6. Write an algorithm for insertion and deletion in a queue using pointers. Write the functions for insertion and deletion operations performed in a de-queue. Consider all possible cases.

7. Write a code for deleting an element from a circular queue.

8. Write a program to implement a priority queue using a linked list.

5.8.3 Multiple Choice Questions

1. New elements in the queue are always inserted from:

   A. Front end

   B. Middle

   C. Rear end

   D. Both (a) and (c)

2. A queue is a _____ data structure.

   A. FIFO

   B. LIFO

   C. FILO

   D. LILO

3. The overflow condition in the circular queue exists when:

   A. Front = MAX – 1 and Rear = 0

   B. Front = 0 and Rear = MAX – 1

   C. Front = 0 and Rear = 0

   D. Front = MAX – 1 and Rear = MAX – 1

4. If the elements P, Q, R, and S are placed in a queue and are deleted one by one, in what order will they be deleted?

   A. PQRS

   B. SRQP

   C. PRQS

   D. SRQP

5. A data structure in which elements are inserted or deleted from the front as well as from the rear end is:

   A. Linear queue

   B. De-queue

   C. Priority Queue

   D. Circular Queue

6. A line outside a movie theater represents a _____.

   A. Linked List

   B. Array

   C. Queue

   D. Stack

7. In a queue, deletion is always done at the _____.

   A. Top end

   B. Back end

   C. Front end

   D. Rear end

8. In a priority queue, two elements with the same priority are processed on a FCFS basis.

   A. False

   B. True

   C. Not possible to comment

9. The function that inserts the elements in a queue is called _____.

   A. Push

   B. En-queue

   C. Pop

   D. De-queue

10. Which of the implementation of queues is better when the size of the queue is not known in advance?

   A. Linked List Representation

   B. Array Representation

   C. Both

   D. None of the above

SEARCHING AND SORTING

In This Chapter

- Introduction to searching
- Linear search or sequential search
- Binary search
- Interpolation search
- Introduction to sorting
- External sorting
- Summary
- Exercises

6.1 Introduction to Searching

As we all know, computer systems are often used to store large numbers. We require some search mechanism to retrieve a specific record from the large amounts of data stored in our computer system. Searching means to find whether a particular data item exists in an array/list or not. *The process of finding a particular value in a list or an array is called searching.* If that particular value is present in the array, then the search is said to be successful and the location of that particular value is returned by the searching process. However, if the value does not exist or we can say that if the value is not present in the array, then searching is said to be unsuccessful. There are many different searching algorithms, but three of the popular searching techniques are as follows:

- Linear Search or Sequential Search

- Binary Search

- Interpolation Search

Hence, we will discuss all these methods in detail.

6.2 Linear Search or Sequential Search

A linear search is also called a sequential search. This is a very simple technique used to search a particular value in an array. *A linear search works by comparing the value of the key being searched for with every element of the array in a linear sequence until a match is found.* A search will be unsuccessful if all the data elements are read and the desired element is not found. The following are some important points:

- It is the simplest way to search an element in the list.

- It searches the data element sequentially, no matter whether the array is sorted or unsorted.

For example – Let us take an array of 10 elements which is declared as follows:

```
int array[10] = {87,   25,   14,   39,   74,   1,   99,   12,
                 30,  67};
```

and the value to be searched for in the array is VALUE = 74, then search to find whether 74 exists in the array or not. If the value is present, then its position is returned. Here the position of VAL = 74 is POS = 4 (index starting from zero) which has been shown by the following figures:

Pass 1 – 87 is compared with 74. Since 87 is not equal to 74, we will move to the next pass.

arr[0]	arr[1]	arr[2]	arr[3]	arr[4]	arr[5]	arr[6]	arr[7]	arr[8]	arr[9]
87	25	14	39	74	1	99	12	30	67

Pass 2 – 25 is compared with 74. Since 25 is not equal to 74, we will move to the next pass.

arr[0]	arr[1]	arr[2]	arr[3]	arr[4]	arr[5]	arr[6]	arr[7]	arr[8]	arr[9]
87	25	14	39	74	1	99	12	30	67

Pass 3 – 14 is compared with 74. Since 14 is not equal to 74, we will move to the next pass.

arr[0]	arr[1]	arr[2]	arr[3]	arr[4]	arr[5]	arr[6]	arr[7]	arr[8]	arr[9]
87	25	14	39	74	1	99	12	30	67

Pass 4 – 39 is compared with 74. Since 39 is not equal to 74, we will move to the next pass.

arr[0]	arr[1]	arr[2]	arr[3]	arr[4]	arr[5]	arr[6]	arr[7]	arr[8]	arr[9]
87	25	14	39	74	1	99	12	30	67

Pass 5 –74 is compared with 74. Since 74 is equal to 74, we will return the position on which 74 is present, which in this case is 4.

arr[0]	arr[1]	arr[2]	arr[3]	arr[4]	arr[5]	arr[6]	arr[7]	arr[8]	arr[9]
87	25	14	39	74	1	99	12	30	67

74 is found at POS = 4

FIGURE 6.1 Working of a linear search.

In this way, a linear search is used to search for a particular value in the array. Now let us understand it further with the help of an algorithm.

Practical Application:

A simple and a real-life example of a linear search is that a person is searching for another person's contact number in a telephone directory. So, if the person does not know the exact name of that person but knows that the name starts with A, then he/she will start searching from the beginning of the telephone directory.

Algorithm for a Linear Search

Let *ARR* be an array of n elements, ARR[1], ARR[2], ARR[3], . . . ARR[n] such that VAL is the element to be searched. Then the algorithm will find the position POS of the VAL in the array ARR.

```
Step 1: START
Step 2: Set I = 0, POS = -1
Step 3: Repeat while I<N
            IF (ARR[I] = VAL)
            POS = I
            PRINT POS
            Go to Step 5
            [End of IF]
            [End of Loop]
Step 4: IF (POS = -1)
            PRINT "VALUE NOT FOUND, SEARCH
            UNSUCCESSFUL"
            [End of IF]
Step 5: EXIT
```

In Step 2 of the algorithm, we are initializing the value of I and POS. In Step 3 a while loop is executed in which a check is made, that is, whether a match is found between the current array element and VAL. If the match is found, then the position of that element is printed. In the last step, if all the elements have been compared and there is no match found, the search will be unsuccessful, that is, the value is not present in the array.

Complexity of a Linear Search Algorithm

The execution time of a linear search is O(n), where n is the number of elements in the array. The algorithm is called a linear search because its complexity can be expressed as a linear function, which is that the number of comparisons to find the target item increases linearly with the size of the data. The best case of a linear search is when the data element to be searched for is equal to the first element of the array. Obviously, the worst case will happen when the data element to be searched for is equal to the last element in the array. However, in both the cases n comparisons have to be made.

6.2.1 Drawbacks of a Linear Search

- It is a very time-consuming process, as it works sequentially.

- It can be applied only to a small amount of data.

- It is a very slow process as almost every data element is accessed in this process, especially when the data element is located near the end.

Write a program to search an element in an array using a linear search technique.

```
# include <stdio.h>
# include <conio.h>
intlinear_search( intarr[], int n, int value ) ;
void main()
{
 intarr[10], n, i, r, value ;
 clrscr() ;
 printf("***LINEAR SEARCH***") ;
 printf("\nenter no of elements") ;
 scanf("%d", &n) ;
 printf("enter the elements of array") ;
 for( i=0 ; i<n ; i++ )
   {
     printf("\nenter element %d", i+1) ;
     scanf("%d", &arr[i]) ; //Accepting the elements of
                             array
   }
```

```
printf("\nenter value to search") ;
scanf("%d", &value) ;
r = linear_search(arr, n, value) ;
if(r == -1)
printf("value not found") ;
else
printf("%d value found at %d", value, r+1) ;
getch() ;
}
intlinearsearch( intarr[], int n, int value )
{
  int i;
  for( i=0 ; i<n ; i++ )
    {
      if(arr[i] == value)
      return i ;
    }
  return (-1);
}
```

Output

```
***LINEAR SEARCH***
Enter no of elements  9

Enter elements of array
Enter element 1:  8
Enter element 2:  2
Enter element 3:  9
Enter element 4:  10
Enter element 5:  1
Enter element 6:  3
Enter element 7:  23
Enter element 8:  69
Enter element 9:  17

Enter value to search   23
23 value found at 7th position
```

Frequently Asked Questions

Q. Explain how a linear search technique is used to search for an element.

Answer.

Suppose that ARR is an array having N elements. ITEM is the value to be searched. Then we have the following cases:

Case 1: Unsorted List – The ITEM is compared with every element of the array. If the element is found, then no further comparison is required. If all the elements are compared and checked, then the ITEM is not found.

Case 2: Sorted List – The ITEM is greater than the first element and smaller than the last element of the list, so searching is performed by comparing each element in the list with ITEM; otherwise, ITEM is reported as "**Not Found**."

6.3 Binary Search

A binary search is an extremely efficient searching algorithm when it is compared to a linear search. *A binary search works only when the array/list is already sorted*. In a binary search, we first compare the value VAL with the data element in the middle position of the array. If the match is found, then the position POS of that element is returned; otherwise, if the value is less than that of the middle element, then we begin our search in the lower half of the array and vice versa. So, we repeat this process on the lower and upper half of the array.

6.3.1 Binary Search Algorithm

Let us now understand how this binary search algorithm works in an array.

1. Find the middle element of the array, that is, n/2 is the middle element of the array containing n elements.

2. Now, compare the middle element of the array with the data element to be searched.

a) If the middle element is the desired element, then the search is successful.

b) If the data element to be searched for is less than the middle element of the array, then search only the lower half of the array, that is, those elements which are on the left side of the middle element.

c) If the data element to be searched for is greater than the middle element of the array, then search only the upper half of the array, that is, those elements which are on the right side of the middle element.

Repeat these steps until a match is found.

Practical Application:

A real-life application of a binary search is that when we search for a particular word in a dictionary, we first open the dictionary somewhere in the middle. Now we will compare the desired word with the first word on that page. If the desired word comes after the first word on an open page then we will look in the second half of the dictionary; otherwise, we will look in the first half. Now, we will again open a page in the second half and compare the desired word with the first word on that page, and the same process is repeated until we have found the desired word.

Algorithm for a Binary Search

```
Binary_Search(ARR, Lower_bound, Upper_bound, VAL)
Step 1: START
Step 2: Set BEG = lower_bound, END = upper_bound, POS = -1
Step 3: Repeat Steps 4 & 5 while BEG <= END
Step 4: Set MID = (BEG+END)/2
Step 5: IF (ARR[MID] = VAL)
            POS = MID
            PRINT POS
            Go to Step 7
```

```
                  ELSE IF (ARR[MID] > VAL)
                  Set END = MID - 1
                  ELSE
                  Set BEG = MID + 1
                  [End of If]
                  [End of Loop]
Step 6:  IF (POS = -1)
                  PRINT "VALUE NOT FOUND, SEARCH
                  UNSUCCESSFUL"
                  [End of IF]
Step 7:  EXIT
```

In Step 2 of the algorithm, we are initializing the values of BEG, END, and POS. In Step 3 a while loop is executed. In Step 3, the value of MID is calculated. In Step 4 we will check if the value to be searched for is equal to the array value at MID. If the match is found, then the position of that element is printed. If the match is not found and the value to be searched for is less than that of the array value at MID, then the END is modified; otherwise, if the value to be searched for is greater than that of the array value at MID, then the BEG is modified. In the last step, if all the elements have been compared and there is no match found, the search has been unsuccessful, that is, the value is not present in the array.

For Example:

Let us now consider an example to search for a particular value in a sorted array.

Consider an array of 10 elements which is declared as:

```
int array[10] = {0, 10, 20, 30, 40, 50, 60, 80,
                 90, 100};
```

and the value to be searched for is VAL = 20. Then the algorithm will proceed as follows:

Solution

Pass 1 –
BEG = 0, END = 10
MID = (BEG + END)/2
     = (0 + 10)/2 = 5

Now, VAL = 20 and ARR[MID] = ARR[5] = 50

As ARR[5] = 50 > VAL = 30, therefore we will now search for the value in the lower half of the array. So now the values of END and MID are modified, and we move to the next pass.

Pass 2 –

Now, END = MID – 1 = 4
MID = (0 + 4)/2 = 2

Now VAL = 20 and ARR[MID] = ARR[2] = 20.

20 is found at POS = 2

Figure 6.2. Working of a binary search.

Hence, the search is successful and VAL = 20 is found at POS = 2.

6.3.2 Complexity of a Binary Search Algorithm

In a binary search algorithm, we can see that with each comparison, the size of the search area is reduced by half. So, we can claim that the efficiency of the binary search in the worst case is $O(\log_{10}n)$, where n is the total number of elements in the array. Obviously, the best case will happen when the value to be searched for is equal to the value of the array in the middle.

6.3.3 Drawbacks of a Binary Search

• A binary search requires that the data elements in the array be sorted; otherwise, a binary search will not work.

- A binary search cannot be used where there are many insertions and deletions of data elements in the array.

Write a program to search for an element in an array using the binary search technique.

```
# include<stdio.h>
# include<conio.h>
intbinary_search (intarr[], int n, intval) ;
void main()
{
  intarr[10], n, i, r, val ;
  clrscr() ;
  printf("***BINARY SEARCH***") ;
  printf("\nenter no of elements") ;
  scanf("%d", &n) ;
  printf("enter the elements of array") ;
  for( i=0; i<n ; i++)
    {
      printf("\nenter element %d", i+1) ;
      scanf("%d", &arr[i]) ;
    }
  printf("\nenter value to search") ;
  scanf("%d", &val) ;
  r = binary_search(arr, n, val) ;
  if(r == -1)
  printf("value not found") ;
  else
  printf("%d value found at %d", val, r+1) ;
  getch() ;
}
intbinary_search(intarr[], int n, intval)
{
  int start = 0, end = n-1, mid ;
  while(start <= end)
    {
      mid = (start+end)/2 ;
      if(arr[mid] == val)
      return mid;
      else if(arr[mid] <val)
      start=mid+1 ;
```

```
        else
        end=mid-1 ;
     }
  return (-1);
}
```

Output

```
***BINARY SEARCH***
Enter no of elements  8

Enter elements of array
Enter element 1:  1
Enter element 2:  5
Enter element 3:  9
Enter element 4:  15
Enter element 5:  27
Enter element 6:  35
Enter element 7:  43
Enter element 8:  60

Enter value to search: 35
35 value found at 6th position
```

Frequently Asked Questions

Q. What is a binary search? Explain.

Answer.
A binary search is one of the searching techniques which is used to find the element in an array. It works very efficiently with a sorted list. In a binary search, the element to be searched for is compared with the middle element of the array. If the value to be searched for is less than the middle element, we will search in the lower half of the array and vice versa.

6.4 Interpolation Search

An interpolation search, also known as an extrapolation search, is a technique for searching a particular value in an ordered array. This searching technique is more efficient than a binary search if the elements in the array are sorted. The technique of an interpolation search is similar to when we are searching for "Abhishek" in the telephone directory; we don't start in the middle, because we know that it will be near the extreme left, so we start from the front and work from there. That is the main idea of an interpolation search, that is, instead of dividing the list into fixed halves, we cut it by an amount that seems most likely to succeed.

Practical Application:

If we want to search for "Ayush" in the directory, then we will always search in the extreme left of the directory.

6.4.1 Working of the Interpolation Search Algorithm

In each step of this searching technique, the remaining search area for the value to be searched for is calculated. The calculations are done on the values at the bounds of the search area and the value which is to be searched. Therefore, the value found at this position will now be compared with the value to be searched. If both values are equal, then the search is said to be successful. If both values are unequal, then depending upon the comparison done, the remaining search area is reduced to the part just before or after the initial position.

Consider an array ARR of n elements in which the elements are arranged in a sorted manner. Initially low is set to 0 and high is set to n-1. Now we are searching a value VAL in ARR between ARR[LOW] and ARR[HIGH]. Then, in this case, MID will be calculated by the following formula:

MID = LOW + (HIGH - LOW) X ((VAL – ARR[LOW] / ARR[HIGH] – ARR[LOW]))

If the value VAL is found at MID, then the search is complete; otherwise, if the value is lower than ARR[MID], reset HIGH = MID – 1, and if the value is greater than ARR[MID], reset LOW = MID + 1. Repeat these steps until the value is found.

Hence, we can say that the interpolation search is very much similar to the binary search technique. The main difference between the techniques is that in a binary search the value selected is always the middle value of the list, and it discards half the values based on the comparison between the value to be searched for and the value found at the estimated position. Let us understand the interpolation search with the help of an algorithm:

Algorithm for an Interpolation Search

```
INTERPOLATION_SEARCH(ARR, Lower_bound, Upper_bound, VAL)

Step 1: START
Step 2: Set LOW = lower_bound, HIGH = upper_
        bound, POS = -1
Step 3: Repeat Steps 4 & 5 while LOW<= HIGH
Step 4: Set MID = LOW + (HIGH - LOW) X ((VAL -
        ARR[LOW] / ARR[HIGH] - ARR[LOW]))
Step 5: IF (ARR[MID] = VAL)
            POS = MID
            PRINT POS
            Go to Step 7
            ELSE IF (ARR[MID] > VAL)
            Set HIGH = MID - 1
            ELSE
            Set LOW = MID + 1
            [End of If]
            [End of Loop]
Step 6: IF (POS = -1)
            PRINT "VALUE NOT FOUND, SEARCH UNSUCCESSFUL"
            [End of IF]
Step 7: EXIT
```

For Example: Consider an array of 7 numbers which is declared as:

```
int array[] = {5, 16, 23, 34, 45, 56, 65} ;
```

and the value to be searched for is 45.

Solution –

Pass 1 –

LOW = 0, HIGH = 7 - 1= 6, VAL =45

ARR[LOW] = ARR[0] = 5, ARR[HIGH] = ARR[6] = 65

Now MID = LOW + (HIGH - LOW) X ((VAL – ARR[LOW]) / (ARR[HIGH] – ARR[LOW]))

$$= 0 + (6 – 0) \text{ X } ((45 – 5) / (65 – 5))$$

$$= 0 + 6 \text{ X } (40 / 60) = 4$$

45 is found at POS = 4

If(VAL == ARR[MID]) i.e. 45 == ARR[4] =45, 45 = 45

Figure 6.3. Working of the interpolation search.

Hence, the value is found.

6.4.2 Complexity of the Interpolation Search Algorithm

The interpolation search makes about $log_{10}(log_{10} n)$ comparisons when there is n number of elements in the list and the elements are uniformly distributed. Obviously, the worst case will happen when the number of elements is increased exponentially; then, in that case, the algorithm can take up to O(n) comparisons.

Write a program to search for an element in an array using the interpolation search technique.

```
# include<stdio.h>
# include<conio.h>
intinterpolation_search (intarr[], int n, intval) ;
void main()
{
```

```
intarr[10], n, i, r, val ;
clrscr() ;
printf("***INTERPOLATION SEARCH***") ;
printf("\nenter no of elements") ;
scanf("%d", &n) ;
printf("enter the elements of array") ;
for( i=0; i<n ; i++)
  {
    printf("\nenter element %d", i+1) ;
    scanf("%d", &arr[i]) ;
  }
printf("\nenter value to search") ;
scanf("%d", &val) ;
r = interpolation_search(arr, n, val) ;
if(r == -1)
printf("value not found") ;
else
printf("%d value found at %d", val, r+1) ;
getch() ;
}
intinterpolation_search(intarr[], int n, intval)
{
  int low = 0, high = n-1, mid ;
  while(low <= high)
    {
      mid = low + (high - low) X ((val - arr[low]) /
      (arr[high] - arr[high]))
      if(arr[mid] == val)
      return mid;
      else if(arr[mid] <val)
      low = mid+1 ;
      else
      high = mid-1 ;
    }
  return (-1);
}
```

Output

INTERPOLATION SEARCH
Enter no of elements 7

Enter elements of array
Enter element 1: 15
Enter element 2: 25
Enter element 3: 35
Enter element 4: 45
Enter element 5: 55
Enter element 6: 65
Enter element 7: 75

Enter value to search: 35
35 value found at 3rd position

6.5 Introduction to Sorting

Sorting refers to the process of arranging the data elements of an array in a specified order, that is, either in ascending or descending order. For example, it will be practically impossible for us to find a name in the telephone directory if the names in it are not in alphabetical order. However, this same thing can be true for dictionaries, book indexes, bank accounts, and so on. Hence, the convenience of having sorted data is unquestionable. Retrieval of information becomes much easier when the data is stored in some specified order. Therefore, sorting is a very important application in computer science.

Let us take an array which is declared and initialized as:

```
int array[] = {10, 25, 17, 8, 30, 3} ;
```

Then, the array after applying the sorting technique is:

```
array[] = {3, 8, 10, 17, 25, 30} ;
```

A sorting algorithm can be defined as an algorithm which puts the data elements of an array/list in a certain order, that is, either numerical order or any predefined order. There are many sorting algorithms which are available and are widely used according to the different environments required by the different sorting methods.

The two basic categories of sorting methods are:

1. **Internal Sorting** – It refers to the sorting of the data elements stored in the computer's main memory.

2. **External Sorting** – It refers to the sorting of the data elements stored in the files. It is applied when the amount of data is large and cannot be stored in the main memory.

6.5.1 Types of Sorting Methods

The various sorting methods are:

1. Selection Sort

2. Insertion Sort

3. Merge Sort

4. Bubble Sort

5. Quick Sort

Let us discuss all of them in detail.

1. Selection Sort

Selection sort is a sorting technique that works by finding the smallest value in the array and placing it in the first position. After that, it then finds the second smallest value and places it in the second position. This process is repeated until the whole array is sorted. Thus, the selection sort works by finding the smallest unsorted element remaining in the entire array and then swapping it with the element in the next position to be filled. It is a very simple technique and it is also easier to implement than other sorting techniques. Selection sort is used for sorting files with large records.

Selection Sort Technique

Let us take an array ARR with N elements in it. Now, the selection sort technique works as follows:

First of all, we will find the smallest value in the entire array, and we will place that value in the first position of the array. Then, we will find the second smallest value in the array and we will place it in the second position of the array. Now, we will repeat this process until the whole array is sorted.

Pass 1 – Find the position POS of the smallest value in the array of N elements and interchange ARR[POS] with ARR[0]. Hence, ARR[0] is sorted.

Pass 2 – Find the position POS of the smallest value in the array of N-1 elements and interchange ARR[POS] with A[1]. Hence, A[1] is sorted.

.

.

.

Pass N-1 – Find the position POS of the smaller of the elements of ARR[N-2] and ARR[N-1] and interchange ARR[POS] with ARR[N-2]. Hence, ARR[0], ARR[1], . . . ARR[N-1] is sorted.

Let us discuss it with the help of a detailed algorithm.

Algorithm for a Selection Sort

Consider an array ARR having N elements from ARR[0] to ARR[N-1]. I and J are the looping variables, and POS is the swapping variable.

```
SELECTION SORT(ARR, N)

Step 1: START
Step 2: Repeat Steps 3 & 4 for I = 1 to N - 1
Step 3: Call MIN(ARR, I, N, POS)
Step 4: Swap ARR[I] with ARR[POS]
          [End of Loop]
Step 5: EXIT

MIN(ARR, I, N, POS)

Step 1: Set SMALLEST = ARR[I]
Step 2: Set POS = I
Step 3: Repeat Step 4 for J = I + 1 to N - 1
Step 4: IF (ARR[J] < SMALLEST)
            Set SMALLEST = ARR[J]
            Set POS = J
            [End of IF]
            [End of Loop]
Step 5: Return POS
```

For Example – Sort the given array using selection sort.

arr[0]	arr[1]	arr[2]	arr[3]	arr[4]
4	14	29	11	35

Solution:

Pass	POS	Array[0]	Array[1]	Array[2]	Array[3]	Array[4]
1	4	4	14	29	11	35
2	3	4	11	29	14	35
3	3	4	11	14	29	35
4	3	4	11	14	29	35
5	4	4	11	14	29	35

Figure 6.4. Working of selection sort.

Hence, after sorting the new array is:

arr[0]	arr[1]	arr[2]	arr[3]	arr[4]
4	11	14	29	35

Complexity of the Selection Sort Algorithm

Selection sort is the simple technique of sorting. In this method, if there are n elements in the array then (n-1) comparisons or iterations are made. Thus, *the selection sort technique has a complexity of $O(n^2)$.*

Write a program to sort an array using the selection sort method.

```c
# include <stdio.h>
# include <conio.h>
void main()
{
  int i, j, min, pos, arr[10], n, temp;
  clrscr();
  printf("enter no of elements in the array") ;
  scanf("%d", &n) ;
  printf("\nelements in the array are ") ;
  for( i=0 ; i<n ; i++ )
    {
```

```
        printf("\nenter element %d", i+1) ;
        scanf("%d", &arr[i]);
    }
  printf("Selection Sort") ;
  for( i=1 ; i<n ; i++ )
    {
      min = arr[ i-1 ] ;
      pos = i-1;
      for( j=I ; j<n ; j++ )
        {
          if( arr[j] < min )
            {
              min = arr[j] ;
              pos = j ;
            }
        }
      if( pos != i-1 )//Swapping of variables is done
        {
          temp = arr[pos] ;
          arr[pos] = arr[i-1] ;
          arr[i-1] = temp ;
        }
    }
  printf("after sorting new array is") ;
  for( i=0 ; i<n ; i++ )
    {
      printf(" \t%d ", arr[i]) ;
    }
  getch() ;
}
```

Output -

```
Enter number of elements 5
Enter elements of array
Enter element 1    12
Enter element 2    78
Enter element 3    36
Enter element 4    94
Enter element 5    10
Selection Sort
After sorting new array is
  10   12   36   78   94
```

Frequently Asked Questions

Q. Define the selection sort technique.

Answer.
Selection sort is a sorting technique which works by finding the smallest element from the array and placing it in the first position. It then finds the second smallest element and places it in the second position. Hence, this procedure is repeated until the whole array is sorted.

2. Insertion Sort

Insertion Sort is another very simple sorting algorithm which works just like its name suggests, that is, it inserts each element into its proper position in the concluding list. To limit the wastage of memory or, we can say, to save memory, most implementations of an insertion sort work by moving the current element past the already sorted elements and repeatedly swapping or interchanging it with the preceding element until it is placed in its correct position.

Practical Application:

We usually use this technique while ordering a deck of cards while playing a game called bridge.

Insertion Sort Technique

Pass 1 – Initially there is only one element in the list which is already sorted. Hence, we proceed to the next steps.

Pass 2 – During the first iteration, the first and the second element of the list are compared. The smaller value occupies the first position of the list.

Pass 3 – During the second iteration, the first three elements of the list are compared. The smaller value will occupy the first position in the list. The second position will be occupied by the second smallest element, and so on.

.

.

This procedure is repeated for all the elements of the array up to (n-1) iterations.

Algorithm for an Insertion Sort

```
INSERTION SORT(ARR, N)
Step 1: START
Step 2: Repeat Steps 3 to 6 for I = 1 to N - 1
Step 3: Set POS = ARR[I]
Step 4: Set J = I - 1
Step 5: Repeat while POS <= ARR[J]
            Set ARR[J + 1] = ARR[J]
            Set J = J - 1
            [End of Inner while loop]
Step 6: Set ARR[J + 1] = POS
            [End of Loop]
Step 7: EXIT
```

In the previous algorithm, in Step 2, a for loop is executed which will be repeated for every element in the array. In Step 3, we are storing the value of the Ith element in POS. In Step 5, again a loop is executed in which the new elements after sorting are placed. At last, the element is stored at the (J+1)[th] position.

For Example – Consider the following array. Sort the given values in the array using the insertion sort technique.

Solution – ☐ sorted   ☐ unsorted

Pass 1 – Initially, ARR[0] is sorted. Move to the next pass.

39	54	10	28	95	7

Pass 2 – Now 39 and 54 are compared. 39 < 54, so ARR[0] = 39 and ARR[1] = 54.

39	54	10	28	95	7

Pass 3 – 39, 54, and 10 are compared. 10 < 39 and 54, so ARR[0] = 10, now 39 < 54 hence ARR[1] = 39 and ARR[2] = 54.

10	39	54	28	95	7

Pass 4 – As 28 < 39 and 54, so ARR[1] = 28.

10	28	39	54	95	7

Pass 5 – In this case, 95 is greater than all the values, so there is no need for swapping.

10	28	39	54	95	7

Pass 6 – 7 is the smallest value, so ARR[0] = 7.

Therefore, after sorting the new array is:

7	10	28	39	54	95

Figure 6.5. Working of an insertion sort.

Complexity of an Insertion Sort

In an insertion sort, the best case will happen when the array is already sorted, and in that case the running time of the algorithm is O(n) (i.e., linear running time). Obviously, the worst case will happen when the array is sorted in the reverse order. Thus, in that case the running time of the algorithm is O(n²) (i.e., quadratic running time).

Write a program to sort an array using the insertion sort method.

```c
# include <stdio.h>
# include <conio.h>
void main()
{
  int i, j, min, arr[10], n, temp;
  clrscr();
  printf("enter no of elements in the array") ;
  scanf("%d", &n) ;
  printf("\nelements in the array are ") ;
  for( i=0 ; i<n ; i++ )
    {
      printf("\nenter element %d", i+1) ;
      scanf("%d", &arr[i]);
    }
  printf("Insertion Sort") ;
  for( i=1 ; i<n ; i++ )
    {
      temp = arr[i] ;
      j = i -1;
      while(( temp <arr[j] && (j >= 0))
        {
          arr[j + 1] = arr[j] ;
          j-- ;
        }
      arr[j + 1] = temp ;
    }
  printf("after sorting new array is") ;
  for( i=0 ; i<n ; i++ )
    {
      printf(" \t%d ", arr[i]) ;
    }
  getch() ;
}
```

Output –

Enter number of elements 7
Enter elements of array
Enter element 1   58
Enter element 2   12
Enter element 3   20
Enter element 4   8
Enter element 5   11
Enter element 6   99
Enter element 7   63

Insertion Sort
After sorting new array is
811   12   20   58   63   99

3. Merge Sort

Merge sort is a sorting method which follows the divide and conquer approach. The divide and conquer approach is a very good approach in which divide means partitioning the array having n elements into two sub-arrays of n/2 elements each. However, if there are no elements present in the list/array or if an array contains only one element, then it is already sorted. However, if an array has more elements, then it is divided into two sub-arrays containing equal elements in them. Conquer is the process of sorting the two sub-arrays recursively using merge sort. Finally, the two sub-arrays are merged into one single sorted array.

Merge Sort Techniques

1. If the array has zero or one element in it, then there is no need to sort that array as it is already sorted.

2. Otherwise, if there are more elements in the array, then divide the array into two sub-arrays containing equal elements.

3. Each sub-array is now sorted recursively using merge sort.

4. Finally, the two sub-arrays are merged into a single sorted array.

Algorithm of Merge Sort

MERGE SORT(ARR, BEG, END)

Step 1: START
Step 2: IF (BEG < END)
Step 3: Set MID = (BEG + END)/2
Call MERGE SORT (ARR, BEG, END)
Call MERGE SORT (ARR, MID + 1, END)
Call MERGE (ARR, BEG, MID, END)
[End of If]
Step 4: EXIT

MERGE(ARR, BEG, MID, END)

Step 1: START
Step 2: Set I = BEG, J = MID + 1, K = 0
Step 3: Repeat while (I <= MID) && (J <= END)
IF (ARR[I] > ARR[J])
Set TEMP[K] = ARR[J]
Set J = J + 1
Set K = K + 1
ELSE IF (ARR[J] > ARR[I])
Set TEMP[K] = ARR[I]
Set I = I + 1
Set K = K + 1
ELSE
Set TEMP[K] = ARR[J]
Set J = J + 1
Set K = K + 1
Set TEMP[K] = ARR[I]
Set I = I + 1
Set K = K + 1
[End of If]
[End of Loop]
Step 4: (Copying the remaining elements of left sub
array if any)
Repeat while (I <= MID)
Set TEMP[K] = ARR[I]
Set I = I + 1
Set K = K + 1
[End of Loop]

```
Step 5: (Copying the remaining elements of right
        sub array if any)
                Repeat while (J <= END)
                Set TEMP[K] = ARR[J]
                Set I = I + 1
                Set K = K + 1
                [End of Loop]
Step 6: Set IND = 0
Step 7: Repeat while (IND < K)
                Set ARR[IND] = ARR[IND]
                Set IND = IND + 1
                [End of Loop]
Step 8: EXIT
```

For Example – Sort the following array using merge sort.

```
int array[] = { 40, 10, 86, 44, 93, 26, 69, 17 }
```

Solution –

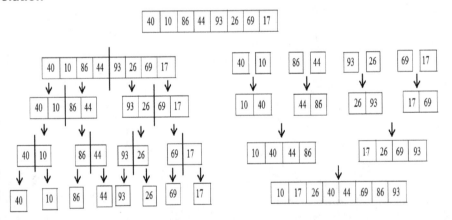

Divide and Conquer Process   Merging the sub arrays into one sorted array

Figure 6.6. Working of a merge sort.

From the previous example, we can see how the merge sort algorithm works. First, the merge sort algorithm recursively divides the array into smaller sub-arrays. After dividing the array into smaller parts, we call the function Merge() to merge all the sub-arrays to form a single sorted array.

Complexity of Merge Sort

The running time of the merge sort algorithm is O(n log$_{10}$n). This runtime remains the same in the average as well as in the worst case of the merge sort algorithm. Although it has an optimal time complexity, sometimes this runtime can be O(n).

Write a program to sort an array using the merge sort method.

```c
# include<stdio.h>
# include<conio.h>
void merge(intarr[], int i1, int j1, i2, int j2) ;
void merge_sort(intarr[], int beg, int end)
{
  int mid ;
  if(beg < end)
    {
      mid=(beg+end)/2;
      merge_sort(arr, beg, mid) ;
      merge_sort(arr, mid+1, end) ;
      merge(arr, beg, mid, mid+1, end) ;
    }
}
void merge(intarr[], int i1, int j1, int i2, int j2)
{
  int temp[20] ;
  int i, j, k ;
  i = i1 ;
  j = i2 ;
  k = 0 ;
  while(i < j1 && j < j2)
    {
      if(arr[i] <arr[j])
        {
          temp[k] = arr[i] ;
          k++ ;
          i++ ;
        }
      else if(arr[i] >arr[j])
        {
```

```
                temp[k] = arr[j] ;
                k++ ;
                j++ ;
              }
          else
            {
              temp[k] = arr[j] ;
              k++ ;
              j++ ;
              temp[k] = arr[i] ;
              k++ ;
              i++ ;
            }
        }
    while(i < j1)
      {
        temp[k] = arr[i] ;
        k++ ;
        i++ ;
      }
    while(j < j2)
      {
        temp[k] = arr[j] ;
        k++ ;
        j++ ;
      }
    for(i = i1, j = 0 ; i <= j2 ; i++, j++)
      {
        arr[i] = temp[j] ;
      }
}
int main()
{
  int i, n, arr[10] ;
  clrscr() ;
  printf("enter no of elements: ") ;
  scanf("%d", &n) ;
  printf("\nelements of array are:") ;
  for(i=0; i<n; i++)
    {
      printf("\nenter element %d", i+1) ;
```

```
    scanf("%d", &arr[i]) ;
  }
merge_sort(arr, 0, n-1) ;
printf("\nafter merge sort new array is:") ;
for(i=0; i<n; i++)
  {
    printf("\t%d", arr[i]) ;
  }
return 0 ;
}
```

Output -

```
Enter number of elements: 8
Enter elements of array:
Enter element 1   3
Enter element 2   15
Enter element 3   69
Enter element 4   32
Enter element 5   10
Enter element 6   87
Enter element 7   21
Enter element 8   45

After merge sort new array is:
  10  15  21  32  45  69  87
```

4. Bubble Sort

Bubble sort, also known as exchange sort, is a very simple sorting method. It works by repeatedly moving the largest element to the highest position of the array. In bubble sort, we are comparing two elements at a time, and swapping is done if they are wrongly placed. If the element at lower index or position is greater than the element at a higher index, then in that case both the elements are interchanged so that the smaller element is placed before the bigger one. This process is repeated until the list becomes sorted. Bubble sort gets its name from the way that the smaller elements "bubble" to the top of the array. This sorting technique only uses comparisons to operate on the elements. Hence, we can also call it a comparison sort.

Bubble Sort Technique

The basic idea applied for a bubble sort is to let us assume if an array ARR contains n elements, then the number of iterations required to sort the array will be $(n - 1)$.

Pass 1 – During the first iteration, the largest value in the array is placed at the last position.

Pass 2 – During the second iteration, the second largest value of the array is placed in the second last position.

Pass 3 – During the third iteration, the third largest value of the array is placed in the third last position and so on.

This procedure is repeated until all the elements in the array are scanned and are placed in their correct position, which means that the array is sorted.

Algorithm of a Bubble Sort

```
BUBBLE SORT(ARR, N)

Step 1: START
Step 2: Repeat Step 3 for I = 0 to N - 1
Step 3: Repeat for J = 0 to N - 1
Step 4: IF (ARR[J] > ARR[J+1])
            INTERCHANGE ARR[J] & ARR[J + 1]
            [End of Inner Loop]
            [End of Outer Loop]
Step 5: EXIT
```

For Example – Consider the following array. Sort the given values in the array using the bubble sort technique.

arr[0]	arr[1]	arr[2]	arr[3]	arr[4]
40	50	20	90	30

Solution – In the given array, the number of elements in the array is 5, so the number of iterations will be $(n - 1) = 4$.

Pass 1 –

40	50	20	90	30

a) 40 and 50 are compared. Since 40 < 50, no swapping is done.

40	50	20	90	30

b) 50 and 20 are compared. Since 50> 20, swapping will be done.

40	20	50	90	30

c) 50 and 90 are compared. Since 50 < 90, no swapping is done.

40	20	50	90	30

d) 90 and 30 are compared. Since 90 > 30, swapping is done.

40	20	50	30	90

At the end of the first pass, the largest element in the array is placed at the highest position in the array, but all the other elements are still unsorted. Let us now proceed to Pass 2.

Pass 2 –

40	20	50	30	90

a) 40 and 20 are compared. Since 40 > 20, swapping is done.

20	40	50	30	90

b) 40 and 50 are compared. Since 40 < 50, no swapping will be done.

20	40	50	30	90

c) 50 and 30 are compared. Since 50 > 30, swapping is done.

20	40	30	50	90

At the end of the second pass, the second largest element in the array is placed at the second last position in the array, but all the other elements are still unsorted. Let us now proceed to Pass 3.

Pass 3 –

20	40	30	50	90

a) 20 and 40 are compared. Since 20 < 40, no swapping is done.

20	40	30	50	90

b) 40 and 30 are compared. Since 40 > 30, swapping will be done.

20	30	40	50	90

At the end of the third pass, the third largest element in the array is placed at the third largest position in the array, but all the other elements are still unsorted. Let us now proceed to Pass 4.

Pass 4 –

20	40	30	50	90

a) 20 and 40 are compared. Since 20 < 40, no swapping is done.

At the end of the fourth pass, we can see that all the elements in the list are sorted. Hence, after sorting the new array will be:

20	40	30	50	90

Figure 6.7. Working of bubble sort.

Complexity of the Bubble Sort

The bubble sort is the most inefficient sorting algorithm, and hence it is not commonly used. In the best case, the running time of the bubble sort is $O(n)$, that is, when the array is already sorted. Otherwise, its level of complexity in average and worst cases is extremely poor, that is, $O(n^2)$.

Write a program to sort an array using the bubble sort method.

```c
# include <stdio.h>
# include <conio.h>
void main()
{
 int  i , n, temp, j, arr[10] ;
 clrscr() ;
 printf("\n enter the number of elements: ") ;
 scanf ("%d", &n) ;
 printf ("\ n enter the elements of array:") ;
 for(i=0 ; i<n ; i++)
   {
    printf("\nenter element %d", i+1) ;
    scanf("%d" , &arr[i]) ;
   }
 for(i=0 ; i<n ; i++)
   {
    for(j=0 ; j<=n ; j++)
      {
       if(arr[j] >arr[j+1])
         {
          temp= arr[j]
          arr[j] = arr[j+1] ;
          arr[j+1] = temp ;
         }
      }
   }
 printf("\nThe Array Sorted In Ascending Order Is\n :")
;
 for(i=0 ; i<n ; i++)
   {
    printf("%d\t" , arr[i]) ;
   }
 getch() ;
}
```

Output -

Enter number of elements: 6
Enter elements of array:

```
Enter element 1   63
Enter element 2   78
Enter element 3   10
Enter element 4   9
Enter element 5   33
Enter element 6   47

The Array Sorted In Ascending Order Is:
9   10   33   47   63   78
```

5. Quick Sort

Quick sort, also known as partition exchange sort and developed by C. A. R. Hoare, is a widely used sorting algorithm which also uses the divide and conquer approach as we have discussed in merge sort. Here also, we will divide a single unsorted array into its two smaller sub-arrays. The divide and conquer method means dividing the bigger problem into two smaller problems, and then those two smaller problems into smaller problems, and so on. Like merge sort, if there are no elements in the array or if an array is containing only one element, then it is already sorted. A quick sort algorithm is faster than all the other sorting algorithms which have time complexity $O(n \log_{10} n)$.

Working of Quick Sort

1. An element called pivot is selected from the array elements.

2. After choosing the pivot element, all the elements of the array are rearranged such that all the elements less than the pivot element will be on left side, and all the elements greater than the pivot element will be placed on the right side of the pivot element. After rearranging all the elements, the pivot is now placed in its final position. Thus, this process is known as partitioning.

3. Now, the two sub-arrays obtained will be recursively sorted.

Quick Sort Technique

1. Initially set the index of the first element to LEFT and POS. Similarly, set the index of the last element to RIGHT. Now, LEFT = 0, POS = 0, RIGHT = N − 1 (assuming n elements in the array).

2. We will start with the last element which is pointed to by RIGHT, and we will traverse each element in the array from right to left, comparing each element with the first element pointed to by POS. ARR[POS] should always be less than ARR[RIGHT].

If ARR[POS] is less than ARR[RIGHT] then continue comparing until RIGHT = POS. If RIGHT = POS then it means that pivot is placed in its correct position.

If ARR[RIGHT] < ARR[POS], then swap the two values and go to the next step.

Set POS = RIGHT.

3. We will start from the first element which is pointed to by LEFT, and we will traverse every element in the array from left to right, comparing each element with the element pointed to by POS. ARR[POS] should always be greater than ARR[LEFT].

If ARR[POS] is greater than ARR[RIGHT] then continue comparing until LEFT = POS. If LEFT = POS then it means that pivot is placed in its correct position.

If ARR[LEFT] > ARR[POS], then swap the two values and go to the previous step.

Set POS = LEFT.

Algorithm of Quick Sort

```
QUICK SORT(ARR, BEG, END)
Step 1: START
Step 2: IF (BEG < END)
            Call PARTITION (ARR, BEG, END, POS)
            Call QUICK SORT (ARR, BEG, POS - 1)
            Call QUICK (ARR, POS + 1, END)
            [End of If]
Step 3: EXIT
```

```
PARTITION(ARR, BEG, END, POS)
Step 1: START
Step 2: Set LEFT = BEG, RIGHT = END, POS = BEG,TEMP = 0
Step 3: Repeat Steps 4 to 7 while TEMP = 0
Step 4: Repeat while ARR[RIGHT] >= ARR[POS]&& POS
        != RIGHT
            Set RIGHT = RIGHT - 1
            [End of Loop]
Step 5: IF (POS = RIGHT)
            Set TEMP = 1
            ELSE IF (ARR[POS] > ARR[RIGHT])
            INTERCHANGE ARR[POS] with ARR[RIGHT]
            Set POS = RIGHT
            [End of If]
Step 6: IF TEMP = 0
            Repeat while ARR[POS] >= ARR[LEFT] &&
            POS != LEFT
            Set LEFT = LEFT + 1
            [End of Loop]
Step 7: IF (POS = LEFT)
            Set TEMP = 1
            ELSE IF (ARR[LEFT] > ARR[POS])
            INTERCHANGE ARR[POS] with ARR[LEFT]
            Set POS = LEFT
            [End of If]
            [End of If]
            [End of Loop]
Step 8: EXIT
```

For Example – Sort the values given in the array using the quick sort algorithm.

arr[0]	arr[1]	arr[2]	arr[3]	arr[4]	arr[5]
25	7	39	17	30	52

Solution –

Step 1 – First element is chosen as the pivot. Now, set POS = 0, LEFT = 0, RIGHT = 5.

25	7	39	17	30	52

POS, LEFT RIGHT

Step 2 – Traverse the list from right to left. Since ARR[POS] < ARR[RIGHT], that is, 25 < 52,   RIGHT = RIGHT – 1 = 4.

25	7	39	17	30	52

POS, LEFT   RIGHT

Step 3 – Since ARR[POS] < ARR[RIGHT], that is, 25 < 30, RIGHT = RIGHT – 1 = 3.

25	7	39	17	30	52

POS, LEFT   RIGHT

Step 4 – Since ARR[POS] > ARR[RIGHT], that is, 25 < 17, we will swap the two values and set POS = RIGHT.

17	7	39	25	30	52

LEFTRIGHT, POS

Step 5 – Traverse the list from left to right. Since ARR[POS] > ARR[LEFT], that is, 25 > 17, LEFT = LEFT + 1.

17	7	39	25	30	52

LEFT   RIGHT, POS

Step 6 – Since ARR[POS] > ARR[LEFT], that is, 25 > 7, LEFT = LEFT + 1.

17	7	39	25	30	52

LEFT   RIGHT, POS

Step 7 – Since ARR[POS] < ARR[LEFT], that is, 25 < 39, we will swap the values and set POS = LEFT.

17	7	25	39	30	52

LEFT, POS RIGHT

(*Continue...*)

Step 8 – Traverse the list from right to left. Since ARR[POS] < ARR[LEFT], RIGHT = RIGHT - 1.

17	7	25	39	30	52

LEFT, POS, RIGHT

Figure 6.8. Working of quick sort.

Now, RIGHT = POS, so now the process is over and the pivot element of the array, that is, 25, is placed in its correct position. Therefore, all the elements which are smaller than 25 are placed before it and all the elements greater than 25 are placed after it. Hence, 17 and 7 are the elements in the left sub-array and 39, 30, and 52 are the elements in the right sub-array, which both are sorted.

Complexity of Quick Sort

The running time efficiency of quick sort is $O(n \log_{10} n)$ in the average and the best case. However, the worst case will happen if the array is already sorted and the leftmost element is selected as the pivot element. In the worst case, its efficiency is $O(n^2)$.

Write a program to sort an array using the quick sort method.

```c
# include <stdio.h>
# include <conio.h>
# define size 100
int part(intarr[], int beg , int end) ;
void quick_sort( intarr[ ] , int beg , int end) ;
void main()
{
  intarr[size], i, n ;
  printf("\n enter the number of elements: ") ;
  scanf ("%d", &n) ;
  printf ("\ n enter the elements of array :") ;
  for(i=0 ; i<n ; i++)
    {
      printf("\n enter element %d", i+1) ;
```

```
      scanf("%d" , &arr[i]) ;
    }
  quick_sort(arr , 0 , n-1) ;
  printf("\nThe sorted array is :\n") ;
  for (i=0 ; i<n ; i++)
    {
      printf(" %d \t ", arr[i]) ;
    }
  getch() ;
}

int part (int arr[], int beg, int end)
{
  int left , right , temp , pos , flag ;
  pos = left = beg ;
  right = end ;
  flag = 0 ;
  while( flag ! = 1)
    {
      while ( ( a[pos] < = arr[right ] && (loc != right ))
      right-- ;
      if(pos == right)
      flag = 1 ;
      else if (arr[pos] >arr[right])
        {
          temp = arr[pos] ;
          arr[pos] = arr[right] ;
          arr[right] = temp ;
          pos  = right ;
        }
      if ( flag != 1)
        {
          while (( arr[pos] >= arr[left] && (pos != left))
          left ++ ;
          if( pos == left )
          flag = 1 ;
          else if (arr[pos] <arr[left])
            {
              temp = arr[pos] ;
              arr[pos]= arr[left] ;
              arr[left]= temp ;
```

```
                pos = left ;
            }
        }
    }
  return pos ;
}
void quick sort (int arr[], int beg, int end)
{
  int pos ;
  if(beg < end)

    {
      pos = part(arr, beg , end) ;
      quick_sort(arr, beg, loc-1) ;
      quick_sort(arr, loc+1, end) ;
    }
}
```

Output -

Enter number of elements: 5
Enter elements of array:
Enter element 1   52
Enter element 2   78
Enter element 3   16
Enter element 4   01
Enter element 5   86

The sorted array is :
01   16   52   78   86

6.6 External Sorting

External Sorting is a sorting technique which is used when the amount of data is very massive. When a large amount of data have to be sorted, it is not possible to bring them into main memory (RAM). Therefore, in that situation a secondary memory needs to be used. Also, at the same time, some portion of data is brought into the main memory from the secondary memory for sorting based on the availability of storage space of the main memory. After the data is sorted, it is sent back to the secondary memory. Now, the next portion of the data is brought into the main memory, and after sorting it is sent back to the secondary memory. This procedure is repeated until all the data is sorted. Here, each portion is called a segment. The time required for sorting is more because the time will be spent while transferring the data from secondary memory to main memory. The merge sort algorithm is widely and commonly used in external sorting, which has been already discussed.

External sorting is used in database applications for performing different kinds of operations like join, union, projection, and many more. It is also used to update a master file from a transaction file. For example, if we are updating the company file based on the new employees, existing employees, locations, and so on. Duplicate records or data can also be removed from external sorting.

6.7 Summary

- The process of finding a particular value in a list or an array is called searching. If that particular value is present in the array, then the search is said to be successful and the location of that particular value is retrieved by the searching process.

- Linear search, binary search and interpolation search are the commonly used searching techniques.

- Linear search works by comparing the values to be searched for with every element of the array in a linear sequence until a match is found.

- Binary search works efficiently when the list is sorted. In a binary search, we first compare the value VAL with the data element in the middle position of the array.

- Interpolation search, also known as extrapolation search, is a technique for searching a particular value in an ordered array. In each step of this searching technique, the remaining search area for the value to be searched for is calculated. The calculations are done on the values at the bounds of the search area and the value which is to be searched.

- Sorting refers to the technique of arranging the data elements of an array in a specified order, that is, either in ascending or descending order.

- Selection sort is a sorting technique that works by finding the smallest value in the array and placing it in the first position. After that, it then finds the second smallest value and places it in the second position. This process is repeated until the whole array is sorted.

- Insertion sort works by moving the current data element past the already sorted data elements and repeatedly interchanging it with the preceding element until it is in the correct place.

- Merge sort is a sorting method which follows the divide and conquer approach. Divide means partitioning the array having n elements into two sub-arrays of n/2 elements each. Conquer is the process of sorting the two sub-arrays recursively using merge sort. Finally, the two sub-arrays are merged into one single sorted array.

- Bubble sort, also known as exchange sort, is a very simple sorting method. It works by repeatedly moving the largest element to the highest position of the array.

- Quick sort is an algorithm which selects a pivot element and rearranges the values in such a way that all the elements less than the pivot element appear before it and the elements greater than pivot appear after it.

- External sorting is a sorting technique which is used when the amount of data is very massive.

6.8 Exercises

6.8.1 Theory Questions

1. Define sorting. Write the importance of sorting.

2. What are the different types of sorting techniques? Discuss each of them in detail.

3. Define searching. Which searching technique will you prefer while searching an element in an array?

4. Explain selection sort and merge sort with suitable examples. Show various stages.

5. How is linear search used to find an element? Explain the working of insertion sort with a suitable example.

6. Explain different types of searching techniques. Give a suitable example to illustrate binary search.

7. Why is quick sort known as "quick"?

8. Explain the concept of external sorting.

9. Differentiate between binary search and interpolation search. Give a suitable example.

10. Discuss the limitations and advantages of insertion sort.

11. Explain the working of bubble sort with a suitable example. Why is bubble sort called "bubble"?

6.8.2 Programming Questions

1. Write a program to implement the bubble sort technique.

2. Write an algorithm to implement the interpolation search technique.

3. Write an algorithm to perform a merge sort. Show various stages in merge sorting over the data: 11, 2, 9, 13, 57, 25, 17, 1, 90, 3.

4. Write a program to implement an insertion sort.

5. Write a program to search an element using the binary search technique.

6. Write a program to perform a comparison sort.

7. Write an algorithm to perform a partition exchange sort technique. Show various stages over the data: 24, 52, 98, 12, 45, 6, 59, 90.

8. Write an algorithm/program to implement a linear search technique.

6.8.3 Multiple Choice Questions

1. A binary search algorithm cannot be applied to _____.

    A. Sorted array

    B. Sorted linked list

    C. Unsorted linked list

    D. Binary trees

2. In a merge sort algorithm, which term refers to "sorting the sub-arrays recursively"?

    A. Conquer

    B. Combine

    C. Divide

    D. All of these

3. The time complexity of a bubble sort algorithm is:

    A. $O(\log n)$

    B. $O(n)$

    C. $O(n.\log n)$

    D. $O(n^2)$

4. Which sorting algorithm is known as a partition and exchange sort?

    A. Selection Sort

    B. Merge Sort

    C. Quick Sort

    D. Bubble Sort

5. Which case would exist when the element to be searched for using linear search is equal to the first element of the array?

    A. Best Case

    B. Worst Case

    C. Average Case

    D. None of these

6. Quick sort is faster than _____.

    A. Bubble Sort

    B. Selection Sort

C. Insertion Sort

D. All of the above

7. When the amount of data is massive, which type of sorting is preferred?

    A. Internal Sorting

    B. External Sorting

    C. Both of these

    D. None of these

8. Which of the searching techniques will be best when the value to be searched for is present in the middle?

    A. Linear Search

    B. Interpolation Search

    C. Binary Search

    D. All of these

9. The complexity of a binary search algorithm is _____.

    A. $O(n^2)$

    B. $O(\log n)$

    C. $O(n)$

    D. $O(n \log n)$

10. Does a selection sort have a linear running time complexity?

    A. True

    B. False

    C. Not possible to comment

STACKS

In This Chapter

- Introduction
- Definitions of a stack
- Overflow and underflow in stacks
- Operations on stacks
- Implementation of stacks
- Applications of stacks
- Summary
- Exercises

7.1 Introduction

A stack is an important data structure which is widely used in many computer applications. A stack can be visualized with many examples from our day to day life which we are already familiar with. A very simple illustration of a stack is a pile of books where one book is placed on top of another as in Figure 7.1. Now, when we want to remove a book, we remove the topmost book first. Hence, we can add or remove an element (i.e., book) only at or from one position, which is the topmost position. Similarly, there are many daily life examples in which we can see how the stack is implemented. Hence, we observe that whenever we talk about a stack, we see that the element at the last position will be served first. Thus, a stack can be described as a LIFO (last in, first out) data structure, that is, the element which is inserted last will be the first one to be taken out. Now, let us discuss stacks in detail.

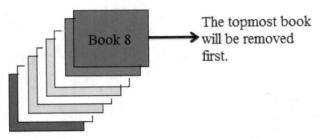

The topmost book will be removed first.

FIGURE 7.1 Stack of books.

7.2 Definition of a Stack

A Stack is a linear collection of data elements in which the element inserted last will be the element taken out first (i.e., a stack is a LIFO data structure). The stack is an abstract data structure, somewhat similar to queues. Unlike queues, a stack is open only from one end. *The stack is a linear data structure in which the insertion, as well as deletion of an element, is done only from the end called TOP.* One end is always closed, and the other end is used to insert and remove data.

Stacks can be implemented by using arrays or linked lists. We will discuss the implementation of stacks using arrays and linked lists in this section.

FIGURE 7.2 Representation of a stack.

Practical Application:

1. A real-life example of a stack is a pile of dishes where one dish is placed on top of another. Now, when we want to remove a dish, we remove the topmost dish first.

2. Another real-life example of a stack is a pile of disks where one disk is placed on top of another. Now, when we want to remove a disk, we remove the topmost disk first.

7.3   Overflow and Underflow in Stacks

Let us discuss both overflow and underflow in stacks in detail:

1. **Overflow in stacks** – The overflow condition is one in a stack which occurs when we try to insert the elements in the stack, but the stack is already full. Hence, in that case, the new elements cannot be inserted in the stack. This is known as an overflow condition in stacks. If an attempt is made to insert a value in the stack that is already full, an overflow message is printed. It can be checked by the following formula:

   If $TOP = MAX - 1$, where MAX is the size of the stack.

2. **Underflow in stacks** – The underflow condition is one in a stack which occurs when we try to remove the elements from the stack, but the stack is already empty. Hence, in that case no deletions can take place from the stack. This is known as an underflow condition in stacks. If an attempt is made to delete a value from the stack that is already empty, an underflow message is printed. It can be checked by the following formula:

   If $TOP = NULL$, where MAX is the size of the stack.

Frequently Asked Questions

Q. Define a stack and what are the operations performed on stacks?

Answer.
A stack is a linear data structure, in which the insertion as well as deletion of an element is done only from the end called TOP. It is LIFO in nature (i.e., Last In First Out). Different operations that can be performed on stacks are:

a. Push operation

b. Pop Operation

c. Peek Operation

7.4   Operations on Stacks

The three basic operations that can be performed on stacks are:

1. PUSH

Push operation is the process of adding new elements in the stack. However, before inserting any new element in the stack, we must always check for the overflow condition, which occurs when we try to insert an element in the stack which is already full. An overflow condition can be checked as follows, If TOP = MAX − 1, where MAX is the size of the stack. Hence, if the overflow condition is true, then an overflow message is displayed on the screen; otherwise, the element is inserted into the stack.

For Example – Let us take a stack which has five elements in it. Suppose we want to insert another element, 10, in it; then TOP will be incremented by 1. Thus, the new element is inserted at the position pointed to by TOP. Now, let us see how a push operation occurs in the stack in the following figure:

arr[0]	arr[1]	arr[2]	arr[3]	arr[4]	arr[5]	arr[6]	arr[7]	arr[8]	arr[9]
7	9	21	25	35					

TOP

After inserting 10 in it, the new stack will be:

arr[0]	arr[1]	arr[2]	arr[3]	arr[4]	arr[5]	arr[6]	arr[7]	arr[8]	arr[9]
7	9	21	25	35	10				

TOP

FIGURE 7.3 Stack after inserting a new element.

Algorithm for a push operation in a stack

```
Step 1: START
Step 2: IF TOP = MAX - 1
            Print OVERFLOW ERROR
            Go to Step 5
            [End of If]
Step 3: Set TOP = TOP + 1
Step 4: Set STACK[TOP] = ITEM
Step 5: EXIT
```

In the previous algorithm, first we check for the overflow condition. In Step 3, TOP is incremented so that it points to the next location. Finally, the new element is inserted in the stack at the position pointed to by TOP.

2. POP

The pop operation is the process of removing elements from the stack. However, before deleting an element from the stack, we must always check for the underflow condition, which occurs when we try to delete an element from the stack which is already empty. An underflow condition can be checked as follows, If TOP = NULL. Hence, if the underflow condition is true, then an underflow message is displayed on the screen; otherwise, the element is deleted from the stack.

For Example – Let us take a stack which has five elements in it. Suppose we want to delete an element, 35, from a stack; then TOP will be decremented by 1. Thus, the element is deleted from the position pointed to by TOP. Now, let us see how the pop operation occurs in the stack in the following figure:

After deleting 35 from it, the new stack will be:

FIGURE 7.4 Stack after deleting an element.

Algorithm for pop operation in a stack

```
Step 1: START
Step 2: IF TOP = NULL
            Print UNDERFLOW ERROR
            Go to Step 5
            [End of If]
Step 3: Set ITEM = STACK[TOP]
Step 4: Set TOP = TOP - 1
Step 5: EXIT
```

In the previous algorithm, first we check for the underflow condition, that is, whether the stack is empty or not. If the stack is empty then no deletion takes place; otherwise, TOP is decremented to the previous position in the stack. Finally, the element is deleted from the stack.

3. PEEK

Peek is an operation that returns the value of the topmost element of the stack. It does so without deleting the topmost element of the array. However, the peek operation first checks for the underflow condition. An underflow condition can be checked as follows, If TOP = NULL. Hence, if the underflow condition is true, then an underflow message is displayed on the screen; otherwise, the value of the element is returned.

arr[0]	arr[1]	arr[2]	arr[3]	arr[4]	arr[5]	arr[6]	arr[7]	arr[8]	arr[9]
7	9	21	25						

TOP

FIGURE 7.5 Stack returning the topmost value.

Algorithm for pop operation in a stack

```
Step 1: START
Step 2: IF TOP = NULL
            Print UNDERFLOW ERROR
            Go to Step 4
            [End of If]
Step 3: Return STACK[TOP]
Step 4: EXIT
```

Write a menu-driven program for stacks performing all the operations.

```c
# include<stdio.h>
# include<conio.h>
# define MAX 10
void push(int stack[], int item) ;
void pop(int stack[], int item) ;
int peek(int stack[]) ;
void display(int stack[]) ;
int top = -1 ;
void main()
{
  int stack[MAX], item, ch ;
  while(1)
    {
      clrscr() ;
```

```c
        printf("\n***MENU***") ;
        printf("\n1. PUSH") ;
        printf("\n2. POP") ;
        printf("\n2. PEEK") ;
        printf("\n4. DISPLAY") ;
        printf("\n5. EXIT") ;
        printf("\nenter your choice: ") ;
        scanf("%d", &ch) ;
        switch(ch)
          {
            case 1 :
            printf("enter value to push: ") ;
            scanf("%d", &item) ;
            push(stack, item) ;
            break ;

            case 2 :
            pop(stack) ;
            break ;

            case 3 :
            item = peek(stack) ;
            if(item != 1)
            printf("The value at the top of stack is %d",
            item) ;
            break ;

            case 4 :
            display(stack) ;
            break ;

            case 5 :
            printf("!!Exit!!") ;
            exit(0) ;

            default :
            printf("wrong choice") ;
          }
      }
}
```

```c
void push(int stack[], int item)
{
  //Case 1 is for inserting an element in the stack
  if(top == MAX - 1)
    {
      printf("\noverflow error") ;
    }
  else
    {
      top++ ;
      stack[top] = item ;
      printf("Success!!") ;
      getch() ;
    }
}

void pop(int stack[], int item)
{
  //Case 2 is for deleting an element from the stack
  if(top == -1)
    {
      printf("\nunderflow error") ;
    }
  else
    {
      item = stack[top] ;
      top -- ;
      printf("deleted value is %d", item) ;
    }
  getch();
}

int peek(int stack[])
{
  //Case 3 is for displaying the topmost element of the
  //stack
  if(top == -1)
    {
      printf("Empty Stack") ;
    }
  else
  return(stack[top]) ;
```

```
}
void display(int stack[])
{
  int i ;
  //Case 4 is for displaying the elements of the stack
  front = front + 1 ;
  for(i = rear ; i > front ; i--)
    {
      printf("\n%d", stack[i]) ;
    }
  getch() ;
}
```

Output –

    MENU

    1: PUSH

    2: POP

    3: PEEK

    4: DISPLAY

    5: EXIT

    Enter your choice: 1

    Enter value to insert: 125

    Success!!

7.5 Implementation of Stacks

Stacks can be represented by two data structures:

1. Representation of stacks using arrays.

2. Representation of stacks using a linked list.

Now, let us discuss both of them in detail.

7.5.1 Implementation of Stacks Using Arrays

Stacks can be easily implemented using arrays. Initially, the TOP pointer of the stack points at the first position or location of the array. As we insert new elements into the stack, the TOP keeps on incrementing, always pointing to the position where the next element will be inserted. The representation of a stack using an array is shown as follows:

FIGURE 7.6 Array representation of a stack.

7.5.2 Implementation of Stacks Using Linked Lists

We have already studied how a stack is implemented using an array. Now let us discuss the same using linked lists. We already know that in linked lists, dynamic memory allocation takes place, that is, the memory is allocated at runtime. But in the case of arrays, memory is allocated at the start of the program. If we are aware of the maximum size of the stack in advance, then implementation of stacks using arrays will be efficient. But if the size is not known in advance, then we will use the concept of a linked list in which dynamic memory allocation takes place. As we all know a linked list has two parts; the first part contains the information of the node, and the second part stores the address of the next element in the linked list. Similarly, we can also implement a linked stack. Now, the START pointer in the linked list will become the TOP pointer in a linked stack. All insertion and deletion operations will be done at the node pointed to by TOP only.

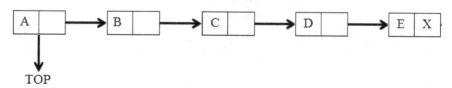

FIGURE 7.7 Linked representation of a stack.

7.5.2.1 Push Operation in Linked Stacks

The push operation is the process of adding new elements in the already existing stack. The new elements in the stack will always be inserted at the topmost position of the stack. Initially, *we will check whether TOP = NULL.* If the condition is true, then the stack is empty; otherwise, the new memory is allocated for the new node. We will understand it further with the help of an algorithm:

Algorithm for inserting a new element in a linked stack

```
Step 1: START
Step 2: Set NEW NODE -> INFO = VAL
        IF TOP = NULL
        Set NEW NODE -> NEXT = NULL
        Set TOP  = NEW NODE
        ELSE
        Set NEW NODE -> NEXT = TOP
        Set TOP  = NEW NODE
        [End of If]
Step 3: EXIT
```

For Example – Consider a linked stack with four elements; a new element is to be inserted in the stack.

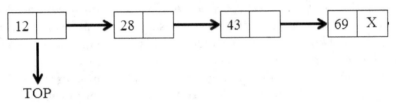

FIGURE 7.8 Linked stack before insertion.

After inserting the new element in the stack, the updated stack becomes as shown in the following figure:

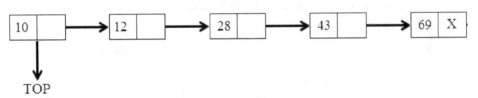

FIGURE 7.9 Linked stack after inserting new node.

7.5.2.2 Pop Operation in Linked Stacks

The pop operation is the process of removing elements from the already existing stack. The elements from the stack will always be deleted from the node pointed to by TOP. Initially, we will check whether TOP = NULL. If the condition is true, then the stack is empty, which means we cannot delete any elements from it. Therefore, in that case an underflow error message is displayed on the screen. We will understand it further with the help of an algorithm:

Algorithm for deleting an element from a linked stack

```
Step 1: START
Step 2: IF TOP = NULL
            Print UNDERFLOW ERROR
            [End of If]
Step 3: Set TEMP = TOP
Step 4: Set TOP = TOP -> NEXT
Step 5: FREE TEMP
Step 6: EXIT
```

For Example – Consider a linked stack with five elements; an element is to be deleted from the stack.

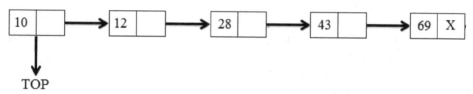

TOP

FIGURE 7.10 Linked stack before deletion.

After deleting an element from the stack, the updated stack becomes as shown in the following figure:

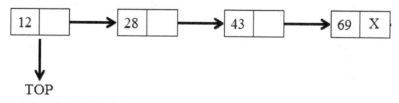

TOP

FIGURE 7.11 Linked stack after deleting topmost node/element.

Write a menu-driven program implementing a linked stack performing push and pop operations.

```c
# include<stdio.h>
# include<conio.h>
struct node
{
  int info ;
  struct node *next ;
} *top = NULL ;
void push(int item) ;
void pop() ;
void display() ;
void main()
{
  int item, choice ;
  while(1)
    {
      clrscr() ;
      printf("\n***MENU***") ;
      printf("\n1. PUSH") ;
      printf("\n2. POP") ;
      printf("\n3. DISPLAY") ;
      printf("\n4. EXIT") ;
      printf("\nenter your choice: ") ;
      scanf("%d", &choice) ;
      switch(choice)
        {
          case 1 :
          printf("enter value to insert: ") ;
          scanf("%d", &item) ;
          push(item) ;
          break ;

          case 2 :
          pop() ;
          break ;

          case 3 :
          display() ;
          break ;
```

```
        case 4 :
        printf("!!Exit!!") ;
        exit(0) ;

        default :
        printf("wrong choice") ;
      }
    }
}

void push(int item)
{
  struct node *Newnode ;
  //Case 1 is for inserting an element in the linked
  //stack
  Newnode = (struct node*)malloc(sizeof(struct node)) ;
  Newnode -> info = item ;
  if(top == NULL)
    {
      Newnode -> next = NULL ;
      top = Newnode
    }
  else
    {
      Newnode -> next = top ;
      top = Newnode ;
    }
  printf("Success!!") ;
  getch() ;
}

void pop()
{
  struct node *temp ;
  //Case 2 is for deleting an element from the linked
  //stack
  temp = top ;
  if(top == NULL)
    {
      printf("\nEmpty stack") ;
    }
```

```
   else
    {
      top = top -> next ;
      printf("deleted value is %d", temp -> info) ;
      free(temp) ;
    }
  getch() ;
}

void display()
{
  struct node *ptr ;
  //Case 3 is for displaying the elements in the linked
  //stack
  if(top == NULL)
    {
      printf("\nEmpty stack") ;
    }
  ptr = top ;
  while(ptr != NULL)
    {
      printf("%d", ptr -> info) ;
      ptr = ptr -> next ;
    }
  getch() ;
}
```

Output –

```
    ***MENU***
    1: PUSH
    2: POP
    3: DISPLAY
    4: EXIT
    Enter your choice: 2
    Empty stack
```

7.6 Applications of Stacks

In this section, we will discuss various applications of stacks. The topics that will be covered in this section are the following:

- Polish and Reverse Polish Notations and their need
- Conversion from Infix Expression to Postfix Expression
- Conversion from Infix Expression to Prefix Expression
- Evaluation of Postfix Expression
- Evaluation of Prefix Expression
- Parenthesis Balancing

Now, let us understand each one of them in detail.

7.6.1 Polish and Reverse Polish Notations and Their Need

a. Polish Notations

Polish notation refers to a notation in which the operator is placed before the operands. Polish notation was named after a Polish mathematician Jan Lukasiewicz. We can also say that the transforming of an expression into a form is called a polish notation. An algebraic expression can be represented in three forms. All these forms refer to the relative position of operators with respect to the operands.

1. **Prefix Form** – In an expression, if the operator is placed before the operands, that is, +XY, then it is said to be in prefix form.

2. **Infix Form** – In an expression, if the operator is placed in the middle of operands, that is, X + Y, then it is said to be in infix form.

3. **Postfix Form** – In an expression, if the operator is placed after the operands, that is, XY+, then it is said to be in postfix form.

b. Reverse Polish Notation

This notation frequently refers to the postfix notation or suffix notation. It refers to the notation in which the operator is placed after its two operands, that is, XY + AF BC°.

c. Need for Polish and Reverse Polish Notation

It is comparatively easy for a computer system to evaluate an expression in polish notation as the system need not check for priority-wise execution of various operators (like the BODMAS rule), as all the operators in prefix or postfix expression will automatically occur in their order of priority.

7.6.2 Conversion from Infix Expression to Postfix Expression

In any expression, we observe that there are two types of parts/components clubbed together. They are operands and operators. The operators are the ones that indicate the operation to be carried out, and the operands are ones on which the operators operate. Operators have their priority of execution. For simplicity of the algorithm, we will use only addition (+), subtraction (-), modulus (%), multiplication (*), and division (/) operators. The precedence of these operators is given as follows:

*, ^, /, % (Higher priority)   +, - (Lower priority)

The order of evaluation of these operators can be changed by using parentheses. For example, an expression X * Y + Z can be solved, as first X * Y will be done and then the result is added to Z. But if the same expression is written with parentheses as X * (Y + Z), now Y + Z will be evaluated first, and then the result is multiplied by X.

We can convert an infix expression to a postfix expression using a stack. First, we start to scan the expression from left side to right side. In an expression, there may be some operators, operands, and parentheses. Hence, we have to keep in mind some of the basic rules which are:

- Each time we encounter an operand, it is added directly to the postfix expression.

- Each time we get an operator, we should always check the top of the stack to check the priority of the operators.

- If the operator at the top of the stack has higher precedence or the same precedence as that of the current operator, then, in that case, it is repeatedly popped out from the stack and added to the postfix expression. Otherwise, it is pushed into the stack.

- Each time when an opening parenthesis is encountered, it is directly pushed into the stack, and similarly, if a closing parenthesis is encountered, we will repeatedly pop out from the stack and add the operators in the postfix expression. Also, the opening parenthesis is deleted from the stack.

Now, let us understand it with the help of an algorithm in which the first step is to push a left parenthesis in the stack and also add a closing parenthesis at the end of the infix expression. The algorithm is repeated until the stack becomes empty.

Algorithm to convert an infix expression into a postfix expression

```
Step 1: START
Step 2: Add ")" parenthesis to the end of infix expres-
        sion.
Step 3: Push''parenthesis on the stack.
Step 4: Repeat the steps until each character in the in-
        fix expression is scanned.
            a) IF "(" parenthesis is found, push it
            onto the stack.
            b) If an operand is encountered, add it to
            the postfix expression.
            c) IF ")" parenthesis is found, then follow
            these steps -
            - Continually pop from the stack and add
            it to the postfix expression until a "(" pa-
            renthesis is encountered.
            - Eliminate the "(" parenthesis.
            d) If an operator is found, then follow
            these steps -
            - Continually pop from the stack and add it
            to the postfix expression which has same or
            high precedence than the current operator.
            - Push the current operator to the stack.
Step 5: Continually pop from the stack to the postfix ex-
        pression until the stack becomes empty.
Step 6: EXIT
```

For Example – Convert the following infix expression into a postfix expression.

a) $(A + B) * C / D$

b) $[((A +B) * (C - D)) + (F - G)]$

Solution:

a)

Character	Stack	Expression
(	(	
A	(	A
+	(+	A
B	(+	AB
)		AB+
✻	✻	AB+
C	✻	AB+C
/	/	AB+C✻
D		AB+C✻D/
		Answer = AB+C✻D/

b)

Character	Stack	Expression
[	[	
(	[(	
(	[((	
A	[((	A
+	[((+	A
B	[((+	AB
)	[(	AB+
✻	[✻	AB+
(	[✻(	AB+
C	[✻(	AB+C
-	[✻(-	AB+C
D	[✻(-	AB+CD
)	[✻	AB+CD-
)	[	AB+CD-✻
+	[+	AB+CD-✻
(	[+(	AB+CD-✻
F	[+(	AB+CD-✻F
-	[+(-	AB+CD-✻F
G	[+(-	AB+CD-✻FG
)	[+	AB+CD-✻FG-
]		AB+CD-✻FG-+
		Answer = AB+CD-✻FG-+

Write a program to convert an infix expression to a postfix expression.

```c
# include<stdio.h>
# include<conio.h>
# include<ctype.h>
# include<string.h>
# define SIZE 50
char stack[SIZE];
int top = -1;
void push( char stack[] ,char);
char pop(char stack[]);
void inftopostf(char src[],char trg[]);
int prior(char);
int main()
{
  char inf[50], postf[50];
  clrscr();
  printf(" \n Enter infix expression of your choice::");
  gets(inf);
  rev(inf);
  strcpy(postf, " ");
  inftopostf( inf, postf);
  printf("\n The postfix expression is:");
  puts(postf);
  getch();
  return 0;
}
void inftopostf(char src[],char trg[])
{
  int p =0,q=0;
  char tmp;
  strcpy( trg , " ");
  while(src[p]!='\0')
    {
      if(src[p]=='(')
        {
          push(stack, src[p]);
          p++;
        }
      else if(src[p]== ')')
        {
          while((top !=-1)&&(stack[top]!='(')
```

```
            {
               trg[q] = pop(stack);
               q++;
            }
         if(top=-1)
            {
               printf(" \n invalid expression");
               exit(1);
            }
         tmp = pop(stack);
         p++;
      }
   else if(isdigit(src[p]) || isalpha(src[p]))
      {
         trg[q]=src[p];
         p++;
      }
   else
      {
         printf("\n wrong element ");
         exit(1);
      }
   }
 while((top!=1)&& (stack[top]!='('))
   {
     trg[q] = pop(stack);
     q++;
   }
 trg[q] ='\0';
}
int prior(char opr)
{
 if(opr== '/' || opr== '*' || opr == '%')
 return 1;
 else if (op == '+' || opr == '-')
 return 0;
}
void push(char stack[], char item)
{
 if(top == SIZE-1)
 printf("\n overflow of stack");
```

```
  else
    {
     top++;
     stack[top] = item;
    }
 }
char pop(char stack[])
{
 char item = ' ';
 if(top==-1)
 printf(" \n underflow of stack");
 else
 item = stack[top];
 top--;
 return item;
}
```

Output –

Enter infix expression of your choice: X / Y – Z

The postfix expression is: XY/Z-

Frequently Asked Questions

Q. Convert the following infix expression into a postfix expression.

(A + B) ^ C – (D * E) / F

Answer.

Character	Stack	Expression
(	(	
A	(	A
+	(+	A
B	(+	AB

		AB+
)		AB+
^	^	AB+
C	^	AB+C
-	-	AB+C^
(	-(	AB+C^
D	-(	AB+C^D
*	-(*	AB+C^D
E	-(*	AB+C^DE
)	-	AB+C^DE*
/	-/	AB+C^DE*
F	-/	AB+C^DE*
		Answer = AB+C^DE*F/-

7.6.3 Conversion from Infix Expression to Prefix Expression

We can convert an infix expression to its equivalent prefix expression with the help of the following algorithm.

Algorithm to convert an infix expression into a prefix expression

```
Step 1:START
Step 2:Reverse the infix expression. Also, interchange
       leftand right parenthesis on reversing the infix
       expression.
Step 3:Obtain the postfix expression of the reversed in-
       fix expression.
Step 4:Reverse the postfix expression so obtained in
       Step 3. Finally, the expression is converted
       into prefix expression.
Step 5:EXIT
```

For Example – Convert the following infix expression into a prefix expression.

a) (X - Y) / (A + B)

b) (X – Y / Z) * (A / B – C)

Solution:

a) After reversing the given infix expression $((B + A) / Y - X)$

Find the postfix expression of $(B + A) / (Y - X)$

Character	Stack	Expression
(	(	
(	((	
B	((	B
+	((+	B
A	((+	BA
)	(	BA+
/	(/	BA+
Y	(/	BA+Y
-	(-	BA+Y/
X	(-	BA+Y/X
)		BA+Y/X-
		BA+Y/X-

Now, reverse the postfix expression so obtained, that is, X/Y+AB

Hence, the prefix expression is **–X/Y+AB**

a) After reversing the given infix expression $(C - B / A) * (Z / Y - X)$

Find the postfix expression of $(C - B / A) * (Z / Y - X)$

Character	Stack	Expression
(	(	
C	(	C
-	(-	C
B	(-	CB
/	(-/	CB
A	(-/	CBA
)		CBA/-
*	*	CBA/-
(	*(	CBA/-
Z	*(	CBA/-Z

/	*(/	CBA/-Z
Y	*(/	CBA/-ZY
-	*(-	CBA/-ZY/
X	*(-	CBA/-ZY/X
)	*	CBA/-ZY/X-
		CBA/-ZY/X-*

Now, reverse the postfix expression so obtained, that is, *–X/ZY-/ABC

Hence, the prefix expression is *–X/ZY-/ABC

Write a program to convert an infix expression to a prefix expression.

```c
# include<stdio.h>
# include<conio.h>
# include<ctype.h>
# include<string.h>
# define SIZE 50
char stack[SIZE];
int top = -1;
void  rev(char string[]);
void push( char stack[] ,char);
char pop(char stack[]);
void inftopostf(char src[],char trg[]);
int prior(char);
char inf[50], postf[50] , temp[50];
int main()
{
  clrscr();
  printf(" \n Enter infix expression of your choice::");
  gets(inf);
  rev(inf);
  strcpy(postf, " ");
  inftopostf(temp, postf);
  printf("\n The postfix expression :");
  puts(postf);
  strcpy(temp, " ");
  rev(postf);
  printf("\n prefix expression is :");
  puts(temp);
```

```
    getch();
    return 0;
}
void rev(char string[])
{
  int length , p=0;q=0;
  length = strlen(string);
  q = length -1;
  while(q>=0)
    {
      if(string[q]== '(')
      temp[p] = ')';
      else if(string[q]== ')')
      temp[p] = '(';
      else
      temp[p] = string[q];
      p++;
      q--;
    }
  temp[p] = '\0';
}
void inftopostf(char src[],char trg[])
{
  int p =0,q=0;
  char tmp;
  strcpy( trg , " ");
  while(src[p]!='\0')
    {
      if(src[p]=='(' )
        {
          push(stack, src[p]);
          p++;
        }
      else if(src[p]== ')')
        {
          while((top !=-1)&&(stack[top]!='(')
            {
              trg[q] = pop(stack);
              q++;
            }
          if(top=-1)
            {
```

```c
            printf(" \n invalid expression");
            exit(1);
        }
      tmp = pop(stack);
      p++;
    }
    else if( isdigit(src[p]) || isalpha(src[p]))
      {
        trg[q]=src[p];
        q++;
        p++;
      }
    else if(src[p] =='+' || src[p]=='-' || src[p]==' '
    || src[p]== '/' || src[p] == '%')
      {
        while((top!=1)&&(stack[top]!='(')&&(prior(stack
        [top]>prior(src[p])))
          {
            trg[p]= pop(stack);
            q++;
          }
        push (stack,src[p]);
        p++;
      }
    else
      {
        printf("\n wrong element ");
        exit(1);
      }
  }
  while((top!=1)&& (stack[top]!='('))
    {
      trg[q] = pop(stack);
      q++;
    }
  trg[q] ='\0';
}
int prior(char opr)
{
  if(opr== '/' || opr== '*' || opr == '%')
```

```
     return 1;
     else if (op == '+' || opr == '-')
     return 0;
  }
  void push(char stack[], char item)
  {
    if(top == SIZE-1)
    printf("\n overflow of stack");
    else
      {
        top++;
        stack[top] = item;
      }
  }
  char pop(char stack[])
  {
    char item = ' ';
    if(top==-1)
    printf("\n underflow of stack");
    else
    item = stack[top];
    top--;
    return item;
  }
```

Output –

Enter infix expression of your choice: W+X-Y*Z

The prefix expression: WX+YZ*-

Prefix expression is: -+WX*YZ

7.6.4 Evaluation of a Postfix Expression

With the help of stacks, any postfix expression can easily be evaluated. Every character in the postfix expression is scanned from left to right. The steps involved in evaluating a postfix expression are given in the algorithm.

Algorithm for evaluating a postfix expression

```
Step 1:START
Step 2:IF an operand is encountered, push it onto the
       stack.
Step 3:IF an operator "op1" is encountered, then follow
       these steps -
            a) Pop the two topmost elements from the
               stack, where X is the topmost element
               and Y is the next top element below X.
            b) Evaluate X op1 Y.
            c) Push the result onto the stack.
Step 4:Set the result equal to the topmost element of
       the stack.
Step 5:EXIT
```

For Example – Evaluate the following postfix expressions.

a) $2\ 3\ 4 + * 5\ 6\ 7\ 8 + * + +$

b) T F T F AND F F F XOR OR AND T XOR AND OR

Solution:

a)

Character	Stack	Operation
2	2	PUSH 2
3	2, 3	PUSH 3
4	2, 3, 4	PUSH 4
+	2, 7	POP 4, 3
		ADD(4 + 3 = 7)
		PUSH 7
*	14	POP 7, 2
		MUL(7 * 2 = 14)
		PUSH 14
5	14, 5	PUSH 5
6	14, 5, 6	PUSH 6
7	14, 5, 6, 7	PUSH 7
8	14, 5, 6, 7, 8	PUSH 8

+	14, 5, 6, 15	POP 8, 7 ADD(8 + 7 = 15) PUSH 15
⊕	14, 5, 90	POP 15, 6 MUL(15 * 6 = 90) PUSH 90
+	14, 95	POP 90, 5 ADD(90 + 5 = 95) PUSH 95
+	109	POP 95, 14 ADD(95 + 14 = 109) PUSH 109
	Answer = 109	

b)

Character	Stack	Operation
T	T	PUSH T
F	T, F	PUSH F
T	T, F, T	PUSH T
F	T, F, T, F	PUSH F
AND	T, F, F	POP F, T AND(F AND T = F) PUSH F
F	T, F, F, F	PUSH F
F	T, F, F, F, F	PUSH F
F	T, F, F, F, F, F	PUSH F
XOR	T, F, F, F, T	POP F, F XOR(F XOR F = T) PUSH T
OR	T, F, F, T	POP T, F OR(T OR F = T) PUSH T
AND	T, F, F	POP T, F AND(T AND F = F) PUSH F
T	T, F, F, T	PUSH T

XOR	T, F, F	POP T, F XOR(T XOR F = F) PUSH F
AND	T, F	POP F, F AND(F AND F = F) PUSH F
OR	T	POP F, T OR(F OR T = T) PUSH T
	Answer = T	

Write a program for evaluation of a postfix expression.

```
# include<stdio.h>
# include<conio.h>
# include<ctype.h>
# define SIZE 50
float stack[SIZE];
int top = -1;
void push( float stack[], float item);
float pop(float stack[]);
float postf(char express[]);
int main()
{
  float item;
  char express[50];
  clrscr();
  printf("\n Enter postfix expression of your choice::");
  gets(express);
  item = postf(express)
  printf("\n Value of postfix expression = %.2f",item);
  getch();
  return 0;
}
float postf(char express[])
{
  int i=0;
  float  opr1,opr2, value;
  while(express[i]!=0)
```

```
      {
      if(isdigit(express[i]))
        {
          push(stack, (float)(express[i]-'0'));
          else
            {
              opr2 = pop(stack);
              opr1 = pop(stack);
              switch(express[i])
                {
                  case '+' :
                  value = opr1+opr2;
                  break;

                  case '-' :
                  value = opr1- opr2;
                  break;

                  case '*' :
                  value = opr1*opr2;
                  break;

                  case '/' :
                  value = opr1/opr2;
                  break;

                  case '%' :
                  value =(int) opr1%(int)opr2;
                  break;
                }
              push(stack, value);
            }
          i++;
        }
      return(pop(stack));
    }
}
void push(float stack[] , float item)
{
  if(top == SIZE-1)
    {
    printf("\n overflow of stack");
```

```
      else
        {
          top++;
          stack[top] = item;
        }
    }
  float pop(float stack[])
    {
      float item =-1;
      if(top ==-1)
      printf("\n underflow of stack");
      else
        {
          item = stack[top];
          top--;
        }
      return item;
    }
}
```

Output –

Enter postfix expression of your choice: 8 7 6 * 5 + 1 + /

Value of postfix expression = 6.00

Frequently Asked Questions

Q. Evaluate the given postfix expression.

2 3 4 * 6 / +

Answer.

Character	Stack
2	2
3	2, 3
4	2, 3, 4
*	2, 12
6	2, 12, 6
/	2, 2
+	4
	Answer = 4

7.6.5 Evaluation of a Prefix Expression

There are a variety of techniques for evaluating a prefix expression. But the simplest of all the techniques are explained in the following algorithm.

Algorithm for evaluating a prefix expression

```
Step 1:START
Step 2:Accept the prefix expression.
Step 3:Repeat the steps 4 to 6 until all the characters
       have been scanned.
Step 4:The prefix expression is scanned from the right.
Step 5:IF an operand is encountered, push it onto the
       stack.
Step 6:IF an operator is encountered, then follow these
       steps -
            a) Pop two elements from the operand stack.
            b) Apply the operator on the popped oper-
               ands.
            c) Push the result onto the stack.
Step 7:EXIT
```

For Example – Evaluate the given prefix expressions.

a) $+ - 4\,6 * 9\,/10\,50$

b) $+ * * + 2\,3\,4\,5 + 6\,7$

Solution:

a)

Character	Stack	Operation
50	50	PUSH 50
10	50, 10	PUSH 10
/	5	POP 10, 50 DIV(50 / 10 = 5) PUSH 5
9	5, 9	PUSH 9
*	45	POP 9, 5 MUL(5 * 9 = 45) PUSH 45
6	45, 6	PUSH 6

4	45, 6, 4	PUSH 4
-	45, 2	POP 4, 6 SUB(6 − 4 = 2) PUSH 2
+	47	POP 2, 45 ADD(45 + 2 = 47) PUSH 47
	Answer = 47	

b)

Character	Stack	Operation
7	7	PUSH 7
6	7, 6	PUSH 6
+	13	POP 6, 7 ADD(7 + 6 = 13) PUSH 13
5	13, 5	PUSH 5
4	13, 5, 4	PUSH 4
3	13, 5, 4, 3	PUSH 3
2	13, 5, 4, 3, 2	PUSH 2
+	13, 5, 4, 5	POP 2, 3 ADD(3 + 2 = 5) PUSH 5
*	13, 5, 20	POP 5, 4 MUL(4 * 5 = 20) PUSH 20
*	13, 100	POP 20, 5 MUL(5 * 20 = 100) PUSH 100
+	113	POP 100, 13 ADD(13 + 100 = 113) PUSH 113
	Answer = 113	

Write a program for evaluation of a prefix expression.

```c
#include<stdio.h>
#include<conio.h>
#include<string.h>
int stack[10];
int top=-1;
void push(int);
int pop();
void main()
{
 char pref[20];
 int length,item,i,op1,op2,result;
 clrscr();
 printf("Enter the prefix Expression :");
 gets(pref);
 length=strlen(pref);
 for(i=length-1;i>=0;i--)
   {
     switch (get(pref[i]))
       {
         case 0:
         item=pref[i]-'0';
         push(item);
         break;

         case 1:
         op1=pop();
         op2=pop();
         switch(pref[i])
           {
             case '+':
             res=opr1+opr2;
             break;
             case '-':
             result=op1-op2;
             break;
             case '*':
             result=op1*op2;
             break;
             case '/':
```

```
            result=op1/op2;
            break;
        }
      push(result);
    }
  }
  printf("Result is %d",stack[0]);
  getch();
}

void push(int item)
{
  stack[++top]=item;
}
int pop()
{
  return(stack[top--]);
}
int get(char ch)
{
  if(ch=='+'||ch=='-'||ch=='*'||ch=='/')
  return 1;
  else
  return 0;
}
```

Output –

Enter the prefix Expression: +-846

Result is 10

7.6.6 Parenthesis Balancing

Stacks can be used to check the validity of parentheses in any arithmetic or algebraic expression. We are already aware that in a valid expression, the parentheses or the brackets occur in pairs, that is, if a parenthesis is opening then it must be closed in an expression. Otherwise, the expression would be invalid. For example, (X + Y – Z is invalid. But (X + Y – Z) looks a valid expression. Hence, there are some key points which are to be kept in mind:

- Each time a "(" parenthesis is encountered, it should be pushed onto the stack.

- Each time a ")" parenthesis is encountered, the stack is examined.

- If the stack is already an empty stack, then the ")" parenthesis does not have a "(" parenthesis and hence, the expression is therefore invalid.

- If the stack is not empty, then we will pop the stack and check whether the popped element corresponds to the ")" parenthesis.

- When we reach the end of the stack, the stack must be empty. Otherwise, one or more "(" parenthesis does not have a corresponding ")" parenthesis and, therefore, the expression will become invalid.

For Example – Check whether the following given expressions are valid or not.

a) ((A – B) * Y

b) [(A + B) – {X + Y} * [C – D]]

Solution:

a)

	Symbol	Stack
1.	(	(
2.	(	(, (
3.	A	(, (
4.	-	(, (
5.	B	(, (
6.	)	(
7.	*	(
8.	Y	(
9.		(

Answer - As the stack is not empty, the expression is not a valid expression.

b)

	Symbol	Stack
1.	[	[
2.	(	[, (
3.	A	[, (
4.	+	[, (
5.	B	[, (
6.	)	[
7.	-	[
8.	{	[, {
9.	X	[, {
10.	+	[, {
11.	Y	[, {
12.	}	[
13.	✿	[
14.	[	[, [
15.	C	[, [
16.	-	[, [
17.	D	[, [
18.	]	[
19.	]	

Answer – As the stack is empty, the given expression is a valid expression.

Write a program to implement parenthesis balancing.

```
#include<stdio.h>
#include<conio.h>
#include<string.h>
# define SIZE 30
int stack[SIZE];
int top=-1;
void push(char);
char pop();
void main()
{
  char express[SIZE], val;
```

```
    int i , temp=1;
    clrscr();
    printf("Enter the Expression :");
    gets(express);
    for(i=0; i<strlen(express); i++)
      {
        if (express[i]== '(' || express[i]== '{' || express[i]==
        '[')
        push(express[i]);
        if(express[i]== ')' || express[i]== '}' || express[i]==
        ']' )
        if(top== -1)
        flag = 0;
        else
          {
            Val = pop( );
            if (express[i]== ')' && (val == '{' || val== '['))
            temp = 0;
            if (express[i]== '}' && (val == '(' || val== '['))
            temp = 0;
            if (express[i]== '}' && (val == '(' || val== '{'))
            temp = 0;
          }
      }
  if(top>=0)
  temp=0;
  if(temp==1)
  printf("\n expression is valid");
  else
  printf("\n expression is invalid");
}
void push(char c)
{
 if(top == (SIZE-1))
 printf("\noverflow of stack");
 else
   {
     top = top+1 ;
     stack[top] = c;
   }
}
```

```
char pop( )
{
  if(top==-1)
  printf("\n underflow of stack");
  else
  return(stack[top--]);
}
```

Output –

Enter the Expression: (X - (Y * Z))

Expression is valid

7.7 Summary

- A stack is a linear collection of data elements in which the element inserted last will be the element taken out first (i.e., stack is a LIFO data structure). The stack is a linear data structure, in which the insertion as well as the deletion of an element is done only from the end called TOP.

- In computer memory, stacks can be implemented by using either arrays or linked lists.

- The overflow condition is one in a stack which occurs when we try to insert the elements in the stack, but the stack is already full.

- The underflow condition is one in a stack which occurs when we try to remove the elements from the stack, but the stack is already empty.

- The three basic operations that can be performed on the stacks are push, pop, and peek operations.

- A push operation is the process of adding new elements in the stack.

- A pop operation is the process of removing elements from the stack.

- A peek operation is the process of returning the value of the topmost element of the stack.

- Polish notation refers to a notation in which the operator is placed before the operands.

- Infix, prefix, and postfix notations are three different but equivalent notations of writing algebraic expressions.

7.8 Exercises

7.8.1 Theory Questions

1. What is a stack? Give its real-life example.

2. What do you understand by stack overflow and stack underflow?

3. What is a linked stack and how it is different from a linear stack?

4. Discuss various operations which can be performed on the stacks.

5. Explain the terms polish notation and reverse polish notation.

6. Define stacks and in what ways a stack can be implemented.

7. What are the various applications of a stack? Explain in detail.

8. Why is a stack known as a Last-In-First-Out structure?

9. What are different notations to represent an algebraic expression? Which one is mostly used in computers?

10. Explain the concept of linked stacks and also discuss how insertion and deletion takes place in it.

11. Draw the stack structure when the following operations are performed one after another on an empty stack.

    A. Push 1, 2, 6, 17, 100

    B. Pop three numbers

    C. Peek

    D. Push 50, 23, 198, 500

    E. Display

12. Convert the following infix expressions to their equivalent postfix expressions.

    A. $A + B + C - D * E / F$

    B. $[A - C] + \{D * E\}$

C. [X / Y] % (A $*$ B) + (C % D)

D. [(A – C + D) % (B – H + G)]

E. 18 / 9 $*$ 3 – 4 + 10 / 2

13. Check the validity of the given algebraic expressions.

A. ((([A – V – D] + B)

B. [(X – {Y $*$ Z})]

C. [A + C + E)

14. Convert the following infix expressions to their equivalent prefix expressions.

A. 18 / 9 $*$ 3 – 4 + 10 / 2

B. X $*$ (Z / Y)

C. [(A + B) – (C + D)] $*$ E

15. Evaluate the given postfix expressions.

A. 1 2 3 $*$ $*$ 4 5 6 7 + + $*$ $*$

B. 12 4 / 45 + 2 3 $*$ +

7.8.2 Programming Questions

1. Write a program to implement a stack using arrays.

2. Write a program to convert an infix expression to a postfix expression.

3. Write a function that performs a peek operation on the stack.

4. Write a program to implement a stack using a linked list.

5. Write a program to input two stacks and compare their contents.

6. Write a program to convert the expression "x + y" into "xy+".

7. Write a program to evaluate a postfix expression.

8. Write a program to evaluate a prefix expression.

9. Write a program to convert "b - c" into "-bc".

10. Write a function that performs a push operation in a linked stack.

7.8.3 Multiple Choice Questions

1. New elements in the stack are always inserted from:

    A. Front end

    B. Top end

    C. Rear end

    D. Both (a) and (c)

2. A stack is a _____ data structure.

    A. FIFO

    B. LIFO

    C. FILO

    D. LILO

3. The overflow condition in the stack exists when:

    A. TOP = NULL

    B. TOP = MAX

    C. TOP = MAX − 1

    D. None of the above

4. The function that inserts the elements in a stack is called _____.

    A. Push()

    B. Peek()

    C. Pop()

    D. None of the above

5. Disks piled up one above the other represent _____.

    A. Queue

    B. Stack

    C. Tree

    D. Linked List

6. Reverse polish notation is the other name for _____.

    A. Postfix expression

    B. Prefix expression

    C. Infix expression

    D. All of the above

7. Stacks can be represented by:

    A. Linked List only

    B. Arrays only

    C. Both a) and b)

    D. None of the above

8. If the numbers 10, 45, 13, 50, and 32 are pushed onto a stack, what does pop return?

    A. 10

    B. 45

    C. 50

    D. 32

9. Which data structure is required for implementing a parenthesis balancer?

    A. Queue

    B. Tree

    C. Stack

    D. Heap

10. The postfix representation of the expression $(2 - b) * (a + 10) / (c * 8)$ will be:

    A. 8 a * c 10 + b 2 - * /

    B. / 2 a c * + b 10 * 9 –

    C. 2 b – a 10 + * c 8 * /

    D. 10 a + * 2 b - / c 8 *

TREES

In This Chapter

- Introduction
- Definitions
- Binary tree
- Binary search tree
- AVL trees
- Summary
- Exercises

8.1 Introduction

In earlier chapters, we have already learned about various data structures such as arrays, linked lists, stacks, and queues. All these data structures are linear data structures. Although linear data structures are flexible, it is quite difficult to use them to organize data into a hierarchical representation. Hence, to overcome this problem or limitation, we create a new data structure which is called a tree. *A tree is a data structure that is defined as a set of one or more nodes which allows us to associate a parent-child relationship.* In trees, one node is designated as the root node or parent node, and all the remaining nodes can be partitioned into non-empty sets, each of which is a subtree of the root. Unlike natural trees, a tree data structure is upside down, having a root at the top and leaves at the bottom. Also, there is no parent of the root node. A root node can only have child nodes. On the contrary, leaf nodes or leaves are those that have no children. *When there are no nodes in the tree, then the tree is known as a null tree or empty tree.* Trees are widely used in various day to day applications. Also, the recursive programming of trees makes the programs optimized and easily understandable. Trees are also used to represent the structure of mathematical formulas. Figure 8.1 represents a tree. In the following tree, A is the root node of the tree. X, Y, and Z are the child nodes of the root node A. They also form the subtrees of the tree. Also, B, C, Y, D, and E are the leaf nodes of the tree as they have no children.

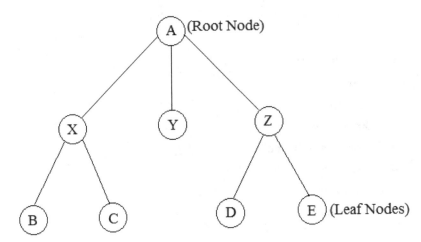

FIGURE 8.1. A tree.

Practical Application:

1. The members of a family can be visualized as a tree in which the root node can be visualized as a grandfather. His two children can be visualized as the child nodes. Then the grandchildren form the left and the right subtrees of the tree.

2. Trees are used to organize information in database systems and also to represent the syntactic structure of the source programs in compilers.

8.2 Definitions

- **Node** – A node is the main component of the tree data structure. It stores the actual data along with the links to the other nodes.

FIGURE 8.2. Structure of a node.

- **Root** – The root node is the topmost node of the tree. It does not have a parent node. If the root node is empty, then the tree is empty.

- **Parent** – The parent of a node is the immediate predecessor of that node. In the following figure, X is the parent of the Y and Z nodes.

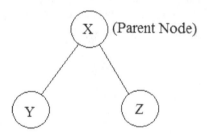

FIGURE 8.3. Parent node.

- **Child** – The child nodes are the immediate successors of a node. They must have a parent node. A child node placed at the left side is called the left child, and similarly, a child node placed at the right side is called a right child. Y is the left child of X and Z is the right child of X.

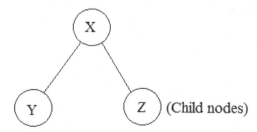

FIGURE 8.4. Child nodes.

- **Leaf/ Terminal nodes** – A leaf node is one which does not have any child nodes.
- **Subtrees** – The nodes B, X, and Y form the left subtree of root A. Similarly, the nodes C and Z form the right subtree of A.

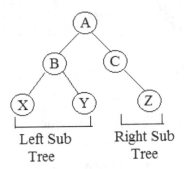

FIGURE 8.5. Subtrees.

- **Path** – It is a unique sequence of consecutive edges which is required to be followed to reach the destination from a given source. The path from root node A to Y is given as A-B, B-Y.

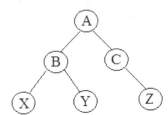

FIGURE 8.6. Path.

- **Level number of a node** – Every node in the tree is assigned a level number. The root is at level 0, the children of the root node are at level 1, and so on.

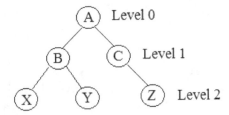

FIGURE 8.7. Node Level Numbers.

- **Height** –The height of the tree is the maximum level of the node + 1. The height of a tree containing a single node will be 1. Similarly, the height of an empty tree will be 0.

- **Ancestors** – The ancestors of a node are any predecessor nodes on the path between the root and the destination. There are no ancestors for the root node. The nodes A and B are the ancestors of node X.

- **Descendants** – The descendants of a node are any successor nodes on the path between the given source and the leaf node. There are no descendants of the leaf node. Here, B, X, and Y are the descendants of node A.

- **Siblings** – The child nodes of a given parent node are called siblings. X and Y are the siblings of B in Figure 8.8.

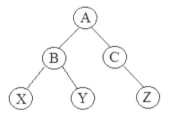

FIGURE 8.8. Siblings.

- **Degree of a node** – It is equal to the number of children that a node has.

- **Out-degree of a node** – It is equal to the number of edges leaving that node.

- **In-degree of a node** – It is equal to the number of edges arriving at that node.

- **Depth** – It is given as the length of the path from the root node to the destination node.

8.3 Binary Tree

A binary tree is a collection of nodes where each node contains three parts, that is, left pointer, right pointer, and the data item. The left pointer points to the left subtree and the right pointer points to the right subtree. The topmost element of the binary tree is known as a root node. The root pointer points to the root node. As the name suggests, *a binary tree can have at most two children, i.e., either a parent can have zero, one, or at most two children.* Also, if root = NULL, then it means that the tree is empty. Figure 8.9 represents a binary tree.

In the following figure, A represents the root node of the tree. B and C are the children of root node A. Nodes B, D, E, F, and G constitute the left subtree. Similarly, nodes C, H, I, and J constitute the right subtree. Now, nodes G, E, F, I, and J are the terminal/leaf nodes of the binary tree as they have no children. Hence, node A has two successors B and C. Node B has two successors D and G. Similarly, node D also has two successors E and F. Node G has no successor. Node C has only one successor H. Node H has two successors I and J. Since nodes E, F, G, I, and J have no successors, they are said to have empty subtrees.

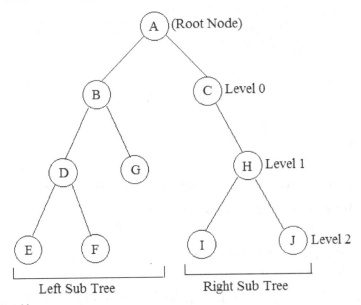

FIGURE 8.9. A binary tree.

8.3.1 Types of Binary Trees

There are two types of binary trees:

1. **Complete Binary Trees** – A complete binary tree is a type of binary tree which obeys/satisfies two properties:

   a. First, every level in a complete binary tree except the last one must be completely filled.

b. Second, all the nodes in the complete binary tree must appear left as much as possible.

In a complete binary tree, the number of nodes at level n is 2^n nodes. Also, the total number of nodes in a complete binary tree of depth d is equal to the sum of all nodes present at each level between 0 and d.

FIGURE 8.10. Complete binary trees.

2. Extended Binary Trees – Extended binary trees are also known as 2T-trees. A binary tree is said to be an extended binary tree if and only if every node in the tree has either zero children or two children. In an extended binary tree, nodes having two children are known as internal nodes. On the contrary, nodes having no children are known as external nodes. In the following figure, the internal nodes are represented by I and the external nodes are represented by E.

FIGURE 8.11. Extended binary trees.

8.3.2 Memory Representation of Binary Trees

Binary trees can be represented in a computer's memory in either of the following ways:

1. Array Representation of Binary Trees

2. Linked Representation of Binary Trees

Now, let us discuss both of them in detail.

Array Representation of Binary Trees

A binary tree is represented using an array in the computer's memory. It is also known as sequential representation. Sequential representation of binary trees is done using one-dimensional (1-D) arrays. This type of representation is static and hence it is inefficient, as the size must be known in advance and it thus requires a lot of memory space. The following rules are used to decide the location of each node in the memory:

a. The root node of the tree is stored in the first location.

b. If the parent node is present at location k, then the left child is stored at location 2k, and the right child is stored at location (2k + 1).

c. The maximum size of the array is given as $(2^h - 1)$, where h is the height of the tree.

For Example – A binary tree is given as follows. Give its array representation in the memory.

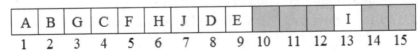

FIGURE 8.12. Binary tree and its array representation.

Linked Representation of Binary Trees

A binary tree can also be represented using a linked list in a computer's memory. This type of representation is dynamic as memory is dynamically allocated, that is, when it is needed, and thus it is efficient and avoids wastage of memory space. In linked representation, every node has three parts:

1. The 1st part is called the left pointer, which contains the address of the left subtree.

2. The 2nd part is called the data part, which contains the information of the node.

3. The 3rd part is called the right pointer, which contains the address of the right subtree.

The structure of the node is declared as follows:

```
struct node
{
  struct node *leftchild ;
  int information ;
  struct node *rightchild ;
}
```

The representation of a node is given in Figure 8.2. When there are no children of a node, then in that case the corresponding pointer fields are NULL.

For Example –A binary tree is given as follows. Give its linked representation in the memory.

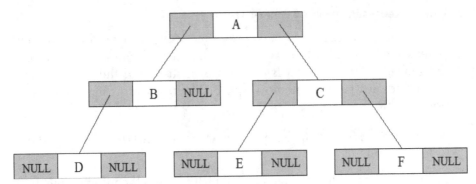

FIGURE 8.13. Binary tree and its linked representation.

8.4 Binary Search Tree

A binary search tree (BST) is a variant of a binary tree. *The special property of a binary search tree is that all the nodes in the left subtree have a value less than that of a root node. Similarly, all the nodes in the right subtree have a value more than that of a root node.* Hence, the binary search tree is also known as an ordered binary tree, because all the nodes in a binary search tree are ordered. Also, the left and the right subtrees are also binary search trees and thus, the same property is applicable on every subtree in the binary search tree. Figure 8.14 represents a binary search tree in which all the keys are ordered.

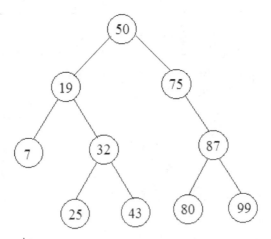

FIGURE 8.14. Binary search tree.

Now, in the previous figure, the root node is 50. The left subtree of the root node consists of the nodes 19, 7, 32, 25, and 43. We can see that all these nodes have smaller values than the root node, and hence it constitutes the left subtree. Similarly, the right subtree of the root node consists of the nodes 75, 87, 80, and 99. Here also, we can see that all these nodes have higher values than the root node and hence it constitutes the right subtree. Also, each of the subtrees is also ordered. Thus, it becomes easier to search an element in the tree and as a result, time is also reduced by a great margin. *Binary search trees are very efficient regarding searching an element.* These trees are already sorted in nature. Thus, these trees have a low time complexity. Now, there are various operations which can be performed on binary search trees, which will be discussed in the upcoming section.

8.4.1 Operations on Binary Search Trees

In this section, we will discuss different operations that are performed on binary search trees, which include:

- Searching a node/key in the binary search tree

- Inserting a node/key in the binary search tree

- Deleting a node/key from the binary search tree

- Deleting the entire binary search tree

- Finding the mirror image of the binary search tree

- Finding the smallest node in the binary search tree

- Finding the largest node in the binary search tree

- Determining the height of the binary search tree

Now, let us discuss all of these operations in detail.

1. **Searching a node/key in the binary search tree** – The searching operation is one of the most common operations performed in the binary search tree. *This operation is performed to find whether a given key exists in the tree or not.* The searching operation starts at the root node. First, it will check whether the tree is empty or not. If the tree is empty, then the node/key for which we are searching is not present in the tree, and the algorithm terminates there by displaying the appropriate message. If the tree is not empty and the nodes are

present in it, then the search function checks the node/value to be searched and compares it with the key value of the current node. If the node/key to be searched is less than the key value of the current node, then in that case, we will recursively call the left child node. On the other hand, if the node/key to be searched is greater than the key value of the current node, then we will recursively call the right child node. Now, let us look at the algorithm for searching for a key in the binary search tree.

Algorithm for searching for a node/key in the binary search tree

```
SEARCH(ROOT, VALUE)
Step 1: START
Step 2: IF(ROOT == NULL)
            Return NULL
            Print "Empty Tree"
            ELSE IF(ROOT -> INFO == VALUE)
            Return ROOT
            ELSE IF(ROOT -> INFO > VALUE)
            SEARCH(ROOT -> LCHILD, VALUE)
            ELSE IF(ROOT -> INFO < VALUE)
            SEARCH(ROOT -> RCHILD, VALUE)
            ELSE
            Print "Value not found"
            [End of IF]
            [End of IF]
            [End of IF]
            [End of IF]
Step 3: END
```

In the previous algorithm, first we check whether the tree is empty or not. If the tree is empty, then we return NULL. If the tree is not empty, then we check whether the value stored at the current node (ROOT) is equal to the node/key we want to search or not. If the value of the ROOT node is equal to the key value to be searched, then we return the current node of the tree, that is, the ROOT node. Otherwise, if the key value to be searched is less than the value stored at the current node, we recursively call the left subtree. If the key value to be searched is greater than the value stored at the current node, then we recursively call the right subtree. Finally, if the value is not found, then an appropriate message is printed on the screen.

For Example –We have been given a binary search tree. Now, search the node with the value 20 in the binary search tree.

Initially the binary search tree is given as:

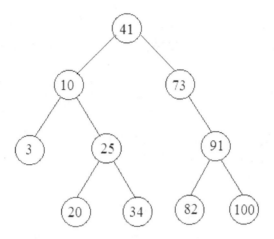

FIGURE 8.15(a)

Step 1: First, the root node, that is, 41, is checked.

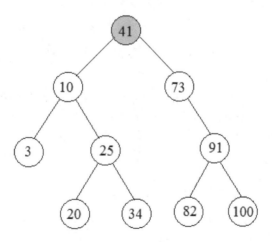

FIGURE 8.15(b)

Step 2: Second, as the value stored at the root node is not equal to the value to be searched, but we know that 20 < 41, thus we will traverse the left subtree.

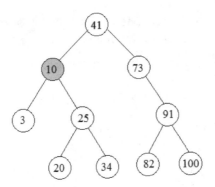

FIGURE 8.15(c)

Step 3: We know that 10 is not the value to be searched, but 20 > 10; thus, we will now traverse the right subtree with respect to 10.

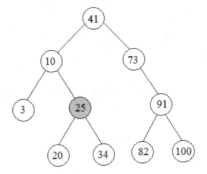

FIGURE 8.15(d)

Step 4: Again 25 is not the value to be searched, but 20 < 25; thus, we will now traverse the left subtree w.r.t to 25.

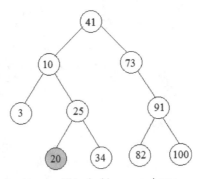

FIGURE 8.15. Searching a node with value 20 in the binary search tree.

Finally, a node having value 20 is successfully searched in the binary search tree.

2. **Inserting a node/key in the binary search tree –** The insertion operation is performed to insert a new node with the given value in the binary search tree. The new node is inserted at the correct position following the binary search tree constraint. It should not violate the property of the binary search tree. The insertion operation also starts at the root node. First, it will check whether the tree is empty or not. If the tree is empty, then we will allocate the memory for the new node. If the tree is not empty, then we will compare the key value to be inserted with the value stored in the current node. If the node/key to be inserted is less than the key value of the current node, then the new node is inserted in the left subtree. On the other hand, if the node/key to be inserted is greater than the key value of the current node, then the new node is inserted in the right subtree. Now, let us discuss the algorithm for inserting a node in the binary search tree.

Algorithm for inserting a node/key in the binary search tree

```
INSERT(ROOT, VALUE)
Step 1: START
Step 2: IF(ROOT == NULL)
            Allocate memory for ROOT node
            Set ROOT -> INFO = VALUE
            Set ROOT -> LCHILD = ROOT -> RCHILD = NULL
            [End of IF]
Step 3: IF(ROOT -> INFO > VALUE)
            INSERT(ROOT -> LCHILD, VALUE)
            ELSE
            INSERT(ROOT -> RCHILD, VALUE)
            [End of IF]
Step 4: END
```

In the previous algorithm, first we check whether the tree is empty or not. If the tree is empty, then we will allocate memory for the ROOT node. In Step 3, we are checking whether the key value to be inserted is less than the value stored at the current node; if so, we will simply insert the new node in the left subtree. Otherwise, the new child node is inserted into the right subtree.

For Example – We have been given a binary search tree. Now, insert a new node with the value 7 in the binary search tree.

Initially, the binary search tree is given as:

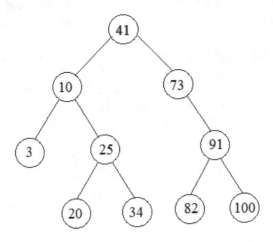

FIGURE 8.16(a)

Step 1: First, we check whether the tree is empty or not. So, we will check the root node. As the root node is not empty, we will begin the insertion process.

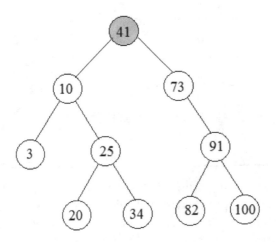

FIGURE 8.16(b)

Step 2: Second, we know that 7 < 41; thus, we will traverse the left subtree to insert the new node.

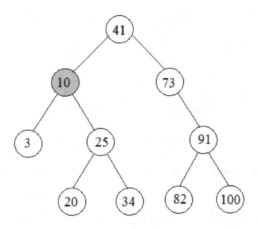

FIGURE 8.16(c)

Step 3: Third, we know that 7<10; thus, we will again traverse the left subtree to insert the new node.

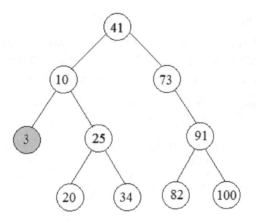

FIGURE 8.16(d)

Step 3: Now, we know that 7> 3, thus the new node with value 7 is inserted as the right child of the parent node 3.

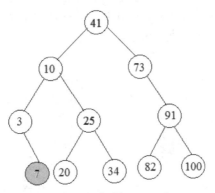

FIGURE 8.16: Inserting a new node with value 7 in the binary search tree.

Finally, the new node with the value 7 is inserted as a right child in the binary search tree.

3. **Deleting a node/key from the binary search tree** – Deleting a node/key from the binary search tree is the most crucial process. We should be careful when performing the deletion operation; while deleting the nodes, we must be sure that the property of the binary search trees is not violated so that we don't lose necessary nodes during this process. The deletion operation is divided into three cases as follows:

Case 1: Deleting a node having no children

This is the simplest case of deletion, as we can directly remove or delete a node which has no children. Look at the binary search tree given in Figure 8.17 and see how deletion is done in this case.

For Example – We have been given a binary search tree. Now, delete a node with the value 61 from the binary search tree.

Initially the binary search tree is given as:

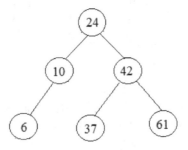

FIGURE 8.17(a)

Step 1: First, we will check whether the tree is empty or not by checking the root node.

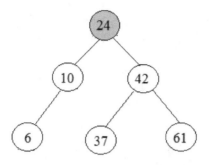

FIGURE 8.17(b)

Step 2: Second, as the root node is present, we will compare the value to be deleted with the value stored at the current node. As 61 > 24, thus, we will recursively traverse the right subtree.

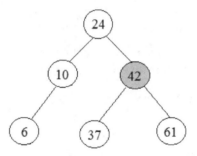

FIGURE 8.17(c)

Step 3: Again, we will compare the value to be deleted with the value stored at the current node. As 61 > 42, thus, we will recursively traverse the right subtree.

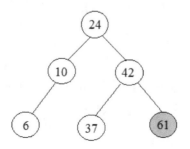

FIGURE 8.17(d)

Step 4: Finally, a node having value 61 is deleted from the binary search tree.

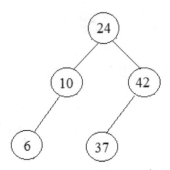

FIGURE 8.17. Deleting the node with value 61 from the binary search tree.

Case 2: Deleting a node having one child

In this case of deletion, the node which is to be deleted, the parent node, is simply replaced by its child node. Look at the binary search tree given in Figure 8.18 and see how deletion is done in this case.

For Example – We have been given a binary search tree. Now, delete a node with the value 10 from the binary search tree.

Initially the binary search tree is given as:

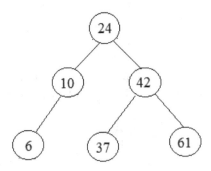

FIGURE 8.18(a)

Step 1: First, we will check whether the tree is empty or not by checking the root node.

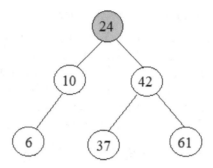

FIGURE 8.18(b)

Step 2: Second, as the root node is present, we will compare the value to be deleted with the value stored at the current node. As 10 < 24, thus, we will recursively traverse the left subtree.

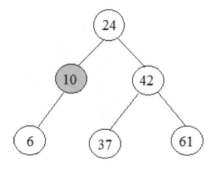

FIGURE 8.18(c)

Step 3: Now, as the node to be deleted is found and has one child, so the node to be deleted is now replaced by its child node, and the actual node is deleted.

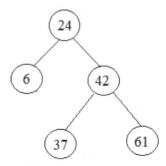

FIGURE 8.18. Deleting the node with value 10 from the binary search tree.

Case 3: Deleting a node having two children

In this case, the node which is to be deleted is simply replaced by its in-order predecessor, that is, the largest value in the left subtree, or by its in-order successor, that is, the smallest value in the right subtree. Also, the in-order predecessor or in-order successor can be deleted using any of the two cases. Now, look at the binary search tree shown in Figure 8.19 and see how the deletion will take place in this case.

Now, let us discuss the algorithm for deleting a node from the binary search tree.

For Example – We have been given a binary search tree. Now, delete a node with the value 42 from the binary search tree.

Initially, the binary search tree is given as:

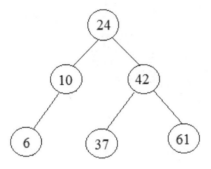

FIGURE 8.19(a)

Step 1: First, we will check whether the tree is empty or not by checking the root node.

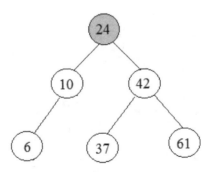

FIGURE 8.19(b)

Step 2: Second, as the root node is present, we will compare the value to be deleted with the value stored at the current node. As 42 <>24, thus, we will recursively traverse the right subtree.

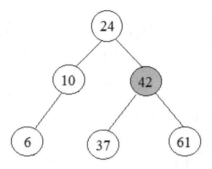

FIGURE 8.19(c)

Step 3: As the node to be deleted is found and has two children, now we will find the in-order predecessor of the current node (42) and replace the current node with its in-order predecessor so that the actual node 42 is deleted.

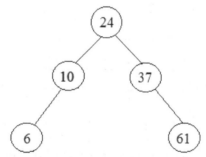

FIGURE 8.19. Deleting the node with value 42 from the binary search tree.

Algorithm for deleting a node/key from the binary search tree

```
DELETE_NODE(ROOT, VALUE)
Step 1: START
Step 2: IF(ROOT == NULL)
            Print "Error"
            [End of IF]
Step 3: IF(ROOT -> INFO > VALUE)
            DELETE_NODE(ROOT -> LCHILD, VALUE)
            ELSE IF(ROOT -> INFO < VALUE)
```

```
                    DELETE_NODE(ROOT -> RCHILD, VALUE)
                    ELSE
                    IF(ROOT -> LCHILD = NULL & ROOT -> RCHILD =
                    NULL)
                    FREE(ROOT)
                    ELSE IF(ROOT -> LCHILD & ROOT -> RCHILD)
                    TEMP = FIND_LARGEST(ROOT -> LCHILD)
                    OR
                    TEMP = FIND_SMALLEST(ROOT -> RCHILD)
                    Set ROOT -> INFO = TEMP -> INFO
                    FREE(TEMP)
                    ELSE
                    IF(ROOT -> LCHILD != NULL)
                    Set TEMP = ROOT -> LCHILD
                    Set ROOT -> INFO = TEMP -> INFO
                    FREE(TEMP)
                    ELSE
                    Set TEMP = ROOT -> RCHILD
                    Set ROOT -> INFO = TEMP -> INFO
                    FREE(TEMP)
                    [End of IF]
                    [End of IF]
                    [End of IF]
Step 4: END
```

In the previous algorithm, first we check whether the tree is empty or not. If the tree is empty, then the node to be deleted is not present. Otherwise, if the tree is not empty, we will check whether the node/value to be deleted is less than the value stored at the current node. If the value to be deleted is less, then we will recursively call the left subtree. If the value to be deleted is greater than the value stored at the current node, then we will recursively call the right subtree. Now, if the node to be deleted has no children, then the node is simply freed. If the node to be deleted has two children, that is, both a left and right child, then we will find the in-order predecessor by calling (TEMP = FIND_LARGEST(ROOT -> LCHILD) or in-order successor by calling (TEMP = FIND_SMALLEST(ROOT -> RCHILD) and replace the value stored at the current node with that of the in-order predecessor or in-order successor. Then, we will simply delete the initial node of either the in-order predecessor or in-order successor. Finally, if the node to be deleted has only one child, the value stored at the current node is replaced by its child node and the child node is deleted.

4. Deleting the entire binary search tree – It is very easy to delete the entire binary search tree. First, we will delete all the nodes present in the left subtrees followed by the nodes present in the right subtree. Finally, the root node is deleted, and the entire tree is deleted.

Algorithm for deleting the entire binary search tree

```
DELETE_BST (ROOT)
Step 1: START
Step 2: IF(ROOT != NULL)
            DELETE_BST(ROOT -> LCHILD)
            DELETE_BST(ROOT -> RCHILD)
            FREE(ROOT)
            [End of IF]
Step 3: END
```

5. Finding the mirror image of the binary search tree – This is an exciting operation to perform in the binary search tree. The mirror image of the binary search tree means interchanging the right subtree with the left subtree at each and every node of the tree.

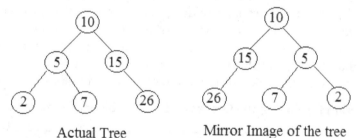

Actual Tree   Mirror Image of the tree

FIGURE 8.20. Binary search tree and its mirror image.

Algorithm for finding the mirror image of the binary search tree

```
MIRROR_IMAGE (ROOT)
Step 1: START
Step 2: IF(ROOT != NULL)
            MIRROR_IMAGE(ROOT -> LCHILD)
            MIRROR_IMAGR(ROOT -> RCHILD)
            Set TEMP = ROOT -> LEFT
            ROOT -> LEFT = ROOT -> RIGHT
            Set ROOT -> RIGHT = TEMP
            [End of IF]
Step 3: END
```

6. **Finding the smallest node in the binary search tree** – We know that it is the basic property of the binary search tree that the smallest value always occurs in the extreme left of the left subtree. If there is no left subtree, then the value of the root node will be the smallest. Hence, to find the smallest value in the binary search tree, we will simply find the value of the node present at the extreme left of the left subtree.

Algorithm for finding the smallest node in the binary search tree

```
SMALLEST_VALUE (ROOT)

Step 1: START
Step 2: IF(ROOT = NULL OR ROOT -> LCHILD = NULL)
            Return NULL
            ELSE
            Return SMALLEST_VALUE(ROOT)
            [End of IF]
Step 3: END
```

7. **Finding the largest node in the binary search tree** – We know that it is the basic property of the binary search tree that the largest value always occurs in the extreme right of the right subtree. If there is no right subtree, the value of the root node will be the largest. Hence, to find the largest value in the binary search tree, we will simply find the value of the node present at the extreme right of the right subtree.

Algorithm for finding the largest node in the binary search tree

```
LARGEST_VALUE (ROOT)
Step 1: START
Step 2: IF(ROOT = NULL OR ROOT -> RCHILD = NULL)
            Return NULL
            ELSE
            Return LARGEST_VALUE(ROOT)
            [End of IF]
Step 3: END
```

8. **Determining the height of the binary search tree** –The height of the binary search tree can easily be determined. We will first calculate the heights of the left subtree and the right subtree. Whichever height is greater, 1 is added to that height; that is, if the height of the left subtree

is greater, then 1 is added to the height of the left subtree. Similarly, if the height of the right subtree is greater, then 1 is added to the height of the right subtree.

Algorithm for determining the height of the binary search tree

```
CALCULATE_HEIGHT(ROOT)
Step 1: START
Step 2: IF ROOT = NULL
            Print "Can't find height of the tree."
            ELSE
            Set LHEIGHT = CALCULATE_HEIGHT(ROOT -> LCHILD)
            Set RHEIGHT = CALCULATE_HEIGHT(ROOT -> RCHILD)
            IF(LHEIGHT < RHEIGHT)
            Return (RHEIGHT) + 1
            ELSE
            Return (LHEIGHT) + 1
            [End of IF]
            [End of IF]
Step 3: END
```

8.4.2 Binary Tree Traversal Methods

Traversing is the process of visiting each node in the tree exactly once in a particular order. We all know that a tree is a non-linear data structure, and therefore a tree can be traversed in various ways. There are three types of traversals, which are:

- Pre-Order Traversal
- In-Order Traversal
- Post-Order Traversal

Now, we will discuss all of these traversals in detail.

Pre-Order Traversal

In pre-order traversal, the following operations are performed recursively at each node:

1. Visit the root node.

2. Traverse the left subtree.

3. Traverse the right subtree.

The word "pre" in pre-order determines that the root node is accessed before accessing any other node in the tree. Hence, it is also known as a DLR traversal, that is, Data Left Right. Therefore, in a DLR traversal, the root node is accessed first followed by the left subtree and right subtree. Now, let us see an example for pre-order traversal.

For Example – Find the pre-order traversal of the given binary tree of the word EDUCATION.

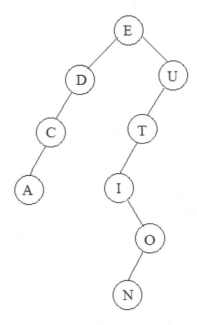

The pre-order traversal of the previous binary tree is:

E D C A U T I O N

Now, let us look at the function for pre-order traversal.

Function for pre-order traversal

```
void pre-order(struct BST * root)
{
  if(root != NULL)
    {
      printf("%d", root -> info) ;
```

```
    pre-order(root ->lchild) ;
    pre-order(root ->rchild) ;
  }
}
```

In-Order Traversal

In in-order traversal, the following operations are performed recursively at each node:

1. Traverse the left subtree.

2. Visit the root node.

3. Traverse the right subtree.

The word "in" in "in-order" determines that the root node is accessed in between the left and the right subtrees. Hence, it is also known as an LDR traversal, that is, Left Data Right. Therefore, in an LDR traversal, the left subtree is traversed first followed by the root node and the right subtree. Now, let us see an example for an in-order traversal.

For Example – Find the in-order traversal of the given binary tree of the word EDUCATION.

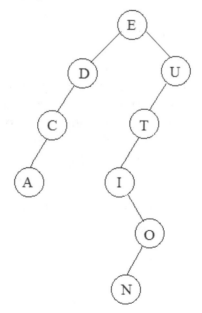

The in-order traversal of the previous binary tree is:

$$\boxed{\text{A C D E I N O T U}}$$

Now, let us look at the function for an in-order traversal.

Function for an in-order traversal

```
void in-order(struct BST * root)
{
  if(root != NULL)
    {
      in-order(root ->lchild) ;
      printf("%d", root -> info) ;
      in-order(root ->rchild) ;
    }
}
```

Post-Order Traversal

In a post-order traversal, the following operations are performed recursively at each node:

1. Traverse the left subtree.

2. Traverse the right subtree.

3. Visit the root node.

The word "post" in post-order determines that the root node will be accessed last after the left and the right subtrees. Hence, it is also known as an LRD traversal, that is, Left Right Data. Therefore, in an LRD traversal, the left subtree is traversed first followed by the right subtree and the root node. Now, let us see an example for a post-order traversal.

For Example – Find the post-order traversal of the given binary tree of the word EDUCATION.

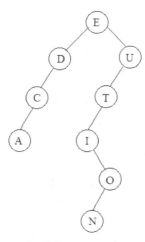

The post-order traversal of the previous binary tree is:

A C D N O I T U E

Now, let us look at the function of the post-order traversal.

Function for post-order traversal

```
void post-order(struct BST * root)
{
  if(root != NULL)
    {
    post-order(root ->lchild) ;
    post-order(root ->rchild) ;
    printf("%d", root -> info) ;
    }
}
```

Write a program to create a binary search tree and perform different operations on it.

```
#include<stdio.h>
#include<malloc.h>
#include<conio.h>
struct node
```

```
{
  int info;
  struct node *lchild;
  struct node *rchild;
};
struct node *BST;

void create_BST(struct node *);
struct node *insert_value(struct node*,int);
void in-order_traversal(struct node *);
void post-order_traversal(struct node*);
void pre-order_traversal(struct node *);
struct node *delete_value(struct node *,int);
intcalculate_height(struct node*);
struct node *delete_BST(struct node *);

int main()
{
  struct node *root;
  int choice, item;
  create_BST(BST);
  clrscr();
  while(1)
    {
      printf("\n\t***MENU***");
      printf("\n 1. Insert Value ");
      printf("\n 2. In-order traversal of the tree");
      printf("\n 3. post-order traversal of the tree");
      printf("\n 4. Pre-order traversal of the tree");
      printf("\n 5. Delete value");
      printf("\n 6. Calculate height ");
      printf("\n 7. Delete BST");
      printf("\n 8. Exit");
      printf("\nEnter your choice : ");
      scanf(" %d",&choice);
      switch(choice)
        {
          case 1:
          printf("\n Enter the new value to be inserted: ");
          scanf("%d", &item);
          BST = insert_value(BST, item);
          break;
```

```
        case 2:
        printf("\n In-order traversal of the tree is : ");
        in-order_traversal(BST);
        break;

        case 3:
        printf("\n Post-order  traversal  of  the  tree  is
        : ");
        post-order_traversal( BST);
        break;

        case 4:
        printf("\n Pre-order traversal of binary tree is
        : ");
        pre-order_traversal(BST);
        break;

        case 5:
        printf("\n Enter the value to delete : ");
        scanf(" %d",&item);
        BST=delete_value(BST,item);
        break;

        case 6:
        printf("\nHeight  of  tree  is  %d",calculate_
        height(BST);
        break;

        case 7;
        BST = delete_BST(BST);
        break;

        case 8:
        printf("Wrong Choice!!!");
        exit(0);
      }
   }
 getch();
 return0;
}
```

```c
void create_BST(struct node*BST)
{
 BST = NULL:
}

struct node *insert_value(struct node *BST, int item)
{
 struct node *root , *node_root , *parent_root;
 root=(struct node*)malloc(sizeof(struct node));
 root->info = item;
 root->lchild = NULL;
 root->rchild= NULL;
 if(BST == NULL)
   {
     BST = root;
     BST->lchild == NULL;
     BST->rchild == NULL;
   }
 else
   {
     parent_root = NULL:
     node_root = BST;
     while(node_root!=NULL)
       {
         parent_root= node_root;
         if(item < (node_root->info))
         node_root=node_root->lchild;
         else
         node_root=parent_root->rchild;
       }
     if(item < (parent_root->info))
     parent_root->lchild = root;
     else
     parent_root->rchild = root;
   }
  return BST;
}

void in-order_traversal(struct node *BST)
  {
```

```
   if(BST != NULL)
    {
      in-order_traversal(BST->lchild);
      printf("%d\t",BST->info);
      in-order_traversal(BST->rchild);
    }
}

void post-order_traversal(struct node *BST)
{
  if( BST!= NULL)
    {
      post-order_traversal(BST->lchild);
      post-order_traversal(BST->rchild);
      printf("%d\t", BST ->info);
    }
}

void pre-order_traversal(struct node *BST)
{
  if(BST!= NULL)
    {
      printf("%d\t",BST->info);
      pre-order_traversal(BST->lchild);
      pre-order_traversal(BST->rchild);
    }
}

struct tree *delete_value(struct node*BST,int item)
{
  struct node *current,*parent,*succ,*psucc,*ptr;
  if(BST->lchild==NULL)
    {
      printf("\n The tree is empty");
      return(BST);
    }
  parent = BST;
  current = BST->lchild;
  while(current !=NULL && item!= current->info)
    {
      parent = current;
```

```
      current = (item<current -> info) ? current ->lchild:
      current ->rchild);
   }
  if(current == NULL)
   {
     printf("\n Item to be deleted is not in the binary
     tree");
     return(BST);
   }
  if(current ->lchild == NULL)
  ptr= current ->rchild;
  else if (current ->rchild == NULL)
  ptr = c->lchild;
  else
   {
     //Finding in-order successor and its parent
     psucc= current;
     current = current ->lchild;
     while(succ->lchild!=NULL)
       {
         psucc = succ;
         succ = succ->lchild;
       }
     if(current == psucc)
       {
         //Case A
         succ->lchild = current ->rchild;
       }
     else
       {
         //case B
         succ->lchild = current ->lchild;
         psucc->lchild= succ->rchild;
         succ->rchild = current ->rchild;
       }
     ptr= succ;
       {
         if(parent ->lchild == current)
         parent ->lchild =ptr;
         else
```

```
                parent ->rchild =ptr;
                free(current);
                return BST;
              }

    intcalculate_height(struct node*BST)
    {
      intlheight, rheight;
      if(BST== NULL)
      return 0;
      else
        {
          lheight = calculate_height(BST->lchild);
          rheight = calculate_height(BST->rchild);
          if(lheight>rheight)
          return (lheight+1);
          else
          return(rheight+1);
        }
    }

    struct node *delete_BST(struct  node*BST)
    {
      if(BST!= NULL)
        {
          delete_BST(BST->lchild);
          delete_BST(BST->rchild);
          free(BST);
        }
    }
```

Output –

    MENU

1) Insert value

2) In-order traversal of the tree

3) Post-order traversal of the tree

4) Pre-order traversal of the tree

```
5) Delete value
6) Calculate height
7) Delete BST
8) Exit

Enter your choice: 1
Enter the value to be inserted: 95
Enter the value to be inserted: 20
Enter your choice: 4
Pre-order traversal of binary tree is: 95  20
Enter your choice : 5
Enter the value to delete : 20
Enter your choice : 8
Wrong Choice!!!
```

8.4.3 Creating a Binary Tree Using Traversal Methods

A binary tree can be constructed if we are given at least two of the traversal results, provided that one traversal should always be an in-order traversal and the second is either a pre-order traversal or a post-order traversal. An in-order traversal determines the left and right child nodes of the binary tree. Pre-order or post-order traversal determines the root node of the binary tree. Hence, there are two different ways of creating a binary tree, which are:

1. In-order and pre-order traversal

2. In-order and post-order traversal

Now, we have pre-order and in-order traversal sequences. Then, the following steps are followed to construct a binary tree:

Step 1: The pre-order traversing sequence is used to determine the root node of the binary tree. The first node in the pre-order sequence will be the root node.

Step 2: The in-order traversing sequence is used to determine the left and the right subtrees of the binary tree. Keys toward the left side of the root node in the in-order sequence form the left subtree. Similarly, keys toward the right side of the root node in the in-order sequence form the right subtree.

Step 3: Now, each element from the pre-order traversing sequence is recursively selected and the left and the right subtrees are created from the in-order traversing sequence.

For Example – Create a binary tree from the given traversing sequences.

In-order –A C D E I N O T U

Pre-order – E DCAU T I O N

Now, we will construct the binary tree.

1. The first node in the pre-order sequence is the root node of the tree. Hence, E is the root node of the binary tree.

Root Node

2. Now, we can easily determine the left and right subtrees from the in-order sequence. Keys toward the left side of the root node, that is, A, C, and D, form the left subtree. Similarly, elements on the right side of the root node, that is, I, N, O, T, and U, form the left subtree.

Root Node

Left Sub-Tree

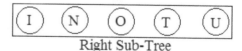
Right Sub-Tree

3. Now, the left child of the root node will be the first node in the pre-order traversing sequence after the root node E. Thus, D is the left child of the root node E.

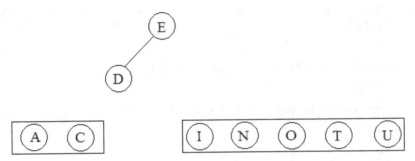

4. Similarly, the right child of the root node will be the first node in the pre-order traversing sequence after the nodes of the left subtree. Thus, U is the right child of the root node E.

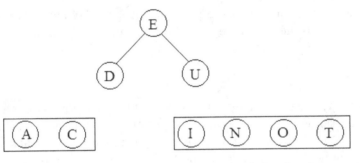

5. In the in-order sequence, A and C are on the left side of D. So, A and C will form the left subtree of D.

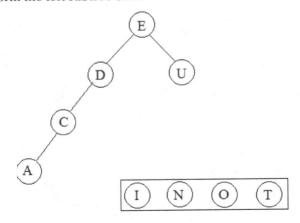

6. Now, the next elements in the pre-order sequence are T and I. Also, in the in-order sequence, T and I are on the left side of U. So, T and I will form the left subtree of U.

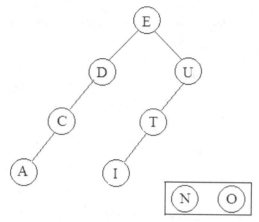

7. The next element in the pre-order sequence is O. In the in-order sequence, O is on the right side of I. So, O will form the right subtree of I. The last element in the pre-order sequence is N. N is on the left side of O in the in-order sequence. Thus, N will form the left subtree of O.

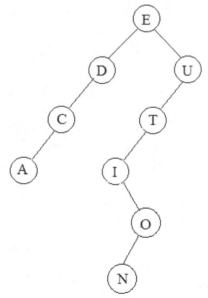

Finally, the binary tree is created from the given traversing sequences.

Frequently Asked Questions

Q. Create a binary tree from the given traversing sequences.

    In-order – d b e a f c g

    Pre-order – a b d e c f g

Answer.

Step 1: a is the root node of the binary tree.

Step 2: d, b, and e are on the left side of the a node in the in-order sequence. Hence, d, b, and e are the left subtrees of root a. Also, d is the left subtree of b and e is the right subtree of b.

Step 3: f, c, and g are on the right side of root a in the in-order sequence. Hence, f, c, and g are the right subtrees of root a. Also, f is the left subtree of c and g is the right subtree of c.

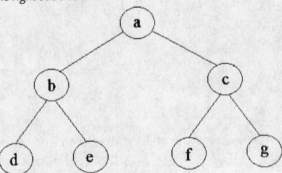

8.5 AVL Trees

The AVL tree was invented by Adelson-Velski and Landis in 1962. The AVL tree is so named in honor of its inventors. The AVL tree was the first balanced binary search tree. It is a self-balancing binary search tree. The AVL tree is also known as a height-balanced tree because of its property that the heights of the two subtrees of a node can differ at most by one. AVL trees are very efficient in performing searching, insertion, and deletion operations, as they take O(log n) time to perform all these operations.

8.5.1 Need of Height-Balanced Trees

AVL trees are very similar to binary search trees but with a small difference. AVL trees have a special variable which is known as a balance factor associated with them. Every node in the AVL tree has a balance factor associated with it. The balance factor is determined by subtracting the height of the right subtree from the height of the left subtree. Thus, *a node with a balance factor of -1, 0, or 1 is said to be a height-balanced tree.* The primary need for the height-balanced tree is that the process of searching becomes very fast. This balancing condition also ensures that the depth of the tree is O(logn). The balance factor is calculated as follows:

Balance Factor = Height(Left sub-tree) – Height(Right sub-tree)

- If the balance factor of the tree is -1, then it means that the height of the right subtree of that node is one more than the height of the left subtree of that node.

- If the balance factor of the tree is 0, then it means that the height of the left and the right subtrees of a node are equal.

- If the balance factor of the tree is 1, then it means that the height of the left subtree of that node is one more than the height of its right subtree.

Thus, the overall benefit of the height-balanced tree is to assist in fast searching.

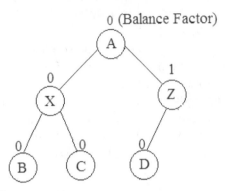

FIGURE 8.21. Balanced AVL tree.

8.5.2 Operations on an AVL Tree

In this section, we will discuss various operations which are performed on the AVL trees. These are:

- Searching a node in an AVL Tree

- Inserting a new node in an AVL Tree

Now, let us discuss both of them in detail.

1. Searching a node in an AVL Tree

The process of searching a node in an AVL tree is the same as for a binary search tree.

2. Inserting a new node in an AVL Tree

The process of inserting a new node in an AVL tree is quite similar to that of binary search trees. The new node is always inserted as a terminal/leaf node in the AVL tree. But the insertion of a new node can disturb the balance of the AVL tree, as the balance factor may be disturbed. Thus, for the tree to remain balanced, the insertion process is followed by a rotation process. The rotation process is usually done to restore the balance factor of the tree. If the balance factor of each node is -1, 0, or 1 after the insertion process, then the rotation is not required as the tree is already balanced; otherwise, rotation is required. Now, let us look at the given example and see how insertion is done without rotations.

For Example – In the given AVL tree, insert a new node with value 60 in the tree.

Initially, the AVL tree is given as:

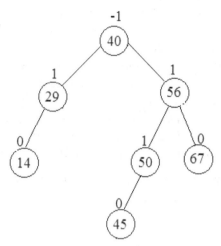

FIGURE 8.22. AVL tree before insertion.

Now, we will insert 60 into the AVL tree.

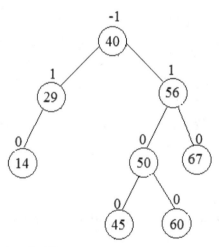

FIGURE 8.23. AVL tree after inserting 60.

Hence, after insertion, there are no nodes in the tree which are unbalanced. Thus, there is no need to apply rotation here. However, now we will discuss how the rotation process is performed in AVL trees.

AVL Rotations

Rotation is done when the balance factor of the node becomes disturbed after inserting a new node. We know that the new node which is inserted will always have a balance factor of 0, as it will be the leaf node. Hence, the nodes whose balance factors will be disturbed are the ones which lie in the path of the root node to the newly inserted node. So, we will perform the rotation process only on those nodes whose balance factors will be disturbed. In the rotation process, our first work is to find the critical node in the AVL tree. The critical node is the nearest ancestor node from the newly inserted node to the root node which does not has a balance factor of -1, 0, or 1. First, let us understand the concept of the critical node with the help of an example.

For Example – Find the critical node in the given AVL tree.

Initially, the AVL tree is given as follows:

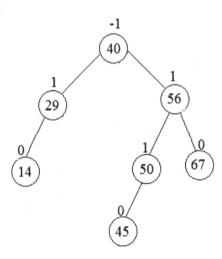

FIGURE 8.23. AVL tree.

Now, we will insert a new node with value 42 in the tree.

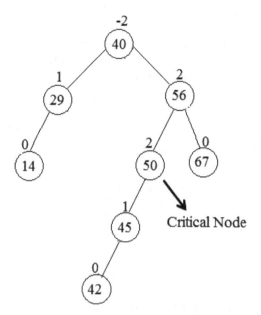

FIGURE 8.24. AVL tree.

After inserting 42 in the AVL tree, we can see that there are three nodes in the tree which have balance factors equal to -2, 2, and 2. Now, the critical node is the one which is the nearest to the newly inserted node with a disturbed balance factor. We can see that 50 is the nearest node to 42, and 50 has a balance factor of 2. Thus, 50 is the critical node in this AVL tree. However, to restore the balance factor of the previous AVL tree, rotations are performed. There are four types of rotations which are:

1. **Left-Left Rotation (LL Rotation)** – New node is inserted in the left subtree of the left subtree of the critical node.

2. **Right-Right Rotation (RR Rotation)** – New node is inserted in the right subtree of the right subtree of the critical node.

3. **Right-Left Rotation (RL Rotation)** – New node is inserted in the left subtree of the right subtree of the critical node.

4. **Left-Right Rotation (LR Rotation)** – New node is inserted in the right subtree of the right subtree of critical node.

Now, let us discuss all of these rotations in detail.

LL Rotation

The LL rotation is also known as the Left-Left rotation, as the new node is inserted in the left subtree of the left subtree of the critical node. It is a single rotation. Let us take an example and perform an LL rotation in it.

For Example –

Initially, the AVL tree is given as:

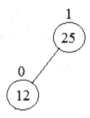

FIGURE 8.25(a)

Insert new node 5 in the AVL tree.

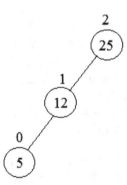

FIGURE 8.25(b)

After inserting 5 in the AVL tree, the balance factor of 25 is disturbed. Thus, 25 is the critical node. Hence, we will apply the LL rotation to restore the balance factor of the tree. After rotation node 12 becomes the root node, node 5 and node 25 become the left and the right child of the tree respectively.

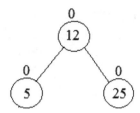

FIGURE 8.25. Showing an LL rotation in an AVL tree.

Therefore, the LL rotation is performed, and the balance factor of each node is also restored.

RR Rotation

The RR rotation is also known as a Right-Right rotation, as the new node is inserted in the right subtree of the right subtree of the critical node. It is also a single rotation. Let us take an example and perform an RR rotation in it.

For Example –

Initially the AVL tree is given as follows:

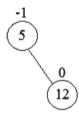

FIGURE 8.26(a)

Insert new node 25 in the AVL tree.

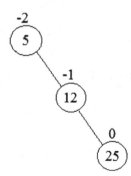

FIGURE 8.26(b)

After inserting 25 in the AVL tree, the balance factor of 5 is disturbed. Thus, 5 is the critical node. Hence, here we will apply an RR rotation to restore the balance factor of the tree. After rotation node 12 becomes the root node, node 5 and node 25 become the left and the right child of the tree respectively.

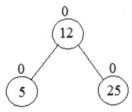

FIGURE 8.26. Showing an RR rotation in an AVL tree.

Therefore, the RR rotation is performed, and the balance factor of each node is also restored.

RL Rotation

The RL rotation is also known as a Right-Left rotation, as the new node is inserted in the left subtree of the right subtree of the critical node. It is a double rotation. Let us take an example and perform an RL rotation in it.

For Example –

Initially, the AVL tree is given as follows:

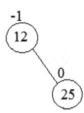

FIGURE 8.27(a)

Insert new node 15 in the AVL tree.

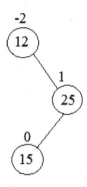

FIGURE 8.27(b)

After inserting 15 in the AVL tree, the balance factor of 12 is disturbed. Thus, 12 is the critical node. Hence, here we will apply an RL rotation to restore the balance factor of the tree. After rotation node 15 becomes the root node, node 12 and node 25 become the left and the right child of the tree respectively.

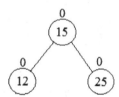

FIGURE 8.27. Showing an RL rotation in an AVL tree.

Therefore, the RL rotation is performed, and the balance factor of each node is also restored.

LR Rotation

The LR rotation is also known as a Left-Right rotation, as the new node is inserted in the right subtree of the left subtree of the critical node. It is also a double rotation. Let us take an example and perform an LR rotation in it.

For Example –

Initially, the AVL tree is given as follows:

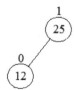

FIGURE 8.28(a)

Insert new node 15 in the AVL tree.

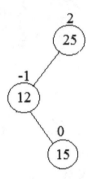

FIGURE 8.28(b)

After inserting 15 in the AVL tree, the balance factor of 25 is disturbed. Thus, 25 is the critical node. Hence, here we will apply an LR rotation to restore the balance factor of the tree. After rotation node 15 becomes the root node, and node 12 and node 25 become the left and the right child of the tree respectively.

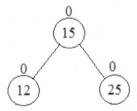

FIGURE 8.28. Showing an LR rotation in an AVL tree.

Therefore, an LR rotation is performed, and the balance factor of each node is also restored.

Frequently Asked Questions

Q. Create an AVL tree by inserting the following elements.

60, 10, 20, 30, 19, 120, 100, 80, 19

Answer.
Step 1: Insert 60.

Step 2: Insert 10. Further, no rebalancing is required.

Step 3: Insert 20. Now, rebalancing is required. We will perform LR rotation.

Step 4: After performing LR rotation, the AVL tree is given as –

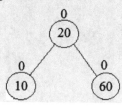

Step 5: Insert 30. No rebalancing is required.

Step 6: Insert 19. Further, no rebalancing is required.

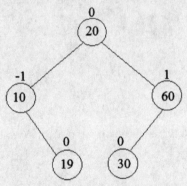

Step 7: Insert 120. No rebalancing is required.

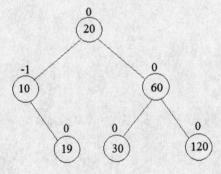

Step 8: Insert 100. No rebalancing is required.

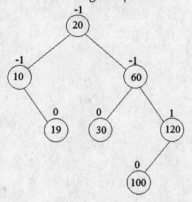

Step 9: Insert 80. Now, rebalancing is required. We will perform LL rotation.

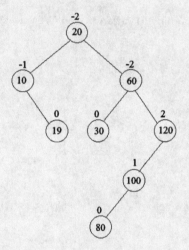

Step 10: After performing LL rotation, the AVL tree is given as –

Step 10: Insert 19. Now, rebalancing is required. We will perform RR rotation.

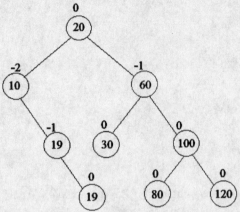

Step 11: After performing RR rotation, the AVL tree is given as –

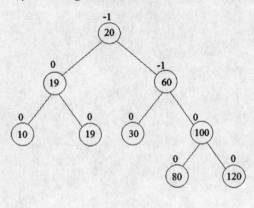

8.6 Summary

- A tree is defined as a collection of one or more nodes where one node is designated as a root node, and the remaining nodes can be partitioned into the left and the right subtrees. It is used to store hierarchical data.

- The root node is the topmost node of the tree. It does not have a parent node. If the root node is empty, then the tree is empty. A leaf node is one which does not have any child nodes.

- A path is a unique sequence of consecutive edges which is required to be followed to reach the destination from a given source.

- The degree of a node is equal to the number of children that a node has.

- A binary tree is a collection of nodes where each node contains three parts, that is, a left pointer, a right pointer, and the data item. A binary tree can have at most 2 children; that is, a parent can have either 0, 1, or at most 2 children.

- There are two types of binary trees, that is, complete binary trees and extended binary trees.

- In a complete binary tree, every level except the last one must be completely filled. Also, all the nodes in the complete binary tree must appear left as much as possible.

- Extended binary trees are also known as 2T-trees. A binary tree is said to be an extended binary tree if and only if every node in the binary tree can have either 0 children or 2 children.

- Binary trees can be represented in the memory in two ways, which are array representation of binary trees and linked representation of binary trees. Array representation, also known as sequential representation, of binary trees is done using one-dimensional (1-D) arrays. Linked representation of binary trees is done using linked lists.

- A binary search tree (BST) is a variant of a binary tree in which all the nodes in the left subtree have a value less than that of a root node. Similarly, all the nodes in the right subtree have a value more than that of a root node. It is also known as an ordered binary tree.

- The searching operation is one of the most common operations performed in the binary search tree. This operation is performed to find whether a particular key exists in the tree or not.

- An insertion operation is performed to insert a new node with the given value in a binary search tree.

- The mirror image of the binary search tree means interchanging the right subtree with the left subtree at every node of the tree.

- Traversing is the process of visiting each node in the tree exactly once in a particular order. A tree can be traversed in various ways which are pre-order traversal, in-order traversal, and post-order traversal.

- The word "pre" in "pre-order" determines that the root node is accessed before accessing any other node in the tree. Hence, it is also known as a DLR traversal, that is, Data Left Right.

- The word "in" in "in-order" determines that the root node is accessed in between the left and the right subtrees. Hence, it is also known as an LDR traversal, that is, Left Data Right.

- The word "post" in "post-order" determines that the root node will be accessed last after the left and the right subtrees. Hence, it is also known as an LRD traversal, that is, Left Right Data.

- A binary tree can be constructed if we are given at least two of the traversal results, provided that one traversal should always be an in-order traversal and the second can be either a pre-order traversal or post-order traversal.

- An AVL is a self-balancing binary search tree. Every node in the AVL tree has a balance factor associated with it. The balance factor is calculated by subtracting the height of the right subtree from the height of the left subtree. Thus, a node with a balance factor of -1, 0, or 1 is said to be a height-balanced tree.

8.7 Exercises

8.7.1 Theory Questions

1. What is a tree? Discuss its various applications.

2. Differentiate between height and level in a tree.

3. Explain the concept of binary trees.

4. In what ways can a binary tree be represented in the computer's memory?

5. What do you understand by 2-T trees? Explain.

6. What do you mean by a binary search tree?

7. List the various operations performed on binary search trees.

8. What are complete binary trees?

9. How can a node be deleted from a binary search tree? Discuss all the cases in detail with an example.

10. Create a binary search tree by inserting the following keys – 76, 12, 56, 31, 199, 17, 40, 76, 75. Also, find the height of the binary search tree.

11. Create a binary search tree by performing following operations:

1. Insert 50, 34, 23, 87, 100, 67, 43, 51, 18, and 95.

2. Delete 100, 34 and 95, 50 from the binary search tree.

3. Find the smallest value in the binary search tree.

12. How can we find the mirror image of a binary search tree?

13. List the various traversal methods of a binary tree.

14. What do you understand by an AVL tree?

15. Explain the concept of balance factor in AVL trees.

16. List the advantages of an AVL tree.

17. Consider the following binary search tree and perform following operations:

1. Find the pre-order and post-order traversals of the tree.

2. Insert 25, 32, 50, 75, 87 in the tree.

3. Find the largest value in the tree.

4. Delete the root node.

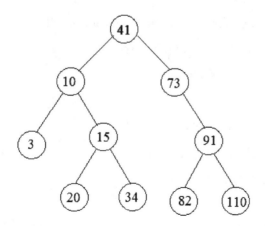

18. Give the linked representation of the binary search tree given above.

19. Construct a binary search tree of the word VIVEKANANDA. Find its pre-order, in-order, and post-order traversal.

20. Create an AVL tree by inserting the following keys – 50, 19, 59, 90, 100, 12, 10, and 150 into the tree.

21. Consider the following AVL search tree and perform various operations in it:

1. Insert 100, 58, 93, 40, and 7 into the tree.

2. Search 93 in the AVL tree.

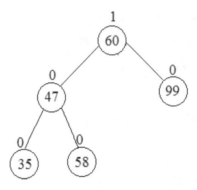

22. Discuss the various types of rotations performed in AVL trees.

23. Which one of the following i) AVL Trees or ii) Binary Search trees is better and why?

24. Consider the following tree and answer the following:

1. Determine the height of the tree.

2. Name the leaf nodes.

3. Siblings of C.

4. Level number of the node J.

5. Root node of the tree.

6. Left and right subtrees.

7. Depth of the tree.

8. Ancestors of E.

9. Descendants of H.

10. Path from node A to F.

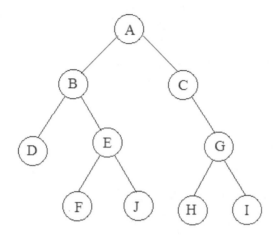

8.7.2 Programming Questions

1. Write a function to find the height of the binary search tree.

2. Write a program to insert and delete nodes from the binary search tree.

3. Write a program to show insertion in AVL trees.

4. Write a function to calculate the total number of nodes in the tree.

5. Write a program to traverse a binary search tree showing all the traversal methods.

6. Write a function to find the largest value in the binary search tree.

7. Write an algorithm showing post-order traversal of a binary search tree.

8. Write an algorithm to find the total number of internal nodes in the binary search tree.

9. Write a function to search a node in the binary search tree.

8.7.3 Multiple Choice Questions

1. The maximum height of a binary tree with n number of nodes is _____.

    A. 0

    B. n

    C. n+1

    D. n-1

2. The degree of a terminal node is always _____.

    A. 1

    B. 2

    C. 0

    D. 3

3. A binary tree is a tree in which _____.

    A. Every node must have two children

    B. Every node must have at least two children

    C. No node can have more than 2 children

    D. All of these

4. What is the post-order traversal of the binary search tree having pre-order traversal as DBAEFGCH and in-order traversal as BEAFDCHG?

    A. EFBAHGCD

    B. EFBAHCGD

    C. EFABHGCD

    D. EFABHCGD

5. How many rotations are required during the construction of an AVL tree if the following keys are to be added in the order given?

    36, 51, 39, 24, 29, 60, 79, 20, 28

    A. 3 Left rotations, 3 Right rotations

    B. 2 Left rotations, 2 Right rotations

C. 2 Left rotations, 3 Right rotations

D. 3 Left rotations, 2 Right rotations

6. A binary tree of height h has at least h nodes and at most _____ nodes.

    A. 2

    B. 2^h

    C. $2^h - 1$

    D. $2^h + 1$

7. How many distinct binary search trees can be created out of 4 distinct keys?

    A. 5

    B. 12

    C. 14

    D. 23

8. Nodes at the same level that also share same parent are called _____.

    A. Cousins

    B. Siblings

    C. Ancestors

    D. Descendants

9. The balance factor of a node is calculated by _____.

    A. $\text{Height}_{\text{left sub-tree}} - \text{Height}_{\text{Right sub-tree}}$

    B. $\text{Height}_{\text{Right sub-tree}} - \text{Height}_{\text{Left sub-tree}}$

    C. $\text{Height}_{\text{left sub-tree}} + \text{Height}_{\text{Right sub-tree}}$

    D. $\text{Height}_{\text{Right sub-tree}} + \text{Height}_{\text{Left sub-tree}}$

10. The following sequence is inserted into an empty binary search tree:

6 11 26 12 5 7 16 8 35

What is the type of traversal is given by:

6 5 11 7 26 8 12 35 16

A. Pre-order traversal

B. In-order traversal

C. Post-order traversal

D. None of these

11. In tree creation, which one will be the most suitable and effective data structure?

A. Stack

B. Linked list

C. Queue

D. Array

12. Binary tree can be represented as:

A. Linked List

B. Arrays

C. Both of the above

D. None of the above

13. A binary tree of n nodes has exactly n+1 edges?

A. True

B. False

C. Not possible to comment

14. The in-order traversal of a tree will yield a sorted listing of the elements of trees in

A. Binary heaps

B. Binary trees

C. Binary search trees

D. All of these

15. Which is the nearest ancestor node on the path from the root node to the newly inserted node of the AVL tree having balance factor -1, 0, or 1?

A. Parent node

B. Child node

C. Root node

D. Critical node

MULTI-WAY SEARCH TREES

In This Chapter

9.1 Introduction

We have already studied binary search trees in which we discussed that in a binary search tree every node contains three parts, that is, an information part and two pointers LEFT and RIGHT which respectively point to the left and right subtrees. The same concept is used for multi-way search trees. *An M-way search tree is a tree which contains (M – 1) values per node*. It also has M subtrees. In an M-way search tree, M is called the degree of the node. For example, if the value of M = 3 in an M-way search tree, then the tree will contain two values per node and it will have three subtrees. When an M-way search tree is not empty, it has following properties:

1. Each node in an M-way search tree is of the following structure:

n	P_0	K_0	P_1	K_1	P_2	K_2 – – – – – –	P_{n-1}	K_{n-1}	P_n

Where $P_0, P_1, P_2, \ldots P_n$ are the pointers to the node's subtrees and $K_0, K_1, K_2, \ldots K_n$ are the key values stored in the node.

2. The key values in a node are stored in ascending order, that is, $K_i < K_{i+1}$, where $i = 0, 1, 2, \ldots n-2$.

3. All the key values stored in the left subtree are always less than the root node.

4. All the key values stored in the right subtree are always greater than the root node.

5. The subtrees pointed to by P_i for $i = 0, 1, 2, \ldots n$ are also M-way search trees.

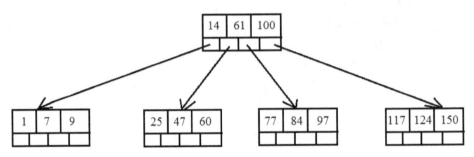

FIGURE 9.1. M-way search tree of order 4.

9.2 B–Trees

A B-tree is a specialized multi-way tree which is widely used for disk access. The B-tree was developed in 1970 by Rudolf Bayer and Ed McCreight. In a B-tree each node may contain large number of keys. A B-tree is designed to store a large number of keys in a single node so that the height remains relatively small. A B-tree of order m has all the properties of a multi-way search tree. In addition, it has the following properties:

1. All leaf nodes are at the bottom level or at the same level.

2. Every node in a B-tree can have at most m children.

3. The root node can have at least two children if it is not a leaf node, and it can obviously have no children if it is a leaf node.

4. Each node in a B-tree can have at least (m/2) children except the root node and the leaf node.

5. Each leaf node must contain at least ceil [(m/2) – 1] keys.

For example – A B-tree of order 5 can have at least ceil [5/2] = 3 children and ceil [(5/2) – 1] = 2 keys. Obviously, the maximum number of children a node can have is 5. Each leaf node must contain at least 2 keys.

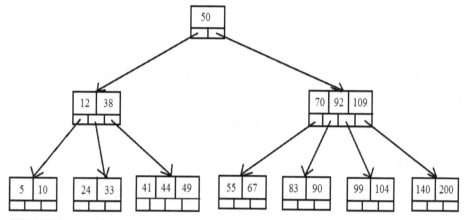

FIGURE 9.2. B-tree of order 4.

Practical Application:

In database programs, the data is too large to fit in memory; therefore, it is stored in secondary storage, that is, tapes or disks.

9.3 Operations on a B-Tree

A B-tree stores sorted data, and we can perform various operations on it which are:

- Inserting a new element in a B-tree

- Deleting an element from a B-tree

So, let's discuss both these operations in detail.

9.3.1 Insertion in a B-Tree

First of all, insertions in a B-tree are done at the leaf-node level. The following are the steps to insert an element in a B-tree:

Step 1 – In Step 1, we will search the B-tree to find the leaf node where the new value or key is to be inserted.

Step 2 – Now, if the leaf node is full, that is, it already contains (m – 1) keys, then follow these steps:

i. Insert the new key into the existing set of keys in order.

ii. Now, the node is split into two halves.

iii. Finally, push the middle (median) element upward to its parent node. Also, if the parent node is full, then split the parent node by following these steps.

Step 3 – If the leaf node is not full, that is, it contains (m – 1) keys, then insert the new key into the node, keeping the elements of the node in order.

Frequently Asked Questions

Q. Construct a B-tree of order 5 and insert the following values into it:

Values to be inserted – B, N, G, A, H, E, J, Q, M, D, V, L, T, Z

Answer.

1. Since order = 5, thus we can store at least 3 values and at most 4 values in a single node. Hence, we will insert B, N, G, A into the B-tree in sorted order.

FIGURE 9.3 (a)

2. Now H is to be inserted between G and N, so now the order will be A B G H N, which is not possible, as at most 4 values can be accommodated in a single node. So now we will split the node and the middle element G will become the root node.

FIGURE 9.3 (b)

3. Now we will insert E J and Q into the B-tree.

FIGURE 9.3 (c)

4. M is to be inserted into the right subtree. But at most 4 values can be stored in the node, so now we will push the middle element, that is, M, into the root node. Thus, the node is split into two halves.

FIGURE 9.3 (d)

5. Now we will insert D V L T into the tree.

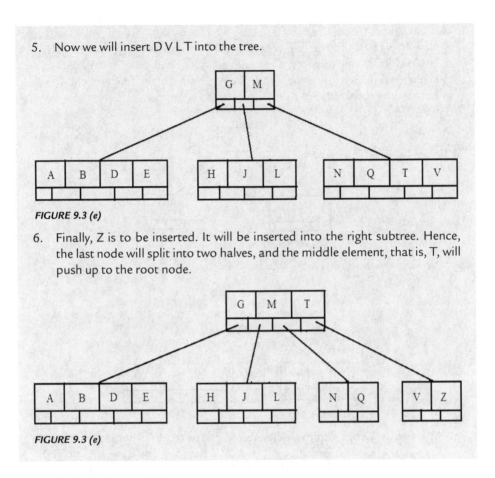

FIGURE 9.3 (e)

6. Finally, Z is to be inserted. It will be inserted into the right subtree. Hence, the last node will split into two halves, and the middle element, that is, T, will push up to the root node.

FIGURE 9.3 (e)

9.3.2 Deletion in a B-Tree

Deletion of keys in a B-tree also first requires traversal in the B-tree, that is, after reaching a particular node, we can come across two cases which are:

1. Node is a leaf node.

2. Node is not a leaf node.

Now, let us discuss both these cases in detail.

a. Node is a leaf node

In this case, if the node has more than minimum number of keys, then deletion can be done very easily. But if the node has a minimum number of keys, then first we will check the number of keys in the adjacent leaf node.

If the number of keys in the adjacent node is more than the minimum number of keys, then the first key of the adjacent leaf node will go to the parent node, and the key present in the parent node will be combined together in a single node. Now if the parent node also has less than the minimum number of keys, then the same steps will be repeated until we get a node which has more than the minimum number of keys present in it.

b. Node is not a leaf node

In this case the key from the node is deleted, and its place will be occupied by either its successor or predecessor key. If both predecessor and successor nodes have keys less than the minimum number, then the keys of the successor and predecessor are combined.

For Example – Consider a B-tree of order 5.

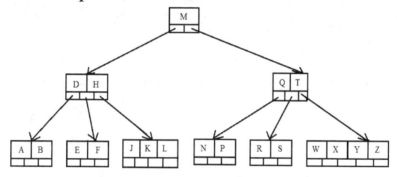

FIGURE 9.4(a)

1. Delete J from the tree. J is in the leaf node, so it is simply deleted from the B-tree.

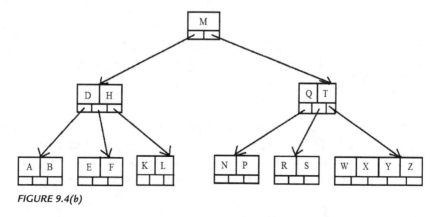

FIGURE 9.4(b)

2. Now T is to be deleted but it is not the leaf node, so we will replace T with its successor, that is, W. Hence, T is deleted.

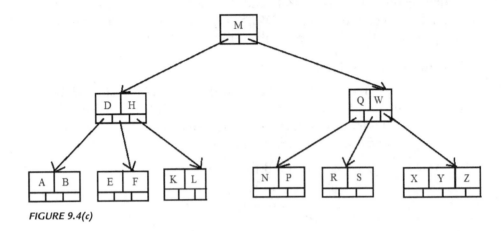

FIGURE 9.4(c)

3. Now delete R; in this case we will borrow keys from the adjacent leaf node.

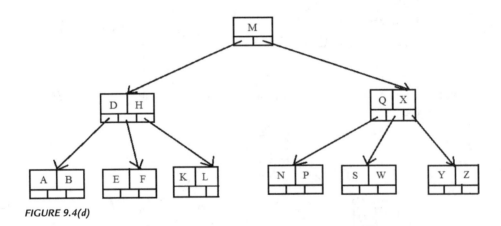

FIGURE 9.4(d)

4. Now we want to delete E. We will also in this case borrow keys from an adjacent node. But we can see that there are no free keys in an adjacent node, so the leaf node has to be combined with one of the two siblings. This includes moving down the parent's key that was between those two leaves.

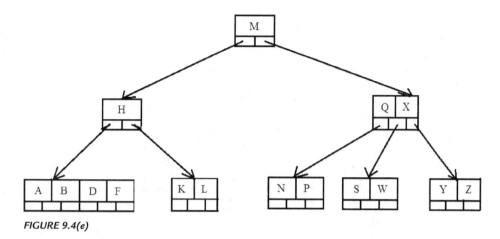

FIGURE 9.4(e)

But we can see that H is still unstable according to the definition. Therefore, the final tree after all deletions is shown as follows:

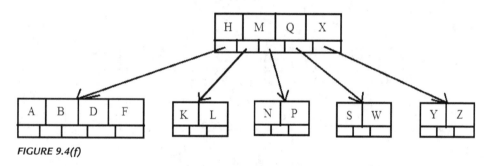

FIGURE 9.4(f)

Frequently Asked Questions

Q. Consider the following B-tree of order 5 and insert 81, 7, 49, 61 and 30 in it.

Answer.

1. Insert 81

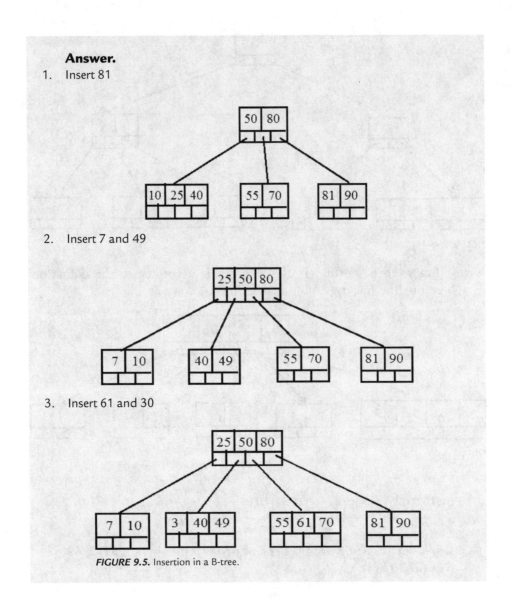

2. Insert 7 and 49

3. Insert 61 and 30

FIGURE 9.5. Insertion in a B-tree.

Frequently Asked Questions

Q. Consider the following B-tree of order 5 and delete the values 95, 200, 176, and 70 from it.

Answer.

1. Delete 95

2. Delete 200

3. Delete 176

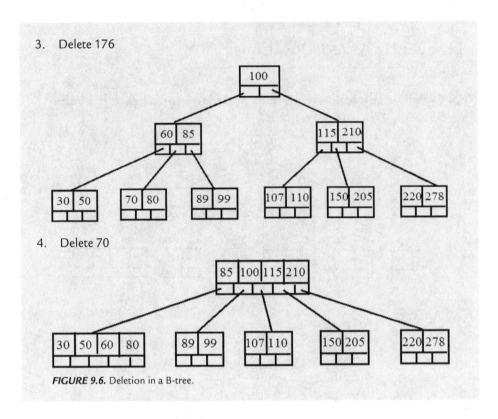

4. Delete 70

FIGURE 9.6. Deletion in a B-tree.

9.4 Application of a B-Tree

The main application of a B-tree is the organization of large amount of data or huge collection of records into a file structure. A B-tree should search the records very efficiently and all the operations such as insertion, deletion, searching, and so on should be done very efficiently; therefore, the organization of records should be very good.

9.5 B+ Trees

A *B+ tree is a variant of a B-tree* which also stores sorted data like a B-tree. The structure of a B-tree is the standard organization for indexes in database systems. Multilevel indexing is done in a B+ tree, that is, leaf nodes constitute a dense index while non-leaf nodes constitute a sparse index. A B+ tree is a slightly different data structure which allows sequential processing of data and stores all the data in the lowest level of the tree. A B-tree can store both records and keys in its interior nodes, while a B+ tree stores all the records in the leaf nodes of the tree and the keys in the interior nodes. In a B+ tree, the leaf nodes are linked to one another like a linked list. It helps in making queries simpler and more efficient. A B+ tree is usually used to store large amounts of data which cannot be stored in the main memory. Hence, in a B+ tree the leaf nodes are stored in the secondary storage while the internal nodes are stored in the main memory.

In a B+ tree, all the internal nodes are called index nodes because they store the index values. Similarly, *all the external nodes are called data nodes* because they store the keys. A B+ tree is always balanced and is very efficient for searching of data as all the data is stored in the leaf nodes. Various advantages of a B+ tree are as follows:

a. A B+ tree is always balanced and the height of the tree always remains less.

b. All the leaf nodes are linked to one another, which make it very efficient.

c. The leaf nodes are also linked to the nodes at an upper level; thus, it can be easily used for a wide range of search queries.

d. The records can be fetched in equal number of disk access.

e. The records can be accessed either sequentially or randomly.

f. Searching of data becomes very easy as all the data are stored only in leaf nodes.

g. Similarly, deletion is also very simple as it will only take place in the leaf nodes.

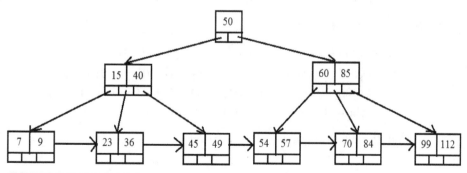

FIGURE 9.7. B+ tree of order 3.

9.6 Summary

- An M-way search tree has M – 1 values per node and M sub trees. M is called the degree of the node.

- A B-tree is a specialized multi-way tree which is widely used for disk access. A B-tree was developed in 1970 and was developed by Rudolf Bayer and Ed McCreight.

- A B-tree of order m has all the properties of a multi-way search tree.

- The main application of a B-tree is the organization of large amount of data or huge collection of records into a file structure.

- A B+ tree is a variant of a B-tree which also stores sorted data like a B-tree. The structure of a B-tree is the standard organization for indexes in database systems. A B+ tree is a slightly different data structure which allows sequential processing of data and stores all the data in the lowest level of the tree.

9.7 Exercises

9.7.1 Review Questions

1. Define

   A. M-way search tree

   B. B-tree

   C. B+ tree

2. Write a difference between B-trees and B+ trees.

3. Give some important applications of a B-tree.

4. Write down some advantages of a B+ tree over a B-tree.

5. Create a B-tree of order 5 on inserting the keys 10, 20, 50, 60 40, 80, 100, 70, 130, 90, 30, 120, 140, 25, 35, 160, 180 inserted in a left-to-right sequence. Show the trees on deleting 190 and 60.

6. Explain the insertion of a node in a B-tree.

7. Explain B+ tree indexing with the help of an example.

8. What do you know about B-trees? Write the steps to create a B-tree. Construct an M-way search tree of order 4 and insert the values 34, 45, 98, 1, 23, 41, 78, 100, 234, 122, 199, 10, 40.

9. Why do we always prefer a higher value of m in a B-tree? Explain.

10. Are B-trees of order 2 full binary trees? Explain.

9.7.2 Multiple Choice Questions

1. B+ trees are preferred to binary trees in databases because:

    A. Disk capacities are greater than memory capacities.

    B. Disk access is much slower than memory access.

    C. Disk data transfer rates are much less than the memory data transfer rates.

    D. Disks are more reliable than memory.

2. In an M-way search tree, M stands for _____.

    A. Degree of the node

    B. External nodes

    C. Internal nodes

    D. None of these

3. A B- A B- tree of order 4 is built. What is the maximum number of keys that a node may accommodate before splitting operations takes place?

    A. 5

    B. 2

    C. 4

    D. 3

4. In a B-tree of order m, every node has at the most _____ children.

   A. M + 1

   B. M – 1

   C. M/2

   D. M

5. Which is the best data structure to search the keys in less time?

   A. B tree

   B. M-way search tree

   C. B+ tree

   D. Binary search tree

6. The best case of searching a value in a binary search tree is:

   A. $O(n^2)$

   B. $O(\log n)$

   C. $O(n)$

   D. $O(n \log n)$

7. External nodes are also called _____.

   A. Index nodes

   B. Data nodes

   C. Value nodes

   D. None of the above

8. A B-tree of order 5 can store at most how many keys?

   A. 3

   B. 4

   C. 5

   D. 6

9. Does a B+ tree store redundant keys?

    A. False

    B. True

    C. Not possible to comment

10. A B-tree of order 3 can store at least how many keys?

    A. 0

    B. 1

    C. 2

    D. 3

HASHING

In This Chapter

- Introduction
- Summary
- Exercises

10.1 Introduction

In the previous chapter, we discussed three types of searching techniques: linear search, binary search, and interpolation search. Linear search has a running time complexity of O(n), whereas binary search has a running time proportional to O(log n), where n is equal to the number of elements in the array. Although searching algorithms discussed within Chapter 6 are efficient. However, their search time is dependent on the number of elements in the array, and none of them can search an element within the constant time equal to O(1). But it is very difficult to achieve in all the searching algorithms like linear search, binary search, and so on, as all these algorithms are dependent on the number of elements present in the array. Also, there are many comparisons involved while searching for an element using the previous searching algorithms. Therefore, our primary need is to search for the element in a constant time along with less key comparisons. Now, let us take an example. Suppose there is an array of size N and all the keys to be stored in the array are unique and also are in the range 0 to N-1.

Now, we will store all the records in the array based on the key where array index and keys are same. Thus, in that case we can access the records in a constant time along with no key comparisons involved in it. This can be further explained by the following figure:

arr[0]	arr[1]	arr[2]	arr[3]	arr[4]	arr[5]	arr[6]	arr[7]	arr[8]	arr[9]
	1		3	4		6		8	

FIGURE 10.1. An array.

In the previous figure, there is an array containing six elements. Note that the keys and the array index are the same, that is, the record with the key value 3 can be directly accessed by array index arr[3]. Similarly, all the records can be accessed through key values and the array index. Thus, this can be done by hashing, where we will convert the key into an array index and store the records in the array. This can be done as follows:

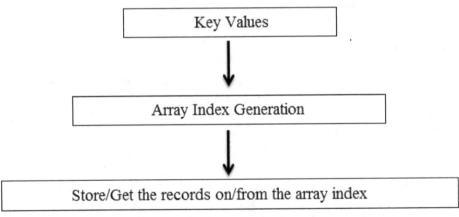

FIGURE 10.2. Array index generation using hashing

The process of array index generation uses a hash function which is used to convert the keys into an array index. The array in which such records are stored is known as a hash table.

Practical Application:

1. A simple real-life example is when we search for a word in the dictionary; then we find the definition or meaning with the help of a key and its index.

2. Driver's license numbers and insurance card numbers are created using hashing from the data item that never changes, that is, date of birth, name, and so on.

Frequently Asked Questions

Q. Explain the term hashing.

Answer.

Hashing is the process of mapping keys to their appropriate locations in the hash table. It is the most effective technique of searching the values in an array or in a hash table.

10.1.1 Difference between Hashing and Direct Addressing

In direct addressing, we store the key at the same address as the value of the key as shown in Figure 10.3. However, in hashing, as shown in Figure 10.4, the address of the key is determined by using a mathematical function known as a hash function. The hash function will operate on the key to determine the address of key. Direct addressing may result in a more random distribution of the key throughout the memory, and hence sometimes leads to more wastage of space when compared with hashing.

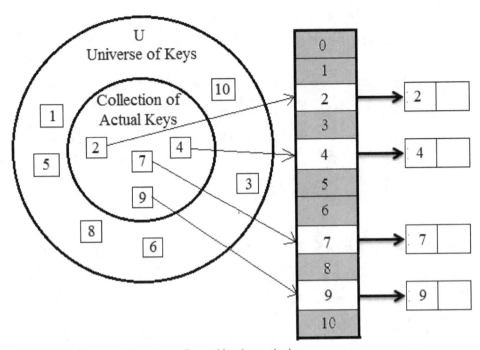

FIGURE 10.3. Mapping of keys using a direct addressing method.

10.1.2 Hash Tables

A hash table is a data structure which supports one of the efficient searching techniques, that is, hashing. A hash table is an array in which the data is accessed through a special index called a key. In a hash table, keys are mapped to the array positions by a hash function. A hash function is a function, or we can say that it is a mathematical formula, which when applied to a key, produces an integer which is used as an index to find a key in the hash table. Thus, a value stored in a hash table can be searched in $O(1)$ time with the help of a hash function. The main idea behind a hash table is to establish a direct mapping between the keys and the indices of the array.

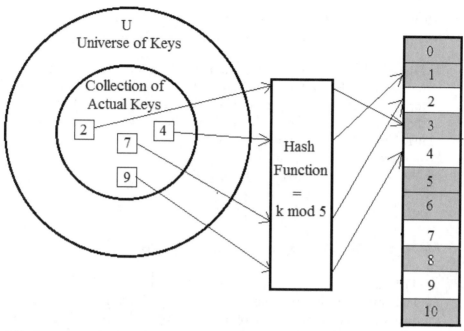

FIGURE 10.4. Mapping of keys to the hash table using hashing.

10.1.3 Hash Functions

A hash function is a mathematical formula which when applied to a key, produces an integer which is used as an index to find a key in the hash table.

Characteristics of the Hash Function

There are four main characteristics of hash functions which are:

1. The hash function uses all the input data.

2. The hash function must generate different hash values.

3. The hash value is fully determined by the data being hashed.

4. The hash function must distribute the keys uniformly across the entire hash table.

Different Types of Hash Functions

In this section, we will discuss some of the common hash functions:

1. **Division Method** – In the division method, a key k is mapped into one of the m slots by taking the remainder of k divided by m. In simple terms, we can say that this method divides an integer, say x, by m and then uses the remainder so obtained. It is the simplest method of hashing. The hash function is given by:

$$h(k) = k \bmod m$$

Address   Key   m no. of slots

For Example, if m = 5 and the key k = 10, then h(k) = 2. Thus, the division method works very fast as it requires only a single division operation. Although this method is good for any value of m, consider that if m is an even number then h(k) is even when the value of k is even, and similarly h(k) is odd when the value of k is odd. Therefore, if the even and odd keys are almost equal, then there will be no problem. But if there is a larger number of even keys, then the division method is not good as it will not distribute the keys uniformly in the hash table. Also, we avoid certain values of m; that is, m should not be a power of 2, because if h(k) = k mod 2^x, then h(k) will extract the lowest x bits of k. The main drawback of the division method is that many consecutive keys map to consecutive hash values respectively, which means that consecutive array locations will be occupied, and hence there will be an effect on the performance.

Frequently Asked Questions

Q. Given a hash table of 50 memory locations, calculate the hash values of keys 20 and 75 using the division method.

Answer.

m = 50, k1 = 10, k2 = 75 hash values are calculated as:

h(10) = 10 % 50 = 10

h(75) = 75 % 50 = 25

2. Mid Square Method – In the mid square method, we will calculate the square of the given key. After getting the number, we will extract some digits from the middle of that number as an address.

For Example, if key k = 5025, then k^2 = 25250625. Thus, h(5025) = 50.

This method works very well as all the digits of the key contribute to the output, that is, all the digits contribute in producing the middle digits. Also in this method, the same r digits must be chosen from all the keys.

Frequently Asked Questions

Q. Given a hash table of 100 memory locations, calculate the hash values of keys 2045 and 1357 using the mid square method.

Answer.

Now, there are 100 memory locations where indices will be from 0 to 99. Hence, only two digits will be taken to map the keys. So, the value of r is equal to 2.

k_1 = 2045, k^2 = 4182025, h(2045) = 20

k_2 = 1357, k^2 = 1841449, h(1357) = 14

Note: The 3rd & 4th digits are chosen to start from the right.

3. Folding Method – In the folding method, we will break the key into pieces such that each piece has the same number of digits except the last one, which may have fewer digits as compared to other pieces. Now, these individual pieces are added. We will ignore the carry if it exists. Hence, the hash value is formed.

For Example, if m = 100 and the key k = 12345678, then the indices will vary from 0 to 99 and thus, each piece of the key must have two digits. Therefore, the given key will be broken into four pieces, that is, 12, 34, 56, and 78. Now we will add all these, that is, 12 + 34 + 56 + 78 = 180. Thus, the hash value will be 80 (ignore the last carry).

Frequently Asked Questions

Q. Given a hash table of 100 memory locations, calculate the hash values of keys 2486 and 179 using the folding method.

Answer.

Now, there are 100 memory locations where indices will be from 0 to 99. Hence, each piece of the key must have 2 digits.

$h(2486) = 24 + 86 = 110$

$h(2486) = 10$ (ignore the last carry)

$h(179) = 17 + 9 = 26$

$h(179) = 26$

10.1.4 Collision

A collision is a situation which occurs when a hash function maps two different keys to a single/same location in the hash table. Suppose we want to store a record at one location. Now, another record cannot be stored at the same location as it is obvious that two records cannot be stored at the same location. Thus, there are methods to solve this problem, which are called collision resolution techniques.

10.1.5 Collision Resolution Techniques

As already discussed, collision resolution techniques are used to overcome the problem of collision in hashing. There are two popular methods which are used for resolving collisions:

1. Collision Resolution by Chaining Method

2. Collision Resolution by Open Addressing Method

Now, we will discuss these methods in detail.

10.1.5.1 Chaining Method

In the chaining method, a chain of elements is maintained which have the same hash address. The hash table here behaves like an array of pointers. Each location in the hash table stores a pointer to the linked list, which contains all the key elements that were hashed to that location. For example, location 5 in the hash table points to the key values that hashed to location 5. If no key value hashes to location 5, then in that case location 5 will contain NULL. The figure given as follows shows how the key values are mapped to the hash table and also how they are stored in the linked list.

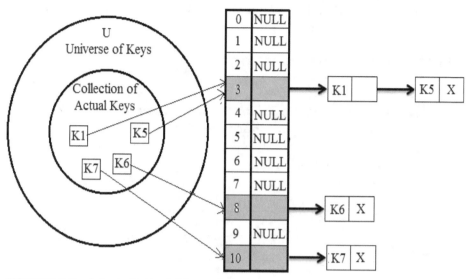

FIGURE 10.5. Keys being hashed by chaining method.

Operations on a Chained Hash Table

1. **Insertion in a Chained Hash Table** – The process of inserting an element is quite simple. First, we get the hash value from the hash function which will map to the hash table. After mapping, the element is inserted in the linked list. The running time complexity of inserting an element in a chained hash table is O(1).

2. **Deletion from a Chained Hash Table** – The process of deleting an element from the chained hash table is same as we did in the singly linked list. First, we will perform a search operation, and then the delete operation as in the case of the singly linked list is performed. The running time complexity of deleting an element from a chained hash table is O(m), where m is the number of elements present in the linked list at that location.

3. **Searching in a Chained Hash Table** – The process of searching for an element in a chained hash table is also very simple. First, we will get the hash value of the key by the hash function in the hash table. Then we will search for the element in the linked list. The running time complexity of searching for an element in a chained hash table is O(m), where m is the number of elements present in the linked list at that location.

Frequently Asked Questions

Q. Insert the keys 4, 9, 20, 35, and 49 in a chained hash table of 10 memory locations. Use hash function h(k) = k mod m.

Answer.
Initially, the hash table is given as:

0	NULL
1	NULL
2	NULL
3	NULL
4	NULL
5	NULL
6	NULL
7	NULL
8	NULL
9	NULL

Now, we will insert 4 in the hash table.

Step 1:
Key to be inserted = 4

h(4) = 4 mod 10

h(4) = 4

Now, we will create a linked list for location 4, and the key element 4 is stored in it.

0	NULL
1	NULL
2	NULL
3	NULL
4		→	4	X
5	NULL
6	NULL
7	NULL
8	NULL
9	NULL

Step 2:

Key to be inserted = 9

h(9) = 9 mod 10

h(9) = 9

Now, we will create a linked list for location 9, and the key element 9 is stored in it.

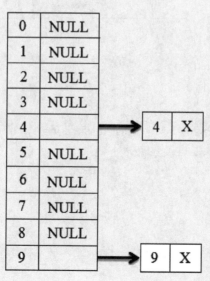

Step 3:

Key to be inserted = 20

$h(20) = 20 \bmod 10$

$h(20) = 2$

Now, we will create a linked list for location 2, and the key element 20 is stored in it.

Step 4:

Key to be inserted = 35

$h(35) = 35 \bmod 10$

$h(35) = 5$

Now, we will create a linked list for location 5, and the key element 35 is stored in it.

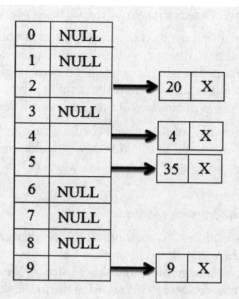

Step 5:

Key to be inserted = 49

h(49) = 49 mod 10

h(49) = 9

Now, we will insert 49 at the end of the linked list of location 9.

Advantages and Disadvantages of the Chained Method

The main advantage of this method is that it completely resolves the problem of collision. It remains effective even when the key elements to be stored in the hash table are higher than the number of locations in the hash table. However, it is quite obvious that with the increase in the number of key elements, the performance of this method will decrease.

The disadvantage of this method is the wastage of storage space as the key elements are stored in the linked list; in addition, the pointers are required for each element to get accessed, which in turn are consuming more space.

10.1.5.2 Open Addressing Method

In the open addressing method, all the elements are stored in the hash table itself. There is no need to provide the pointers in this method, which is the biggest advantage of this method. Once a collision takes place, open addressing computes new locations using the probe sequence, and the next element or next record is stored on that location. Probing is the process of examining the memory locations in the hash table. When we perform the insertion operation in the open addressing method, we first successively probe/examine the hash table until we find an empty slot in which the new key can be inserted. The open addressing method can be implemented using the following:

- Linear Probing
- Quadratic Probing
- Double Hashing

Now, let us discuss all of them in detail.

Linear Probing

Linear Probing is the simplest approach to resolving the problem of collision in hashing. In this method, if a key is already stored at a location generated by the hash function $h(k)$, then the situation can be resolved by the following hash function:

$$h'(k) = (h(k) + i) \bmod m$$

$$\text{where } h(k) = k \bmod m$$

$$i = Probe\ no. = 0,\ 1,\ 2,\ 3\ldots\ldots\ldots(m-1)$$

$$m = no.\ of\ slots$$

Now, let us understand the working of this technique. For a given key k, first the location generated by (h(k) + 0) mod m is probed, because for the first time i = 0. If the location generated is free, then the key is stored in it. Otherwise, the second probe is generated for i = 1 given by the hash function (h(k) + 1) mod m. Similarly, if the location generated is free, then the key is stored in it; otherwise, subsequent probes are generated such as (h(k) + 2) mod m, (h(k) + 3) mod m, and so on, until we find a free location.

Frequently Asked Questions

Q. Given keys k = 13, 25, 14, and 35, map these keys into a hash table of size m = 5 using linear probing.

Answer.
Initially, the hash table is given as:

0	1	2	3	4
NULL	NULL	NULL	NULL	NULL

Step 1:
i = 0

Key to be inserted = 13

h'(k) = (k mod m + i) mod m

h'(13) = (13 % 5 + 0) % 5

h'(13) = (3 + 0) % 5

h'(13) = 3 % 5 = 3

Now, since location T[3] is free, 13 is inserted at location T[3].

0	1	2	3	4
NULL	NULL	NULL	13	NULL

Step 2:

i = 0

Key to be inserted = 25

h'(25) = (25 % 5 + 0) % 5

h'(25) = (0 + 0) % 5

h'(13) = 0 % 5 = 0

Now, since location T[0] is free, 25 is inserted at location T[0].

0	1	2	3	4
25	NULL	NULL	13	NULL

Step 3:

i = 0

Key to be inserted = 14

h'(14) = (14 % 5 + 0) % 5

h'(14) = (4 + 0) % 5

h'(14) = 4 % 5 = 4

Now, since location T[4] is free, 14 is inserted at location T[4].

0	1	2	3	4
25	NULL	NULL	13	14

Step 4:

i = 0

Key to be inserted = 35

h'(35) = (35 % 5 + 0) % 5

h'(35) = (0 + 0) % 5

h'(35) = 0 % 5 = 0

Now, since location T[0] is not free, the next probe sequence, that is, i = 1, is computed as:

i = 1

h'(35) = (35 % 5 + 1) % 5

h'(35) = (0 + 1) % 5

h'(35) = 1 % 5 = 1

Now, since location T[1] is free, 35 is inserted at location T[1].

Thus, the final hash table is shown as:

0	1	2	3	4
25	35	NULL	13	14

Write a program to show the linear probing technique of the collision resolution method.

```c
# include<stdio.h>
# include<conio.h>
# define SIZE 50

intarr[SIZE];
void linear( int,int[]);
void lprob(int k, intarr[SIZE]);
void disp(intarr[SIZE]);
void main( )
{
  int i, k , choice ;
  clrscr();
  for (i=0; i<SIZE; i++)
    {
      arr[i]= '\0';
      do
        {
          printf("\n\t  MENU");
          printf("\n 1. Insert Keys");
          printf("\n 2. Search Keys");
          printf("\n 3. Display Keys");
          printf("\n 4. Exit ");
```

```
        printf("\n Select Operation ");
        scanf("%d" ,&choice);
        switch(choice)
          {
            Case1: do
              {
                printf("\n Enter values of key ");
                scanf( "%d", &k);
                if(k!=-1)
                  {
                    linear(k,arr);
                  }
                while(k!=1);
                disp(arr);
                break;

                case2:
                printf(" \n enter key value to search ");
                scanf("%d",&k);
                lprob(k, arr);
                break;

                case3:
                disp(arr);
                break;
              }
          }
        while(choice!=4);
      }
    }
}

void linear(int k, intarr[SIZE])
{
  int position ;
  position = k%SIZE;
  while(arr[position]!= '\0')
    {
      position = ++ position %SIZE;
      arr[position] = k;
    }
}
```

```
void lprob(int k, intarr[SIZE])
{
  int position ;
  position = k%SIZE;
  while ((arr[position] != k)&& (arr[position] != '\0'))
  position = ++ position %SIZE;
  if(arr[position]!= '\0')
  printf("\n successfully searched at %d", position);
  else
  printf("\n unsuccessfull search");
}

void disp(intarr[SIZE])
{
  int i ;
  printf("\n List of keys :\n");
  for(i=0; i<SIZE; i++)
  printf("%d" , arr[i]);
}
```

Advantages and Disadvantages of Linear Probing

Linear probing is a very good technique, as the algorithm provides good memory caching through good locality of address. But the main disadvantage of this method is that it results in clustering. Due to clustering, there is a higher risk of collisions taking place. Also, the time required for searching also increases with the size of the clusters. Now, we can say that the higher the number of collisions, the higher the number of probes are required to find a vacant location, and the performance is lessened. This is known as primary clustering. We can avoid this clustering by using other techniques such as quadratic probing and double hashing.

Quadratic Probing

Quadratic probing is another approach to resolving the problem of collision in hashing. In this method, if a key is already stored at a location generated by the hash function h(k), then the situation can be resolved by the following hash function:

$$h'(k) = (h(k) + c_1 i + c_2 i^2) \bmod m$$
$$\text{where } h(k) = k \bmod m$$
$$i = Probe \ no. = 0, 1, 2, 3.........(m-1)$$
$$c_1, c_2 = consonants$$
$$(c_1, c_2 \ should \ not \ be \ equal \ to \ zero)$$

The quadratic probing method is better than linear probing, as it terminates the phenomenon of primary clustering because of its searching speed; that is, it is doing a quadratic search. For a given key k, first the location generated by $(h(k) + 0 + 0) \bmod m$ is probed because for the first time $i = 0$. If the location generated is free, then the key is stored in it. Otherwise, subsequent positions probed are offset by the amounts/factors that depend in a quadratic manner on the probe number i. The quadratic probing method works better than linear probing, but to maximize the use of the hash table, the values of m, c_1, and c_2 are constrained.

Frequently Asked Questions

Q. **Given keys k = 25, 13, 14, and 35, map these keys into a hash table of size m = 5 using quadratic probing with c_1 = 1 and c_2 = 3.**

Answer.
Initially, the hash table is given as follows:

0	1	2	3	4
NULL	NULL	NULL	NULL	NULL

Step 1:
i = 0

c1 = 1, c2 = 3

Key to be inserted = 25

$h'(k) = (k \bmod m + c_1 i + c_2 i^2) \bmod m$

$h'(25) = (25 \% 5 + 1 \times 0 + 3 \times (0)^2) \% 5$

$h'(25) = (0 + 0) \% 5$

$h'(13) = 0 \% 5 = 0$

Now, since location T[0] is free, 25 is inserted at location T[0].

0	1	2	3	4
25	NULL	NULL	NULL	NULL

Step 2:

$i = 0$

$c_1 = 1, c_2 = 3$

Key to be inserted = 13

$h'(13) = (13 \% 5 + 1 \times 0 + 3 \times (0)^2) \% 5$

$h'(13) = (3 + 0) \% 5$

$h'(13) = 3 \% 5 = 3$

Now, since location T[3] is free, 13 is inserted at location T[3].

0	1	2	3	4
25	NULL	NULL	13	NULL

Step 3:

$i = 0$

$c_1 = 1, c_2 = 3$

Key to be inserted = 14

$h'(14) = (14 \% 5 + 1 \times 0 + 3 \times (0)^2) \% 5$

$h'(14) = (4 + 0) \% 5$

$h'(14) = 4 \% 5 = 4$

Now, since location T[4] is free, 14 is inserted at location T[4].

0	1	2	3	4
25	NULL	NULL	13	14

Step 4:

$i = 0$

$c_1 = 1, c_2 = 3$

Key to be inserted = 35

$h'(35) = (35 \% 5 + 1 \times 0 + 3 \times (0)^2) \% 5$

$h'(35) = (0 + 0) \% 5$

$h'(35) = 0 \% 5 = 0$

Now, since location T[0] is not free, the next probe sequence, that is, $i = 1$, is computed as:

$i = 1$

$h'(35) = (35 \% 5 + 1 \times 1 + 3 \times (1)^2) \% 5$

$h'(35) = (0 + 1 + 3) \% 5$

$h'(35) = 4 \% 5 = 4$

Again, since location T[4] is not free, the next probe sequence, that is, $i = 2$, is computed as:

$i = 2$

$h'(35) = (35 \% 5 + 1 \times 2 + 3 \times (2)^2) \% 5$

$h'(35) = (0 + 2 + 12) \% 5$

$h'(35) = 14 \% 5 = 4$

Again, since location T[4] is not free, the next probe sequence, that is, $i = 3$, is computed as:

$i = 3$

$h'(35) = (35 \% 5 + 1 \times 3 + 3 \times (3)^2) \% 5$

$h'(35) = (0 + 3 + 27) \% 5$

$h'(35) = 30 \% 5 = 0$

Again, since location T[0] is not free, the next probe sequence, that is, $i = 4$, is computed as:

$i = 4$

$h'(35) = (35 \% 5 + 1 \times 4 + 3 \times (4)^2) \% 5$

$h'(35) = (0 + 4 + 48) \% 5$

$h'(35) = 52 \% 5 = 2$

Now, since location T[2] is free, 35 is inserted at location T[2].

Thus, the final hash table is shown as:

0	1	2	3	4
25	NULL	35	13	14

Write a program to show the quadratic probing technique of the collision resolution method.

```c
# include<stdio.h>
# include<conio.h>
# define SIZE 50

intarr[SIZE];
void quad( int ,int[]);
void qprob(int k, intarr[SIZE]);
void disp(intarr[SIZE);
void main( )
{
  int i, k , choice ;
  clrscr();
  for (i=0; i<SIZE; i++)
    {
      arr[i]= '\0';
      do
        {
          printf("\n\t MENU");
          printf("\n 1. Insert Keys");
          printf("\n 2. Search Keys");
          printf("\n 3. Display Keys");
          printf("\n 4. Exit ");
          printf("\n Select Operation ");
          scanf("%d" ,&choice);
          switch(choice)
            {
              Case1:
              do
                {
```

```
              printf("\n Enter values of key ");
              scanf( "%d", &k);
              if(k!=-1)
                {
                   quad(k,arr);
                }
              while(k!=1);
              disp(arr);
              break;

              case2:
              printf("\n enter value of search key ");
              scanf("%d",&k);
              qprob(k, arr);
              break;

              case3:
              disp(arr);
              break;
            }
        }
      while(choice!=4);
        }
    }
}

void quad(int k, intarr[SIZE])
{
  int position, i=1;
  position = k%SIZE;
  while(arr[position]!= '\0')
    {
      position = (k%SIZE + i*i) % SIZE;
      i++;
    }
  arr[position] = k;
}

void qprob(int k, intarr[SIZE])
{
  int position ;
```

```
  position = k%SIZE;
  while ((arr[position] != k)&& (arr[position] !=-1))
  position = ++ position %SIZE;
  if(arr[position]!= '\0')
  printf("\n successfully searched at %d", position);
  else
  printf("\n unsuccessfull search");
}

void disp(intarr[SIZE])
{
  int i ;
  printf("\n List of keys :\n");
  for(i=0; i<SIZE; i++)
  printf("%d" , arr[i]);
}
```

Advantages and Disadvantages of Quadratic Probing

As already discussed previously, one of the biggest advantages of quadratic probing is that it eliminates the phenomenon of primary clustering. On the contrary, one of the major disadvantages of this method is that a sequence of successive probes may only cover some portion of the hash table, and this portion may be quite small. Therefore, if such a situation occurs, then it will be difficult for us to find an empty location in the hash table despite the fact that the table is not full. Hence, quadratic probing encounters a problem which is known as secondary clustering. In this method, the chance of multiple collisions increases as the hash table become full. This type of situation can be overcome by double hashing.

Double Hashing

Double hashing is one of the best methods available for open addressing. As the name suggests, this method uses two hash functions to operate rather than a single hash function. The hash function is given as follows:

$$h'(k) = (h_1(k) + ih_2(k)) \bmod m,$$

where $h_1(k) = k \bmod m$ and $h_2(k) = k \bmod m'$ are the two hash functions, m is the size of the hash table, m' is less than m (can be (m − 1) or (m − 2)), and i is the probe number that varies from 0 to (m − 1).

Now, let us understand the working of this technique. For a given key k, first the location generated by ($h_1(k)$ mod m) is probed because for the first time i = 0. If the location generated is free, then the key is stored in it. Otherwise, subsequent probes generate locations that are at an offset of ($h_2(k)$ mod m) from the previous location. Also, the offset may vary with every probe depending upon the value generated by the second hash function, that is, ($h_2(k)$ mod m). As a result, the performance of double hashing is very near to the performance of the "ideal" scheme of uniform hashing.

Frequently Asked Questions

Q. Given keys k = 71, 29, 38, 61, and 100, map these keys into a hash table of size m = 5 using double hashing. Take h_1 = (k mod 5) and h_2 = (k mod 4).

Answer.
Initially, the hash table is given as:

0	1	2	3	4
NULL	NULL	NULL	NULL	NULL

Step 1:
i = 0

Key to be inserted = 71

$h'(k) = (h_1(k) + i h_2(k))$ mod m

$h'(k) = (k \bmod m + (i\, k \bmod m'))$ mod m

$h'(71) = (71 \% 5 + (0 \times 71 \% 4)) \% 5$

$h'(71) = (1 + (0 \times 3)) \% 5$

$h'(71) = 1 \% 5 = 1$

Now, since location T[1] is free, 71 is inserted at location T[1].

0	1	2	3	4
NULL	71	NULL	NULL	NULL

Step 2:

i = 0

Key to be inserted = 29

h'(k) = (k mod m + (i k mod m')) mod m

h'(29) = (29 % 5 + (0 X 29 % 4)) % 5

h'(29) = (4 + (0 X 1)) % 5

h'(29) = 4 % 5 = 4

Now, since location T[4] is free, 29 is inserted at location T[4].

0	1	2	3	4
NULL	71	NULL	NULL	29

Step 3:

i = 0

Key to be inserted = 38

h'(k) = (k mod m + (i k mod m')) mod m

h'(38) = (38 % 5 + (0 X 38 % 4)) % 5

h'(38) = (3 + (0 X 2)) % 5

h'(38) = 3 % 5 = 3

Now, since location T[3] is free, 38 is inserted at location T[3].

0	1	2	3	4
NULL	71	NULL	38	29

Step 4:

i = 0

Key to be inserted = 61

h'(k) = (k mod m + (i k mod m')) mod m

h'(61) = (61 % 5 + (0 X 61 % 4)) % 5

h'(61) = (1 + (0 X 1)) % 5

h'(61) = 1 % 5 = 1

Now, since location T[1] is not free, the next probe sequence, that is, i = 1, is computed as:

i = 1

h'(61) = (61 % 5 + (1 X 61 % 4)) % 5

h'(61) = (1 + (1 X 1)) % 5

h'(61) = (1 + 1) % 5

h'(61) = 2 % 5 = 2

Now, since location T[2] is free, 61 is inserted at location T[2].

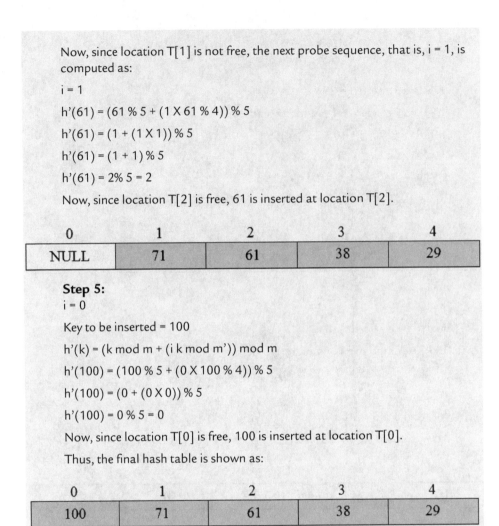

0	1	2	3	4
NULL	71	61	38	29

Step 5:

i = 0

Key to be inserted = 100

h'(k) = (k mod m + (i k mod m')) mod m

h'(100) = (100 % 5 + (0 X 100 % 4)) % 5

h'(100) = (0 + (0 X 0)) % 5

h'(100) = 0 % 5 = 0

Now, since location T[0] is free, 100 is inserted at location T[0].

Thus, the final hash table is shown as:

0	1	2	3	4
100	71	61	38	29

Advantages and Disadvantages of Double Hashing

The double hashing method is free from all the problems of primary clustering and secondary clustering. It also minimizes repeated collisions.

10.2 Summary

- A hash table is an array in which the data is accessed through a special index called a key. In a hash table, keys are mapped to the array positions by a hash function.

- A hash function is a mathematical formula which when applied to a key produces an integer which is used as an index to find a key in the hash table.

- There are different types of hash functions which use numeric keys. Popular methods are the division method, the mid square method, and the folding method.

- In the division method, a key k is mapped into one of the m slots by taking the remainder of k divided by m. The main drawback of the division method is that many consecutive keys map to consecutive hash values respectively which means that consecutive array locations will be occupied, and hence there will be an effect on the performance.

- In the mid square method, we will calculate the square of the given key. After getting the number, we will extract some digits from the middle of that number as an address.

- In the folding method, we will break the key into pieces such that each piece has the same number of digits except the last one, which may have lower digits as compared to other pieces. Now, these individual pieces are added. Hence, the hash value is formed.

- A collision is a situation which occurs when a hash function maps two different keys to a single/same location in the hash table.

- Collision resolution techniques are used to overcome the problem of collision in hashing. There are two popular methods which are used for resolving collisions, which are collision resolution by the chaining method and collision resolution by the open addressing method.

- In the chaining method, a chain of elements is maintained which have same hash address. Hash tables here behave like an array of pointers. In this, each location in the hash table stores a pointer to the linked list which contains all the key elements that were hashed to that location. The disadvantage of this method is the wastage of storage space as the key elements are stored in the linked list, and also for each element to get accessed the pointers are required, which in turn are consuming more space.

- In an open addressing method, all the elements are stored in the hash table itself. There is no need to provide the pointers in this method, which is the biggest advantage of this method. Once a collision takes place, open addressing computes new locations using the probe sequence, and the next element or next record is stored in that location.

- Probing is the process of examining the memory locations in the hash table.

- Linear probing is the simplest approach to resolving the problem of collision in hashing. In this method, if a key is already stored at a location generated by the hash function $h(k)$, then the situation can be resolved by the following hash function:

$$h'(k) = (h(k) + i) \bmod m$$

- Quadratic probing is another approach to resolving the problem of collision in hashing. In this method, if a key is already stored at a location generated by the hash function $h(k)$, then the situation can be resolved by the following hash function:

$$h'(k) = (h(k) + c_1 i + c_2 i^2) \bmod m$$

- Double hashing is one of the best methods available for open addressing. As the name suggests, this method uses two hash functions to operate rather than a single hash function. The hash function is given as:

$$h'(k) = (h_1(k) + ih_2(k)) \bmod m$$

10.3 Exercises

10.3.1 Review Questions

1. What are hash tables?

2. What is hashing? Give some of its practical applications.

3. Define the hash function and also explain the various characteristics of a hash function.

4. What is a collision in hashing and how it can be resolved?

5. Explain the different type of hash functions along with an example.

6. Discuss the collision resolution techniques in hashing.

7. What is clustering in hashing? What are the two types of clustering?

8. What do you understand by double hashing?

9. Define the following terms:

    A. Quadratic Probing

    B. Linear Probing

10. What is the chaining method in hashing and how it can help in resolving collisions?

11. Consider a hash table of size 10. Using linear probing, insert the keys 12, 45, 67, 122, 78, and 34 in it.

12. Consider a hash table of size 9. Using double hashing, insert the keys 4, 17, 30, 55, 90, 11, 54, and 77 in it. Take h_1 = k mod 9 and h_2 = k mod 6.

13. Consider a hash table of size 11. Using quadratic probing, insert the keys 10, 45, 56, 97, 123, and 1 in it.

14. How can the open addressing method be used in resolving collisions?

15. Write a C function to retrieve an item from the hash table using linear probing and quadratic probing.

10.3.2 Multiple Choice Questions

1. Which of the following collision resolution techniques is free from the clustering phenomenon?

    A. Linear Probing

    B. Quadratic Probing

    C. Double hashing

    D. None of these

2. The process of examining a memory location is called _____.

   A. Probing

   B. Hashing

   C. Chaining

   D. Addressing

3. A hash table with chaining as a collision resolution technique degenerates to a:

   A. Tree

   B. Graph

   C. Array

   D. Linked List

4. Which of the probing techniques suffers from the problem of primary clustering?

   A. Quadratic Probing

   B. Linear Probing

   C. Double Hashing

   D. All of these

5. Given the hash function $h(k) = k \bmod 6$, what is the number of collisions to store the following sequence of keys using open addressing?

   A. 1

   B. 3

   C. 2

   D. 5

6. In a hash table, an element with the key k is stored at _____.

   A. k

   B. $h(k^2)$

   C. $h(k)$

   D. $\log h(k)$

7. A good hash function eliminates the problem of collision.

   A. True

   B. False

   C. Not possible to comment

8. Given the hash function of size 7 and hash function $h(k) = k \bmod 7$, what is the number of collisions with linear probing for insertion of the following keys: 29, 36, 16, and 30?

   A. 1

   B. 2

   C. 3

   D. 4

9. _____ is the process of mapping keys to appropriate locations in the hash table.

   A. Probing

   B. Hashing

   C. Collision

   D. Addressing

10. When there is no free location in the hash table, then _____ occurs.

   A. Underflow

   B. Overflow

   C. Collision

   D. None of the above

FILES

In This Chapter

11.1 Introduction

We all know that nowadays in most organizations, a large amount of data is collected in one form or another. Some of the organizations are using various types of data collection applications for collecting the data. When we talk about an organization, it is not only the big ones like schools, colleges, and companies, but also a small bakery shop at the corner of the street; it can be observed that collection and exchange of data take place everywhere. For example, when we get admitted into a school, a lot of data is collected by the school such as name, age, address, parent's name, blood type, and so on. In older times, we all know that the data was collected in the form of paper documents which were very difficult to handle and store. Therefore, to efficiently and effectively analyze the collected data, computers are used to store the data in the form of files. A file in computer terminology is defined as a block of useful data in a persistent storage medium; that is, the file is available for future use. The data is organized in a hierarchical order in the files. The hierarchical order includes items such as records, fields, and so forth, which all are defined as follows.

11.2 Terminologies

- **Data Field** – A data field is a unit which stores a unary fact. It is usually characterized by its type and size. For example, "employee's name" is a data field that stores the names of employees.

- **Record** – The collection of related data fields is called a record. For example, an employee's record may contain various data fields such as name, id, address, contact number, and so on.

- **File** – The collection of related records is called a file. For example, a file of the employees working in an organization.

- **Directory** – The collection of related files is called a directory. Every file in a computer system is stored in a directory.

- **File Name** – The name of a file is a string of characters.

- **Read-only** – A file named read-only cannot be modified or deleted. If we try to delete the file, then a particular message is displayed.

- **Hidden** – A file marked as hidden is not displayed in the directory.

11.3 File Operations

There are various operations which can be performed on the files.

1. **File Creation** – It is the first operation to be performed on the files if the file is not created. A file is created by specifying its name and mode. The records are inserted into the file by opening the file in writing mode.

Once all the records are inserted into the file, the file can be used for future read and write operations. For example, we create a new file named EMPLOYEE.

2. **Updating a File** – It means changing the contents of a file. It is usually done in the following ways:

    a. Inserting into a File – The new record is inserted into the file. For example, if a new employee joins an organization, his/her record is inserted in the EMPLOYEE file.

    b. Modifying a File – The existing records are modified in the file. For example, if the address of an employee is changed, then the new address must be modified in the EMPLOYEE file.

    c. Deleting from a File – The existing record is deleted from the file. For example, if an employee quits a job, then his/her record is deleted from the EMPLOYEE file.

3. **Retrieving from a File** – It refers to the process of extracting some useful data from a file. It is usually done in the following ways:

    a. Enquiring – It retrieves a low amount of data from the file.

    b. Generating a Report – It retrieves a huge amount of data from the file.

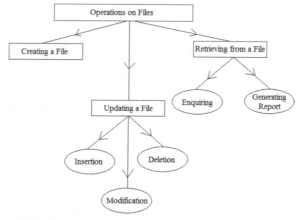

FIGURE 11.1 Operations on files.

11.4 File Classification

A file is classified into two types, which are:

1. Text Files – A text file, often called a flat file, is a file that stores all the numeric or non-numeric data using its corresponding ASCII values. The data can be a string of letters, numbers, or special symbols. Therefore, it is also known as an ASCII file. Usually, a text file has a special marker known as the end of file marker which denotes the end of the file.

2. Binary Files – A binary file is a file that contains all the data in the binary form of 1s and 0s. It stores the data in the same form as that of primary memory. Thus, a binary file is not readable by human beings. Binary files are read by computer programs, and they decode the binary files into something meaningful. Data is efficiently stored in binary files.

11.5 File Organization

File organization refers to the way in which records are physically arranged on a storage device. Further, there may be a single key or multiple keys associated with it. Therefore, based on its physical storage and the keys used to access the records, files are classified as sequential files, relative files, indexed sequential files, and inverted files. There are various factors which should be taken into consideration while choosing a particular type of file organization which are:

1. Ease of retrieval of the records.

2. Economy of storage.

3. Reliability, that is, whether a file organization is reliable or not.

4. Security, that is, whether a file organization is secured or not.

Now, we will discuss some of the techniques which are commonly used for file organization.

11.6 Sequence File Organization

Sequence file organization is the most basic way to organize a collection of records in a file. Sequence file organization is when the file is created when the records are written, one after the other in order, and can be accessed only in that order in which they are written when the file is used for input. All the records are numbered from zero onward. Thus, if there are N records in a file, then the first record is numbered as 0, and the last record will be numbered as N-1. In some cases, records of sequential files are sorted by the value of some field in each record. The field whose value is used to sort the records is known as a sort key. If a file is sorted by the value of a field named "key field," then the record i proceeds record j if and if only if the value of "key field" in record i is less than or equal to the value of "key field" in record j. Also, a file can be sorted in either ascending or descending order by a sort key comprising one or more fields. As the records in a sequential file can only be accessed sequentially, these files are used more commonly in batch processing than in interactive processing. For example, the records of a sequential file are used to generate the white pages of a telephone directory that will be sorted by the subscriber's last name.

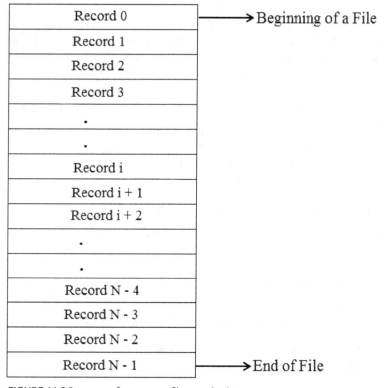

FIGURE 11.2 Structure of a sequence file organization.

Advantages of a Sequence File Organization

1. It is easy to handle.

2. It does not involve extra overheads/problems.

3. Records can be of varying lengths in this organization.

4. It can be stored on magnetic disks as well as tapes.

Disadvantages of Sequence File Organization

1. Records can be accessed only in sequence.

2. It does not support the update operation in between the files.

3. It does not support interactive applications.

11.7 Indexed Sequence File Organization

An indexed sequential file organization is an efficient way of organizing the records when there is a need to access both sequentially by some key values and also to access the records individually by the same key value. It provides the combination of access types that are supported by a sequential file or a relative file. The index has been structured as a binary search tree. This index is used to serve as a request for access to a particular record and the sequential data file alone is used to support sequential access to the entire collection of records. Because of its capability to support both sequential and direct access, indexed sequence file organization is used to support applications that require both batch and interactive processing.

Advantages of Indexed Sequence File Organization

1. Records can be accessed sequentially and randomly.

2. It supports batch as well as interactive oriented applications.

3. It supports the update operation in between records in the file.

Disadvantages of Indexed Sequence File Organization

1. In this organization, files can only be stored on magnetic disks.

2. It involves extra overhead in the form of maintenance.

3. Records can only be of a fixed length, as we maintain the structure of each node like a linked list.

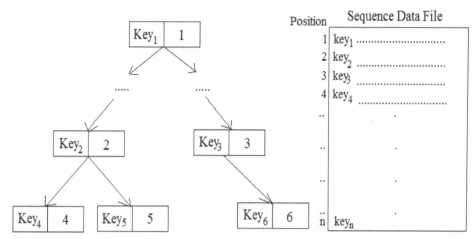

FIGURE 11.3 Use of BST and sequential files to provide indexed sequential access.

11.8 Relative File Organization

Relative file organization provides an effective way of accessing individual records directly. In a relative file organization, there is a predictable relationship between the key and the record's location in the file. The records do not necessarily appear physically in sorted order by their keys. Then how is a given record found? The relationship that will be used to translate between key value and the physical address is designated, for example, R(Key value → address). When a record is to be written into a relative file, the mapping function R is used to translate the record's key to an address, which indicates where the record is to be stored. The fundamental techniques that are used for mapping function R are directory lookup and address calculation (hashing).

- **Directory Lookup Technique** – It is the simplest technique for implementing a mapping function R. The basic idea of this technique is to keep a directory of key values: address pairs. To find a record in a relative file, one locates its key value in the directory, and then the indicated address is used to find the record on the storage device. The directory can be organized as a binary search tree.

- **Address Calculation Technique** – Another common technique for implementing a mapping function R is to perform a calculation on the key value (hashing) such that the result is a relative address.

Advantages of Relative File Organization

1. Records can be accessed out of sequence.

2. It is well suited for interactive applications.

3. It supports an update operation in between the files.

Disadvantages of Relative File Organization

1. It can be only stored on magnetic disks.

2. It also involves extra overhead in the form of maintenance of indexes.

11.9 Inverted File Organization

One fundamental approach for providing a linkage between an index and a file is called inversion. A key's inversion index contains all the values that the key presently has in records of the file. Each key-value entry in the inversion index points to all the data records that have the corresponding value. Then, the file is said to be inverted on that key. The inversion approach for providing multi-key access has been used as the basis for a physical data structure in commercially available relational DBMS such as Oracle, DB2, and so on. These systems were designed to provide rapid access to the records via as many inversion keys as the designer cares to identify. They have user-friendly natural-language-like query languages to assist the user in formulating inquiries. A complete inverted file has an inversion index for every data field. If a file is not completely inverted but has at least one inversion index, then it is said to be a partially inverted file.

Advantages of Inverted File Organization

1. The Boolean query requires only one access per record satisfying the query plus some access to process the indexes.

2. Records can be stored in any way; for example, sequentially ordered by primary key, randomly linked ordered by primary key, and so forth.

3. It also results in space saving as compared with the other file structures.

Disadvantages of Inverted File Organization

Since the index entries are of variable lengths, index maintenance becomes more complex.

11.10 Summary

- A file is a collection of records. It is usually stored on a secondary storage device.

- The data is organized in a hierarchical order in the files. The hierarchical order includes items such as records, fields, and so on.

- File creation is the first operation to be performed on the files if the file is not created. A file is created by specifying its name and mode.

- A file is classified into two types, which are text files and binary files.

- A text file, often called a flat file, is a file that stores all the numeric or non-numeric data using its corresponding ASCII values. The data can be a string of letters, numbers, or special symbols.

- A binary file is a file that contains all the data in the binary form of 1s and 0s. It stores the data in the same form as that of primary memory.

- A file organization refers to the way in which records are physically arranged on a storage device.

- Sequence file organization is the most basic way to organize a collection of records in a file. In sequence file organization the file is created when the records are written, one after the other in order, and can be accessed only in that order in which they are written when the file is used for input. All the records are numbered from zero onward.

- An indexed sequential file organization is an effective way of organizing the records when there is a need to access both sequentially by some key values and also to access the records individually by the same key value. It provides the combination of access types that are supported by a sequential file or a relative file.

- Relative file organization provides an effective way of accessing individual records directly. In a relative file organization, there is a predictable relationship between the key and the record's location in the file.

- One fundamental approach for providing a linkage between an index and a file is called inversion. The inversion approach for providing multi-key access has been used as the basis for the physical data structure.

11.11 Exercises

11.11.1 Review Questions

1. What is a file?

2. Why there is a need to store the data in the files? Explain.

3. What do you understand by the terms record and field?

4. Discuss various operations that can be performed on files.

5. Differentiate between a text file and a binary file.

6. Write a short note on file attributes.

7. What do you understand by file organization? Discuss in detail.

8. Explain sequential file organization.

9. What are inverted files? Discuss.

10. Explain indexed sequential file organization.

11. Give the merits and demerits of indexed sequential file organization.

12. What is relative file organization? Also, discuss the advantages and disadvantages of relative file organization.

11.11.2 Multiple Choice Questions

1. A collection of related fields is called:

   A. Data

   B. Record

   C. Field

   D. File

2. A file marked as _____ can't be modified or deleted.

    A. Hidden

    B. Read-only

    C. Archive

    D. None of these

3. Which of the following is often known as a flat file?

    A. Binary File

    B. Text File

    C. String File

    D. None of these

4. _____ is a collection of data organized in a fashion which facilitates various operations such as updating, retrieving, and so forth.

    A. Record

    B. Data word

    C. Field

    D. File

5. Can relative files be used both for random as well as sequential access?

    A. True

    B. False

    C. Not enough information

6. A file marked as _____ is not displayed in the directory.

    A. Read-only

    B. Archive

    C. Hidden

    D. None of these

7. A data field is characterized by:

   A. Type

   B. Size

   C. Mode

   D. Both (a) and (b)

8. _____ is used to store a collection of files.

   A. Record

   B. Dictionary

   C. Directory

   D. System

# CHAPTER 1

GRAPHS

In This Chapter

- Introduction
- Definitions
- Graph representation
- Graph traversal techniques
- Topological sort
- Minimum spanning tree
- Summary
- Exercises

12.1 Introduction

So far, we have studied various types of linear data structures which are widely used in various applications. But the only non-linear data structure we have studied thus far is trees. In trees, we discussed the parent-child relationship in which one parent can have many children. But in graphs, this parent-child relationship is less restricted, that is, any complex relationship can exist. Thus, a tree can be generalized as a special type of graph. Therefore, a graph is a non-linear data structure which has a wide range of real-life applications. *A graph is a collection of some vertices (nodes) and edges that connect these vertices.* Figure 12.1 represents a graph.

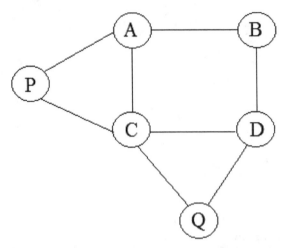

FIGURE 12.1. A graph.

Thus, *a graph G can be defined as an ordered set of vertices and edges (V, E), where V(G) represents the set of vertices and E(G) represents the set of edges that connect these vertices.* In the previous figure, V(G) = {A, B, C, D, P, Q} represents the set of vertices and E(G) = {(A, B), (B, D), (D, C), (C, A), (C, Q), (Q, D), (A, P), (P, C)} represents the set of edges.

Practical Application:

A simple illustration of the graph is that when we connect with our friends on social media, say Facebook, where each user is a vertex and two users connect with each other, it forms an edge.

Now, there are two types of graph:

1. **Undirected Graph** – In an undirected graph, the edges do not have any direction associated with them. As we can see in the following figure, the two nodes A and B can be traversed in both the directions, that is, from A to B or from B to A. Thus, an undirected graph does not give any information about the direction.

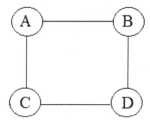

FIGURE 12.2. An undirected graph.

2. Directed Graph – In a directed graph, the edges have directions associated with them. As we can see in the following figure, the two nodes A and B can be traversed in only one direction, that is, only from A to B and not from B to A. Therefore, in the edge (A, B), the node A is known as the initial node and node B is known as the final node.

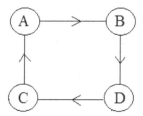

FIGURE 12.3. A directed graph.

12.2 Definitions

- **Degree of a vertex/node** – The degree of a node is the total number of edges incident to that particular node. Here, the degree of the node B is three, as three edges are incident to the node B.

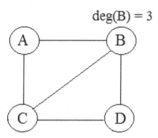

FIGURE 12.4. Graph showing degree of node B.

- **In-degree of a node** – The in-degree of a node is equal to the number of edges arriving at that particular node.

- **Out-degree of a node** – The out-degree is equal to the number of edges leaving that particular node.

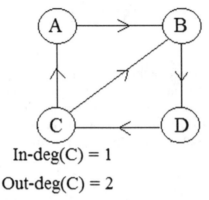

$$\text{In-deg(C)} = 1$$

$$\text{Out-deg(C)} = 2$$

FIGURE 12.5. Graph showing in-degree and out-degree of node C.

- **Isolated Node/Vertex** – A node having zero edges is known as the isolated node. The degree of such a node is zero.

FIGURE 12.6. Two isolated nodes X and Y.

- **Pendant Node/Vertex** – A node having one edge is known as a pendant node. The degree of such a node is one.

FIGURE 12.7. Two pendant nodes X and Y.

- **Adjacent Nodes** – For every edge e = (A, B) that connect nodes A and B, the nodes A and B are said to be the adjacent nodes.

- **Parallel Edges** – If there is more than one edge between the same pair of nodes, then they are known as parallel edges.

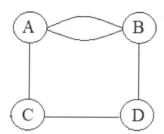

FIGURE 12.8. Parallel edges between A and B.

- **Loop** – If an edge has a starting and ending point at the same node, that is, e = (A, A), then it is known as a loop.

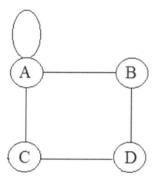

FIGURE 12.9. A loop.

- **Simple Graph** – A graph G(V, E) is known as a simple graph if it does not contain any loop or parallel edge.

- **Complete Graph** – A graph G(V, E) is known as a complete graph if and only if every node in the graph is connected to another node and there is no loop on any of the nodes.

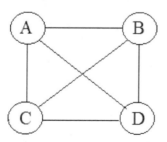

FIGURE 12.10. Complete graph.

- **Regular Graph** – A regular graph is a graph in which every node has the same degree. If every node has a degree r, then the graph is called a regular graph of degree r. In the given figure, all the nodes have the same degree, that is, 2; hence, it is known as the 2-regular graph.

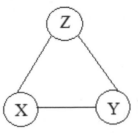

FIGURE 12.11. 2-Regular graph.

- **Multi-graph** - A graph G(V, E) is known as a multi-graph if it contains either a loop, parallel edges, or both.

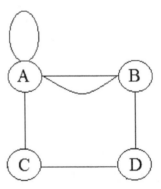

FIGURE 12.12. Multi-graph.

- **Cycle** – It is a path containing one or more edges which starts from a particular node and also terminates at the same node.

- **Cyclic Graph** – A graph which has cycles in it is known as a cyclic graph.

- **Acyclic Graph** – A graph without any cycles is known as an acyclic graph.

- **Connected Graph** – A graph G(V, E) is known as a connected graph if there is a path from any node in the graph to another node in the graph such that for every pair of distinct nodes, there must be a path.

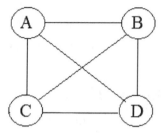

FIGURE 12.13. Connected graph.

- **Strongly Connected Graph** – A directed graph is said to be a strongly connected graph if there exists a dedicated path between every pair of nodes in the graph. For example, if there are two nodes, say P and Q, and there is a dedicated path from P to Q, then there must be a path from Q to P.

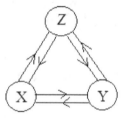

FIGURE 12.14. Strongly connected graph.

- **Size of a graph** – The size of a graph is equal to the total number of edges present in the graph.

- **Weighted Graph** – A graph G(V, E) is said to be a weighted graph if all the edges in the graph are assigned some data. This data indicates the cost of traversing the edge.

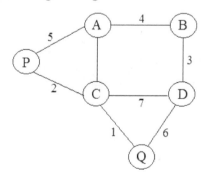

FIGURE 12.15. Weighted graph.

12.3 Graph Representation

Graphs can be represented in a computer's memory in either of the following ways:

1. Sequential Representation of Graphs using Adjacency Matrix

2. Linked Representation of Graphs using Adjacency List

Now, let us discuss both in detail.

12.3.1 Adjacency Matrix Representation

An adjacency matrix is used to represent the information of the nodes which are adjacent to one another. The two nodes will only be adjacent when there is an edge connecting those nodes. For any graph G having n nodes, the dimension of the adjacency matrix will be (n X n). Let G(V, E) be a graph having vertices V = {V_1, V_2, V_3.........V_n}, then the adjacency matrix representation (n X n) will be given by:

$$a_{ij} = \begin{cases} 1 & \text{if there is an edge from } V_i \text{ to } V_j. \\ 0 & \text{otherwise} \end{cases}$$

The adjacency matrix is also known as a bit matrix or Boolean matrix, since it contains only 0s and 1s. Now, let us take few examples to discuss and understand it more clearly.

Example 1 – Consider the given directed graph and find its adjacency matrix.

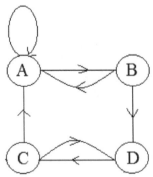

FIGURE 12.16. A directed graph.

The adjacency matrix for the graph will be:

$$
\begin{array}{c c c c c}
 & A & B & C & D \\
A & 1 & 1 & 0 & 0 \\
B & 1 & 0 & 0 & 1 \\
C & 1 & 0 & 0 & 1 \\
D & 0 & 0 & 1 & 0
\end{array}
$$

Example 2 – Now, consider the given undirected graph and find its adjacency matrix.

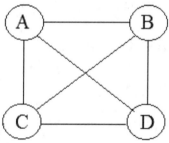

FIGURE 12.17. An undirected graph.

The adjacency matrix for the graph will be:

$$
\begin{array}{c c c c c}
 & A & B & C & D \\
A & 0 & 1 & 1 & 1 \\
B & 1 & 0 & 1 & 1 \\
C & 1 & 1 & 0 & 1 \\
D & 1 & 1 & 1 & 0
\end{array}
$$

Example 3 – Now, consider the given weighted graph and find its adjacency matrix.

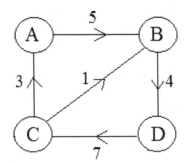

FIGURE 12.18. A directed weighted graph.

The adjacency matrix for the graph will be:

$$
\begin{array}{c c c c c}
 & A & B & C & D \\
A & 0 & 5 & 0 & 0 \\
B & 0 & 0 & 0 & 4 \\
C & 3 & 1 & 0 & 0 \\
D & 0 & 0 & 7 & 0
\end{array}
$$

Example 4 – Consider the given undirected multi-graph and find its adjacency matrix.

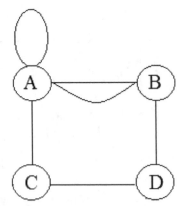

FIGURE 12.19. An undirected multi-graph.

The adjacency matrix for the graph will be:

$$
\begin{array}{c c c c c}
 & A & B & C & D \\
A & 1 & 2 & 1 & 0 \\
B & 2 & 0 & 0 & 1 \\
C & 1 & 0 & 0 & 1 \\
D & 0 & 1 & 1 & 0
\end{array}
$$

From the above examples, we conclude that:

- The memory space needed to represent a graph using its adjacency matrix is n^2 bits.

- The adjacency matrix for an undirected graph is always symmetric.

- The adjacency matrix for a directed graph needs not be symmetric.

- The adjacency matrix for a simple graph having no loops or parallel edges will always contain 0s on the diagonal.

- The adjacency matrix for a weighted graph will always contain the weights of the edges connecting the nodes instead of 0 and 1.

- The adjacency matrix for an undirected multi-graph will contain the number of edges connecting the vertices instead of 1.

12.3.2 Adjacency List Representation

The adjacency matrix representation has some major drawbacks. First, it was very difficult to insert and delete the nodes in/from the graph as the size of the matrix needs to be changed accordingly, which is a very time-consuming process. Also, sometimes the matrix may contain many zeroes (sparse matrix). Hence, it was not a healthy representation. Therefore, adjacency list representation is preferred for representing sparse graphs in the memory. In this representation, every node is linked to its list of all the other nodes which are adjacent to it. Adjacency list representation makes it easier to add or delete nodes. Also, it shows the adjacent nodes of a particular node. Now, let us take a few examples to discuss and understand it more clearly.

Example 1 – Consider the given undirected graph and find its adjacency list representation.

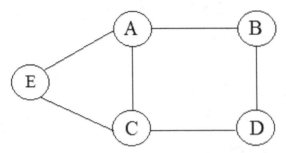

FIGURE 12.20. An undirected graph.

The adjacency list representation of the graph will be:

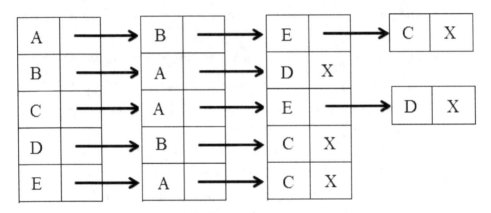

Example 2 – Consider the given directed graph and find its adjacency list representation.

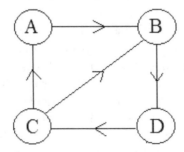

FIGURE 12.21. A directed graph.

The adjacency list representation of the graph will be:

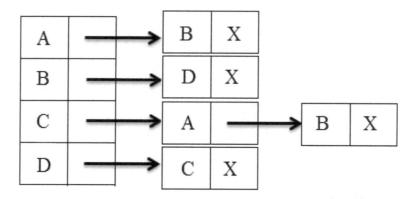

Example 3 – Now, consider the given weighted graph and find its adjacency list representation.

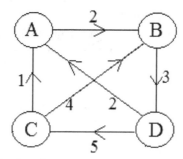

FIGURE 12.22. A directed weighted graph.

The adjacency list representation of the graph will be:

A		→	B	2	X			
B		→	D	3	X			
C		→	A	1	→	B	4	X
D		→	C	5	→	A	2	X

12.4 Graph Traversal Techniques

In this section, we will discuss various types of techniques to traverse a graph. As we all know, a graph is a collection of nodes and edges. Thus, traversing in a graph is the process of visiting each node and edge in some systematic approach. Therefore, there are two types of standard graph traversal techniques, which are:

1. Breadth First Search (BFS)

2. Depth First Search (DFS)

So now, we will discuss both of these techniques in detail.

12.4.1 Breadth First Search

Breadth first search is a traversal technique that uses the queue as an auxiliary data structure for traversing all member nodes of a graph. In this technique, first we will select any node in the graph as a starting node, and then we will take all the nodes adjacent to the starting node. We will maintain the same approach for all the other nodes. Also, we will maintain the status of all the traversed/visited nodes in a queue so that no nodes are traversed again. Now, let us take a graph and apply BFS to traverse the graph.

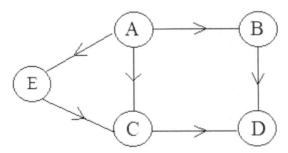

FIGURE 12.23: A sample graph.

Now, we will start the traversal of the graph by taking node A as a starting node of the above sample graph. Then, we will traverse all the nodes adjacent to the starting node A. As we can see, B, C, and E are the adjacent nodes of A. So we will traverse these nodes in any order, say E, C, B. So the traversal is:

$$\boxed{\text{A, E, C, B}}$$

Now, we will traverse all the nodes adjacent to E. Node C is adjacent to node E. But node C has already been traversed, so we will ignore it and we will move to the next step. Now, we will traverse all the nodes adjacent to node C. As we can see, D is the adjacent node of C. So we will traverse node D and the traversal is:

$$\boxed{\text{A, E, C, B, D}}$$

Now, we can see that all the nodes have been traversed and hence, this was the breadth first search traversal by taking node A as a starting node.

Now, we will implement the breadth first search traversal technique with the help of a queue. In this, we will maintain an array which will store all the adjacent unvisited neighbor nodes of a given under consideration. Initially, the front and rear are set to -1. We will also maintain the status of the visited nodes in a Boolean array, which will have value 1 if the node is visited and 0 if it is not visited.

- First, we will en-queue/insert the starting node into the queue.

- Second, the first node/element in the queue is deleted from the queue and all the adjacent unvisited nodes are inserted into the queue. This is repeated until the queue becomes empty.

For Example – Consider the following sample graph and traverse the graph using the breadth first search technique.

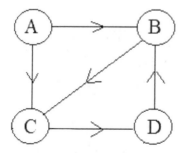

FIGURE 12.24 A sample graph.

The appropriate adjacency list representation of a graph is given as follows:

Node	Adjacency List
A	B, C
B	C
C	D
D	B

In this example, we are taking A as a starting node.

Step 1: First, node A is inserted into the queue.

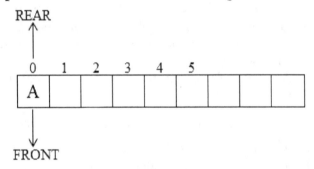

Step 2: Node A is deleted from the queue and FRONT is incremented by 1. Now, insert all the nodes adjacent to A, which are nodes B and C, by incrementing REAR. Also, node A has been traversed.

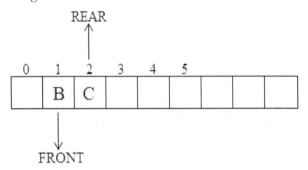

Step 3: Similarly, node B is deleted from the queue and FRONT is incremented by 1. Now, insert all the nodes adjacent to B, which is node C, by incrementing REAR. But C has already been inserted in the queue. So

now in this case, node C is also deleted by incrementing FRONT by 1, and the node adjacent to C, that is, D, is inserted into the queue. Therefore, nodes A, B, and C are traversed.

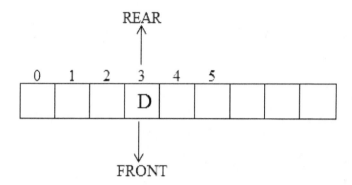

Step 4: Now, we will again delete the front element from the queue which is D. We will insert the adjacent node of D, that is, B. But it is already traversed. Finally, as we delete the front element D, we notice that FRONT > REAR, which is not possible. Hence, we have traversed all the nodes in the graph.

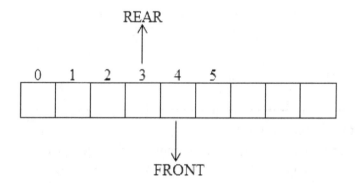

Therefore, the breadth first search traversal of the graph is given as:

$$\boxed{A, B, C, D}$$

Now, let us look at the function for a breadth first search traversal.

Function for breadth first search traversal

```
Breadth_First_Search(int node)
{
  int i , front, rear;
  int queue[SIZE];
  front=rear= -1;
  printf("%d", node);
  visited[node]= 1;
  rear++;
  front++;
  queue[rear]= node ;
  while(front<=rear)
    {
      node = queue[front];
      front++;
      for(i=1; i<=n; i++)
        {
          if(adjacent[node][i]==1) && visited[node]==0)
            {
              printf("%d", node);
              visited[i]=1;
              rear++;
              queue[rear]= i ;
            }
        }
    }
}
```

12.4.2 Depth First Search

Depth first search is another traversal technique that uses the stack as an auxiliary data structure for traversing all the member nodes of a graph. Also in this technique, we first select any node in the graph as a starting node, and then we travel along a path which begins from the starting node. We will visit the adjacent node of the starting node, and again the adjacent node of the previous node, and so on. We will maintain the same approach for all the other nodes. Now, let us take a graph and apply DFS to traverse the graph.

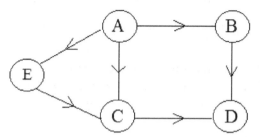

FIGURE 12.25 A Sample Graph.

Now, we will start the traversal of the graph by taking node A as a starting node. Then, we will traverse any of the nodes adjacent to the starting node A. As we can see, B, C, and E are the adjacent nodes of A. If we traverse node E, then we will traverse the node adjacent to E, that is, C. After traversing C, we will traverse the node adjacent to C which is D. Now, there is no adjacent node to D, hence, we have reached the dead end. Thus, the traversal until now is:

$$\boxed{\text{A, E, C, D}}$$

Because of the dead end, we will move backward. Now, we reach node C. We will check if there is any other node adjacent to C. There is no such node and thus, we again move backward. Now, we reach E. We will again check if there is any other node adjacent to E. There is no such node and thus, we again move backward. Now, we reach A. We will check if there is any other node adjacent to A. There are two nodes, B and C, adjacent to node A. As C is already traversed, it will be ignored. Now, we will traverse node B. After traversing B, we will traverse the node adjacent to B which is D, but D is already traversed. Thus, we can't move backward or forward. Thus, we have completed the traversal. The final traversal is given as:

$$\boxed{\text{A, E, C, D, B}}$$

Now, we will implement the depth first search traversal technique with the help of a stack. In this, we will maintain an array which will store all the adjacent unvisited neighbor nodes of a given node. Initially, the top is set to -1. We will also maintain the status of the visited nodes in a Boolean array, which will have value 1 if the node is visited and 0 if it is not visited.

- First, we will push the starting node onto the stack.

- Second, the topmost node/element is popped out from the stack and is traversed. If it is already traversed, then we will ignore it.

- Third, all the adjacent unvisited nodes of the popped node/element are pushed onto the stack. This process is repeated until the queue becomes empty. The steps are repeated until the stack becomes empty.

For Example – Consider the following sample graph and traverse the graph using the breadth first search technique.

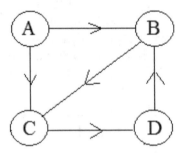

FIGURE 12.26 A sample graph

In this example, we are taking A as a starting node.

Step 1: Push A onto the stack.

$$\boxed{\text{A}}$$

Step 2: Now, pop the topmost element from the stack, that is, A. Thus, A is traversed. Now, push all the nodes adjacent to A, that is, push B and C.

Step 3: Again, pop the topmost element from the stack, that is, C. Thus, C is also traversed. Now, push all the nodes adjacent to C, that is, push D.

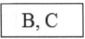

Step 4: Now, again pop the topmost element from the stack, that is, D. Thus, D is also traversed. Now, push all the nodes adjacent to D, that is, push B. But B is already in the stack. Therefore, no push is performed. Thus, the stack becomes:

$$\boxed{\text{B}}$$

Step 5: Again, pop the topmost element from the stack, that is, B. Thus, B is also traversed. Now, push all the nodes adjacent to B, that is, push C. But C is already traversed; hence, the stack becomes empty.

Therefore, the depth first search traversal of the graph is given as follows:

$$\boxed{\text{A, C, D, B}}$$

Now, let us look at the function for the depth first search traversal.

Function for depth first search traversal

```
Depth_First_Search(int node)
{
  inti, stack[SIZE], top = -1, pop ;
  top++ ;
  stack[top] = node ;
  while(top >= 0)
    {
      pop = stack[top] ;
      top-- ;
      if(visited[pop] == 0)
        {
          printf("%d", pop) ;
          visited[pop] = 1;
        }
      else
      continue
      for(i=n; i>=1 ;i--)
        {
          if(adjacent[pop][node] == 1 && visited[node] == 0)
            {
```

```
                top++  ;
                stack[top] = node ;
            }
        }
    }
}
```

Memory Aid:

To remember which of the data structures are used in implementing a breadth first search and depth first search, we can use this memory aid. Breadth first search is implemented using a queue data structure, and depth first search is implemented using a stack data structure, as it can be remembered by alphabetical order. B (Breadth First Search) and Q (Queue) comes before than D (Depth First Search) and S (Stack) in alphabetical order.

12.5 Topological Sort

Topological sort is a procedure to determine the linear ordering of the nodes of an acyclic directed graph also known as (DAG) in which each node comes before all those nodes which have zero predecessors. A topological sort of a DAG is a linear ordering of the vertices of a graph G(V, E) such that if (a, b) is an edge, then a must appear before b in the topological ordering. The main idea behind this is that in a graph, if a vertex has in-degree 0, then that vertex should be selected as the first element in the topological order. Also, a topological sort is possible only in acyclic directed graphs. An acyclic graph is one which does not have any cycles in it. Topological sorting is widely used in scheduling tasks, applications, and so on. Now, let us look at the algorithm of topological sorting.

Algorithm for Topological Sort

```
Step 1: START
Step 2: Find the in-degree of every node.
Step 3: Insert all the nodes/elements having in-degree
        zero in the queue.
Step 4: Repeat Steps 5 and 6 until the queue becomes
        empty.
Step 5: Delete the first node from the queue by increment-
        ing FRONT by 1.
```

```
Step 6: Repeat for each neighbor P of node N –
        a. Delete the edge from P to M by decreasing the
           in-degree by 1.
        b. If in-degree of P is zero, then add P to the
           rear of the queue.
Step 7: END
```

For Example – Consider a given acyclic directed graph and find its topological sort.

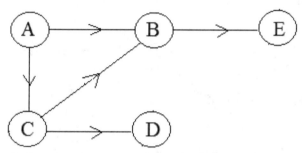

FIGURE 12.27. Acyclic directed graph.

The appropriate adjacency list representation of the previous graph is given as follows:

Node	Adjacency List
A	B, C
B	E
C	B, D
D	-
E	-

Step 1: In-degree of all the nodes -

In-degree (A) – 0

In-degree (B) – 2

In-degree (C) – 1

In-degree (D) – 1

In-degree (E) – 1

Now, we have node A with in-degree = 0; thus A will be added to the queue.

Step 2: Now, insert node A into the queue.

FRONT = 1, REAR = 1, QUEUE = A

Step 3: Now, delete node A from the queue. Also, delete all the edges going from A.

FRONT = 0, REAR = 0, TOPOLOGICAL SORT = A

Thus, the graph becomes:

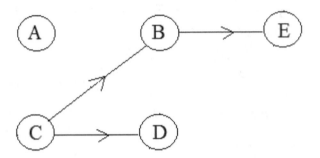

Now, the in-degree of all the nodes -

In-degree (B) – 1

In-degree (C) – 0

In-degree (D) – 1

In-degree (E) – 1

Now, we have node C with in-degree = 0; thus, C will be added to the queue.

Step 4: Now, insert node C into the queue.

FRONT = 1, REAR = 1, QUEUE = C

Step 5: Now, delete node C from the queue. Also, delete all the edges going from C.

FRONT = 0, REAR = 0, TOPOLOGICAL SORT = A, C

Thus, the graph becomes:

Now, the in-degree of all the nodes -

In-degree (B) – 0

In-degree (D) – 0

In-degree (E) – 1

Now, we have two nodes B and D with in-degree = 0; thus, B and D will be added to the queue.

Step 6: Now, insert nodes B and D into the queue.

FRONT = 1, REAR = 2, QUEUE = B, D

Step 7: Now, delete node B from the queue. Also, delete all the edges going from B. There will be no change in the in-degree of the nodes.

FRONT = 1, REAR = 1, TOPOLOGICAL SORT = A, C, B, QUEUE = D

Step 8: Now, delete node D from the queue. Also, delete all the edges going from D.

FRONT = 0, REAR = 0, TOPOLOGICAL SORT = A, C, B, D

Thus, the graph becomes:

Now, the in-degree of all the nodes -

In-degree (E) – 0

Now, we have node E with in-degree = 0. Thus E will be added to the queue.

Step 9: Now, insert node E into the queue.

FRONT = 1, REAR = 1, QUEUE = E

Step 10: Now, delete node E from the queue. Also, delete all the edges going from E.

FRONT = 0, REAR = 0, TOPOLOGICAL SORT = A, C, B, D, E

Now, we have no nodes left in the graph. Thus, the topological sort of the graph will be

$$\boxed{A, C, B, D, E}$$

12.6 Minimum Spanning Tree

A spanning tree of an undirected and connected graph G is a sub-graph which contains all the vertices and edges that connect these vertices and is a tree. The weights/costs can be assigned to the edges, and these weights/costs can be used to calculate the weight/cost of the spanning tree by calculating the sum of the weights/cost of each edge. A graph can have many spanning trees. Thus, a minimum spanning tree (MST) is defined as a spanning tree that has weights/costs associated with the edges such that the total weight/cost of the spanning tree is at a minimum. Although there are various approaches for determining an MST, the two most popular approaches for determining a minimum cost spanning tree of a graph are:

1. Prim's Algorithm

2. Kruskal's Algorithm

Now, let us discuss both of them in detail.

12.6.1 Prim's Algorithm

Prim's algorithm is the algorithm that is used to build a minimum cost spanning tree. This algorithm works in such a way that it builds a tree edge by edge. The next edge to be included is chosen according to some criterion. The steps involved in Prim's algorithm are:

Step 1: Select a starting vertex/node and add it to the spanning tree.

Step 2: During each iteration, select a vertex/node in such a way that the edge connecting vertex V_i to another vertex V_j has the minimum cost/weight assigned to it. Remember, the edge forming a cycle must not be added.

Step 3: End the process when (n-1) number of edges have been inserted into the tree.

Frequently Asked Questions

Q. Consider the given graph and construct a minimum spanning tree using Prim's algorithm.

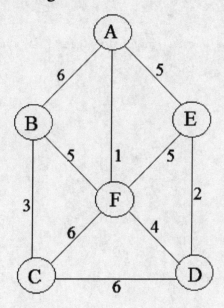

Answer.
Step 1: The starting node is F.

Step 2: The lowest weighted/cost edge is (F, A), that is, 1. Hence, it is added to the tree.

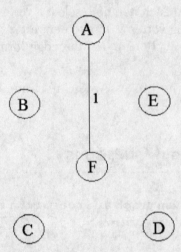

Step 3: Now, the lowest weighted/cost edge is (F, D), that is, 4. Hence, it is added to the tree.

Step 4:

Step 5:

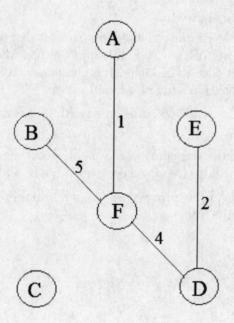

Step 6: Finally the minimum spanning tree is constructed.

12.6.2 Kruskal's Algorithm

Kruskal's algorithm is another approach for determining the minimum cost spanning tree of a graph. In this approach also, the tree is built edge by edge. The next edge to be included is chosen according to some criterion. The steps involved in Kruskal's algorithm are:

Step 1: The weights/costs assigned to the edges are sorted in ascending order.

Step 2: In this step, the lowest weighted/cost edge is added to the tree. Remember, the edge forming a cycle must not be added.

Step 3: End the process when (n-1) number of edges have been inserted into the tree.

Frequently Asked Questions

Q. Consider the given graph and construct a minimum spanning tree using Kruskal's algorithm.

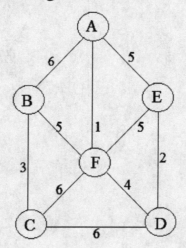

Answer.
Step 1: Initially the tree is given as:

Step 2: Choose edge (F, A).

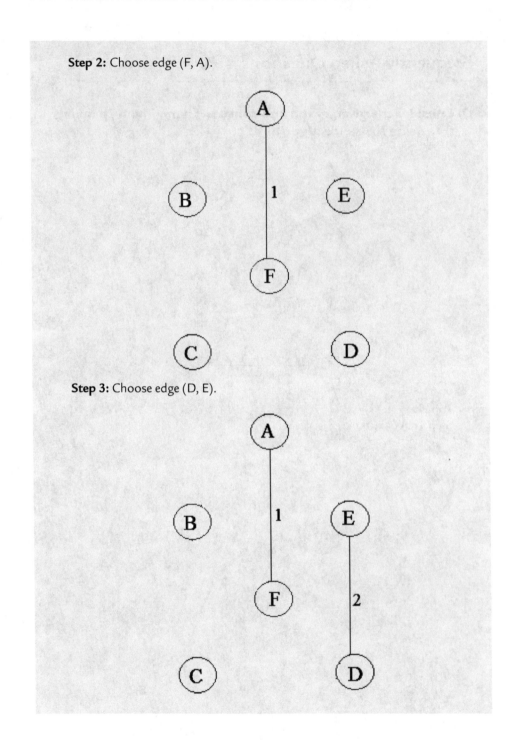

Step 3: Choose edge (D, E).

Step 4: Choose edge (B, C).

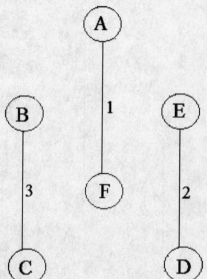

Step 5: Choose edge (F, D).

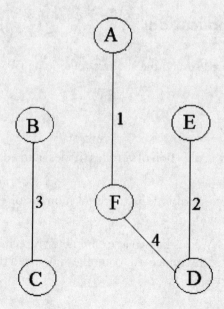

Step 6: Choose edge (F, B).

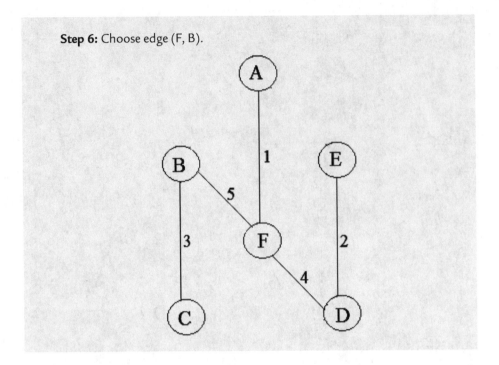

Practical Application:

Graphs are used to find the shortest route using GPS, Google maps, and Yahoo maps.

12.7 Summary

- A graph is a collection of vertices (nodes) and edges that connect these vertices.

- The degree of a node is the total number of edges incident to that particular node.

- A graph G(V, E) is known as a complete graph if and only if every node in the graph is connected to another node and there is no loop on any of the nodes.

- An adjacency matrix is usually used to represent the information of the nodes which are adjacent to one another. The adjacency matrix is also known as a bit matrix or Boolean matrix since it contains only 0s and 1s.

- In adjacency list representation, every node is linked to its list of all the other nodes which are adjacent to it.

- Traversing in a graph is the process of visiting each node and edge in some systematic approach.

- Breadth first search is a traversal technique that uses the queue as an auxiliary data structure for traversing all the member nodes of the graph. In this technique, first we will select any node in the graph as a starting node, and then we will take all the nodes adjacent to the starting node. We will maintain the same approach for all the other nodes.

- Depth first search is another traversal technique that uses the stack as an auxiliary data structure for traversing all the member nodes of the graph. In this also, first we will select any node in the graph as a starting node, and then we will travel along a path which begins from the starting node. We will visit the adjacent node of the starting node, and again the adjacent node of the previous node, and so on.

- Topological sort is a procedure to determine linear ordering of the nodes of an acyclic directed graph also known as (DAG) in which each node comes before all those nodes which have zero predecessors.

- A minimum spanning tree (MST) is defined as a spanning tree that has weights/costs associated with the edges such that the total weight/cost of the spanning tree is at a minimum.

12.8 Exercises

12.8.1 Theory Questions

1. What is a graph? Explain its features.

2. What do you understand by a complete graph?

3. What is a multi-graph?

4. How can a graph be represented in the computer's memory? Discuss.

5. Differentiate between a directed and undirected graph with an example of each.

6. Consider the following graph and find the following:

    A. Adjacency Matrix Representation.

    B. Degree of each node.

    C. Is the graph complete?

    D. Pendant nodes.

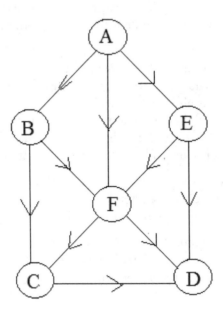

7. Explain why adjacency list representation is preferred for storing sparse matrices over adjacency matrix representation.

8. What are the different types of graph traversal techniques? Explain each of them in detail with the help of an example.

9. What do you understand by topological sort?

10. In what kind of graphs can topological sorting be used?

11. Differentiate between breadth first search and depth first search.

12. Consider the following graph and find out its BFS and DFS traversal.

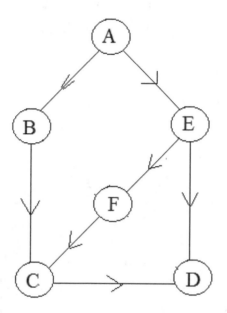

13. Consider the following graph and find out its BFS and DFS traversal.

14. What is a spanning tree?

15. Why is a minimum spanning tree called a spanning tree? Discuss.

16. Consider the given adjacency matrix and draw the directed graph.

	A	B	C	D
A	1	1	0	1
B	1	1	1	0
C	0	1	1	0
D	0	1	1	1

17. Write a short note on Prim's algorithm.

18. Explain Kruskal's algorithm.

19. List some of the real-life applications of graphs.

20. Consider the following graph and find the minimum spanning tree using

    A. Prim's algorithm

    B. Kruskal's algorithm

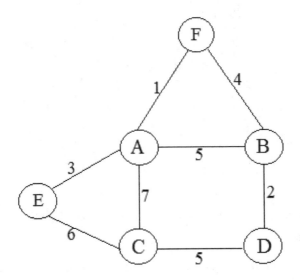

12.8.2 Programming Questions

1. Write a program to create and display a graph.

2. Write an algorithm to perform a topological sort on the graph.

3. Write an algorithm to find the degree of a node N in a graph.

4. Write a program to traverse a graph using depth first search.

5. Write an algorithm to traverse a graph using breadth first search.

6. Write a program to find the shortest path using Prim's algorithm.

7. Write a program to find the shortest path using Kruskal's algorithm.

12.8.3 Multiple Choice Questions

1. To implement Breadth First Search, the data structure used is:

    A. Stack

    B. Queue

    C. Trees

    D. Linked List

2. A graph having multiple edges is known as a _____.

    A. Connected Graph

    B. Complete Graph

    C. Simple Graph

    D. Multi-graph

3. An edge having initial and end points at the same node is called:

    A. Degree

    B. Cycle

    C. Loop

    D. Parallel Edge

4. Adjacency Matrix is also known as:

    A. Bit Matrix

    B. Boolean Matrix

    C. Both of the above

    D. None of the above

5. To implement depth first search, the data structure used is:

    A. Stack

    B. Queue

    C. Trees

    D. Linked List

6. Topological Sort is performed only on:

    A. Cyclic Directed Graphs

    B. Acyclic Directed Graphs

    C. Both of the above

    D. None of the above

7. Which one of the following nodes has a zero degree?

    A. Simple node

    B. Isolated node

    C. Pendant node

    D. None of the above

8. _____ is the total number of nodes in a graph.

    A. Degree

    B. In-degree

    C. Out-degree

    D. Size

9. A graph G can have many spanning trees.

    A. True

    B. False

    C. Not possible to comment

10. The memory use of an adjacency matrix is:

    A. $O(\log n)$

    B. $O(\log n^2)$

    C. $O(n)$

    D. $O(n^2)$

ANSWERS TO SELECTED EXERCISES

Chapter 1: Introduction to Data Structures

Multiple Choice Questions

1 (c)

3. (d)

5. (d)

7. (c)

9. (b)

11. (a)

13. (a)

15. (d)

Chapter 2: Introduction to C Language

Multiple Choice Questions

1 (b)

3. (d)

5. (d)

7. (b)

9. (a)

Chapter 3: Arrays

Multiple Choice Questions

1 (c)

3. (d)

5. (e)

7. (d)

9. (b)

Chapter 4: Linked Lists

Multiple Choice Questions

1 (b)

3. (b)

5. (d)

7. (c)

9. (a)

Chapter 5: Queues

Multiple Choice Questions

1 (c)

3. (b)

5. (b)

7. (c)

9. (b)

Chapter 6: Searching and Sorting

Multiple Choice Questions

1 (b)

3. (d)

5. (a)

7. (b)

9. (b)

Chapter 7: Stacks

Multiple Choice Questions

1 (b)

3. (c)

5. (b)

7. (c)

9. (c)

Chapter 8: Trees

Multiple Choice Questions

1 (d)

3. (c)

5. (d)

7. (c)

9. (a)

11. (b)

13. (b)

15. (d)

Chapter 9: –Multi-Way Search Trees

Multiple Choice Questions

1 (b)

3. (d)

5. (c)

7. (b)

9. (b)

Chapter 10: Hashing

Multiple Choice Questions

1 (c)

3. (d)

5. (c)

7. (b)

9. (b)

Chapter 11: Files

Multiple Choice Questions

1 (b)

3. (b)

5. (b)

7. (d)

Chapter 12: Graphs

Multiple Choice Questions

1 (b)

3. (c)

5. (a)

7. (b)

9. (a)

INDEX